Complementing each essay are evocative black-and-white photographs from United Nations archives and various news sources, and specially drawn maps that allow readers to locate various peacekeeping operations discussed in the text. A guide to U.N. acronyms and a gazetteer of operations provide quick reference to all peacekeeping missions since 1948.

With a preface by United Nations Secretary-General Boutros Boutros-Ghali, *Soldiers for Peace* is a revealing examination of all aspects of peacekeeping, its successes and failures past and present, and its prospects for the future. This engrossing chronicle is written from an historical perspective that sheds light on the ever-evolving goals of the U.N. as it struggles for balance in peacemaking, peacekeeping, peace-enforcement, and peace-building throughout the world today. *Soldiers for Peace* is a must-read for all.

Barbara Benton is Special Projects Editor for *MHQ: The Quarterly Journal of Military History,* where she produced a special section on peacekeeping in 1992. She is the author of *Ellis Island: A Pictorial History* (Facts On File, 1985) and a forthcoming book on women and warfare.

SOLDIERS FOR PEACE

Fifty
Years of
United
Nations
Peacekeeping

SOLDIERS FOR PEACE

BARBARA BENTON,
Editor

Facts On File, Inc.

AN INFOBASE HOLDINGS COMPANY

The publisher wishes to acknowledge the assistance of the United Nations Department of Public Information in preparing this volume. The views expressed are those of the authors and do not necessarily reflect the position of the United Nations or its member states.

Soldiers for Peace

Facts On File, Inc.
11 Penn Plaza
New York, N.Y. 10001

ISBN: 0-8160-3509-1 (hc)
ISBN: 0-8160-3510-5 (pb)
Complete Library of Congress Cataloging-in-Publication Data is available from Facts On File, Inc.

Facts On File books are available at special discounts when purchased in bulk quantities for businesses, associations, institutions, or sales promotions. Please call our Special Sales Department in New York at (212) 967-8800 or (800) 322-8755.

Jacket and book design by Marleen Adlerblum, N.Y.C.

This book is printed on acid-free paper.
Printed in the United States of America.

10 9 8 7 6 5 4 3 2 1

Half-title and title pages: obverse and reverse views of the United Nations medal for peacekeeping personnel. Frontispiece: Cambodian refugees and U.N. helicopter, April 1992.

Contents

United Nations Secretary-General Boutros Boutros-Ghali was surrounded by soldiers of the Egyptian battalion during his visit to Sarajevo in December 1992.

Preface: The Evolution of Peacekeeping Policy

Peacekeeping, an invention of the United Nations, was born of necessity. Because of the Cold War, the vision of collective security embodied in the charter of the United Nations never came to be. The gap was filled by the pragmatic device of peacekeeping, a concept that entailed the deployment of military forces not to prosecute a war, but to help bring about peace.

The instrument of peacekeeping served its purpose well for many years, and a body of doctrine emerged on when and how these "soldiers for peace" should go about their work. Consent, impartiality, and the non-use of force were the watchwords of the organization, and a record of successes, from Asia to the Middle East and the Mediterranean, was built. The calming presence of United Nations peacekeepers, either unarmed observers or lightly armed forces, helped to contain numerous conflicts and created conditions for political talks to go forward.

For most of United Nations history, peacekeeping operations were deployed in situations of interstate conflict, with the mandate to monitor cease-fires and buffer zones between disciplined armies. The end of the Cold War brought new challenges, however, requiring further innovation. Most of today's conflicts are within states, fought not only by regular armies but also by militia and armed civilians with ill-defined chains of command. Cease-fire agreements tend to be fragile and humanitarian emergencies are commonplace, exacerbated by a tendency of warring parties to obstruct relief efforts. Negotiated settlements, when achieved, must cover a wide range of military, political, humanitarian, and other civilian matters. They are not self-executing: Sustained and intensive efforts by peacekeeping missions are essential to ensure compliance. For these settlements to endure, long-term programs are required to address the root causes of the conflict and to promote national reconciliation.

When negotiated settlements cannot be achieved, peacekeeping is not well suited for the task. Nor does it help to give lightly armed peacekeepers a mandate for enforcement, as recent experience in Somalia and Bosnia suggests. For that, a fundamentally different type of operation is required. In such cases, the nature of the international community's involvement must be carefully tailored to the situation at hand. Issues such as the level and type of force, if any, that should be used, as well as the question of who should actually carry out the operation, must be made on a case-by-case basis. There are no cook-book solutions.

One option that has been utilized recently is known as "subcontracting." Where a forceful presence was required, the Security Council authorized military operations by coalitions of member states. Once the situation was stabilized, the coalition operation was followed by a peacekeeping operation under the command and control of the United Nations. Managing these transitions effectively has been a challenge for the international community, and important lessons have been learned. If, in the future, subcontracting.is deemed appropriate to address certain conflicts, some of these lessons should be borne in mind.

First, it is important from the outset to integrate the short- to medium-term "stabilizing actions" of the coalition force with the longer-term efforts of the United Nations to promote lasting reconciliation. In the context of internal conflicts, especially, lasting peace requires the institutionalization of effective channels through which parties can pursue their interests, so that they do not feel compelled to return to the battlefield. This is not an easy process, nor one that can be accomplished if it remains unconnected to the considerations of force and diplomacy of the coalition operation. Hence it is essential from the outset to formulate an integrated strategy incorporating the goals and methods of all players in the peace process.

Second, consultation between the multinational force and the U.N. throughout the intervention is critical to ensure a smooth transition. Consultation should take place both at headquarters and in the field, through such mechanisms as liaison officers and joint task forces.

Third, the transition to the United Nations operation should not occur until the conditions on the ground are conducive to a peacekeeping operation, where the consent and cooperation of the parties can be guaranteed. The transition date, typically, should not be established in advance but rather based on an objective assessment of the conditions on the ground. The U.N. peacekeepers cannot be expected to take over an incomplete enforcement action. In this same vein, difficult tasks that can best be performed under Chapter VII of the charter should not be deferred to the peacekeeping phase. This requires a carefully drafted mandate and the will of the multinational force to execute that mandate.

Fourth, the peacekeepers should be endowed with the mandate and resources to ensure that there is no "vacuum" in the immediate aftermath of an intervention. The parties to a conflict must understand that they have nothing to gain by biding their time until the interventionary force leaves.

Finally, the primacy of the United Nations Security Council, which authorizes coalition forces as well as United Nations operations, is essential. It is what ensure that the efforts are—and are seen to be—legitimate actions for the common good rather than parochial adventures. When this principle is upheld and the other elements cited above are taken into account, it may be possible to exploit an important area of cooperation between the U.N. and other international actors, drawing on the comparative advantage of each and, hopefully, ensuring the further development of the international community's tools for the containment of conflict and the establishment of enduring peace.

Boutros Boutros-Ghali
United Nations Secretary-General
May 2, 1996

Introduction: A Situation Report

The earnest expression on the face of the young soldier on the cover of this volume (and in the uncropped version of the photograph on page 208) is a reflection of the tender soul of peacekeeping. He probably is not more than nineteen or twenty years old himself, and there he is, in the midst of slaughter, rubber-gloved, his weapon slung over his shoulder, stepping around the gashed bodies at his feet as he tries to carry an orphaned child to safety. He has been sent to that refugee camp by his government, through the United Nations, with the best of intentions. He is doing the best he can in an appalling situation. Caught as he is in this image, our soldier is also a metaphor for the state of peacekeeping today. But then, unfortunately, so is the dead soldier being dragged through the streets of Mogadishu, in the photograph on page 180, also a reflection of what can happen to the best of intentions.

Since the end of the Cold War it is hardly possible to pick up a major newspaper and not find a report on United Nations peacekeeping. We who live in relatively stable, affluent countries sift uneasily through these reports and watch perplexedly, often moved to tears of sadness and outrage, at the images of deprivation and desolation that illustrate the evening news. We struggle to make sense of so many deteriorating situations that could undermine international security. United Nations peacekeepers—Blue Helmets, as they have come to be called—seem to be everywhere, and adding to the confusion of information about them and their disputed efficacy is a barrage of acronyms: UNIFIL, UNOSOM, UNPROFOR, etc. What, we wonder, do all those letters stand for? Are the missions they represent doing anything meaningful? (We can get an answer to at least the first question: See "A Guide to Acronyms" on page 8.)

These days we tend not to worry as much as we used to about the possibility of someone dropping a nuclear bomb on us. Instead, our attention is riveted to dozens of "little" wars—most often civil and ethnic in origin, sometimes over territory along disputed borderlines—that require international military and humanitarian intervention to keep them from igniting into larger conflagrations. In the last several years United Nations peacekeepers have been on assignment in Haiti, Costa Rica, El Salvador, Guatemala, Honduras, Nicaragua, Cyprus, Israel, southern Lebanon, the Syrian Golan Heights, Gaza, Iran, Iraq, Kuwait, Cambodia, India, Pakistan, Afghanistan, Georgia, Tajikistan, Namibia, Angola, Western Sahara, Uganda, Rwanda, Somalia, Mozambique, Liberia, Chad, Bosnia and Herzegovina, Croatia, and Macedonia. Thousands of people have been killed in ethnic and civil wars in some of these places and many more made refugees: dispossessed, wounded, starved, and diseased—and, as ever, the majority of victims are innocents.

United Nations efforts to stop the carnage are variably successful. Sometimes, as in Cambodia and Namibia, international efforts to intervene do seem to make a qualitative, lasting difference; sometimes, as in Somalia and Rwanda, they do not; and sometimes, as in the former Yugoslavia, the conduct of the mission itself as well as its outcome are open to question. We are obligated to do something about these wars and the human suffering they bring. Or are we? It is our business to intervene, to stop the senseless destruction. Or is it? We should help by sending food, medicine, relief workers, troops, matériel, and—most of all—money. Or should we? The politicians disagree; the journalists, particularly the editorialists, disagree; the peacekeepers themselves disagree; and historians, especially military historians, are slow to get into print, and if we knew what they thought, they would probably disagree, too. The politicians are accused of self-interest, self-aggrandizement; the journalists of uneven coverage or downright sensationalism; the professional peacekeepers of inept, impacted bureaucracy. With so much filtered information and so many subjective opinions to evaluate, how can we possibly come to objective conclusions about policy? We are mired in a distracted agnosticism. In too many cases, we simply do not know what is right action—what will produce the greatest good for all concerned. Furthermore, peacekeeping costs billions of dollars, and funding for it is running out. How should we proceed, if at all?

Soldiers for Peace is not intended to answer the difficult questions, more to raise them. Its contributors are several award-winning journalists who cover international affairs, three professional peacekeepers, and three military historians—often in provocative disagreement with one another. Although their essays are written from disparate points of view, they constitute, we hope, a balanced study of the state of peacekeeping, against the backdrop of historical precedent.

Five of the essays originally appeared in a special section on peacekeeping in the Autumn 1992 issue of *MHQ: The Quarterly Journal of Military History.* (Part of the mandate of *MHQ*—a hardcover magazine about world history from a military perspective—is to present an informed readership with scholarly but accessibly written examinations of historical antecedents to current military events.) Simultaneous to the publication of that issue of *MHQ*, with its special section, the peacekeeping material was expanded and bound separately in soft-cover–magazine format as *Soldiers for Peace.* Now, this second edition, published in book form by Facts on File, further updates and expands the material to include eight new articles that add background to peacekeeping and cover events since 1992. It is not encyclopedic. It is not definitive. It is a situation report on a worthy but intrinsically problematic enterprise whose importance may only increase.

Barbara Benton
Editor
May 10, 1996

A Guide to Acronyms

United Nations missions are so numerous—and their formal titles so lengthy—that for the sake of efficient communication professional peacekeepers have come to speak and write of them in a complex, confusing jargon of acronyms. The following is a quick reference for the bewildered. It includes the acronym for each mission, followed by its full, formal title; location (site of headquarters, where possible); and inclusive dates. Operations are listed as current or past, in chronological order from date of inception. See page 224 for a complete gazetteer and page 255 for a world map.

Current Peacekeeping Operations

UNTSO: United Nations Truce Supervision Organization; Jerusalem, Israel; June 1948 to present

UNMOGIP: United Nations Military Observer Group in India and Pakistan; India–Pakistan border, in state of Jammu and Kashmir; January 1949 to present

UNFICYP: United Nations Peacekeeping Force in Cyprus; Nicosia; March 1964 to present

UNDOF: United Nations Disengagement Observer Force; Syrian Golan Heights; June 1974 to present

UNIFIL: United Nations Interim Force in Lebanon; Southern Lebanon; March 1978 to present

UNIKOM: United Nations Iraq–Kuwait Observation Mission; Umm Qasr, Iraq, in demilitarized zone between Iraq and Kuawit; April 1991 to present

MINURSO: United Nations Mission for the Referendum in Western Sahara; Laayoune; April 1991 to present

UNOMIG: United Nations Observer Mission in Georgia; Sukhumi; August 1993 to present

UNOMIL: United Nations Observer Mission in Liberia; Monrovia; September 1993 to present

UNMIH: United Nations Mission in Haiti; Port-au-Prince; September 1993 to present

UNAMIR: United Nations Assistance Mission for Rwanda; Kigali; October 1993 to present

UNMOT: United Nations Mission of Observers in Tajikistan; Dushanbe; December 1994 to present

UNAVEM III: United Nations Angola Verification Mission III; Angola; February 1995 to present

UNPREDEP: United Nations Preventive Deployment Force; Skopje, the former Yugoslav Republic of Macedonia; March 1995 to present

UNMIBH: United Nations Mission in Bosnia and Herzegovina; Sarajevo; December 1995 to present

UNTAES: United Nations Transitional Administration for Eastern Slavonia, Baranja and Western Sirmium; Vukovar, Croatia; January 1996 to present

UNMOP: United Nations Mission of

Observers in Prevlaka; Prevlaka peninsula Croatia; January 1996 to present

Past Peacekeeping Operations

UNEF I: First United Nations Emergency Force; Suez Canal, Sinai peninsula, and Gaza; November 1956 to June 1967

UNOGIL: United Nations Observation Group in Lebanon; Lebanese–Syrian border; June 1958 to December 1958

ONUC: United Nations Operation in the Congo (now Zaire); Leopoldville (now Kinshasa); July 1960 to June 1964

UNSF: United Nations Security Force in West New Guinea (now West Irian); Hollandia (now Jayaphra); October 1962 to April 1963

UNYOM: United Nations Yemen Observation Mission; Sana'a; July 1963 to September 1964

DOMREP: Mission of the Representative of the Secretary-General in the Dominican Republic; Santo Domingo; May 1965 to October 1966

UNIPOM: United Nations India–Pakistan Observation Mission; border between Kashmir and the Arabian Sea; September 1965 to March 1966

UNEF II: Second United Nations Emergency Force; Suez Canal and Sinai peninsula; October 1973 to July 1979

UNGOMAP: United Nations Good Offices Mission in Afghanistan and Pakistan; Kabul and Islamabad; April 1988 to March 1990

UNIIMOG: United Nations Iran–Iraq Military Observer Group; Tehran and Baghdad; August 1988 to February 1991

UNAVEM I: United Nations Angola Verification Mission I; Luanda; January 1989 to June 1991

UNTAG: United Nations Transition Assistance Group; Namibia and Angola; April 1989 to March 1990

ONUCA: United Nations Observer Group in Central America; Costa Rica, El Salvador, Guatemala, Honduras, and Nicaragua; November 1989 to January 1992

UNAVEM II: United Nations Angola Verification Mission II; Luanda; June 1991 to February 1995

ONUSAL: United Nations Observer Mission in El Salvador; San Salvador; July 1991 to April 1995

UNAMIC: United Nations Advance Mission in Cambodia; Phnom Penh; October 1991 to March 1992

UNPROFOR: United Nations Protection Force; Bosnia and Herzegovina, Croatia, the Federal Republic of Yugoslavia (Serbia and Montenegro), and the former Yugoslav Republic of Macedonia; March 1992 to December 1995

UNTAC: United Nations Transitional Authority in Cambodia; Phnom Penh; March 1992 to September 1993

UNOSOM I: United Nations Operation in Somalia I; Mogadishu; April 1992 to April 1993

ONUMOZ: United Nations Operation in Mozambique; Maputo; December 1992 to December 1994

UNOSOM II: United Nations Operation in Somalia II; Mogadishu; May 1993 to March 1995

UNOMUR: United Nations Observer Mission Uganda–Rwanda; Kabale, Uganda, on Uganda–Rwanda border; June 1993 to September 1994

UNASOG: United Nations Aouzou Strip Observer Group; Aouzou Strip, Republic of Chad; May 1994 to June 1994

UNCRO: United Nations Confidence Restoration Operation in Croatia; Zagreb; March 1995 to January 1996

French troops intervene in Upper Silesia, May 22, 1921. A year later, the League of Nations successfully mediated a compromise between Poland and Germany, dividing the wealth of the region.

The "Prehistory" of Peacekeeping

by Thomas F. Arnold & Heather R. Ruland

International military cooperation to promote and even enforce peace is older than the United Nations. The "prehistory" of peacekeeping stretches back to anti-noble peasant militias of the middle ages, and includes the nineteenth-century effort to suppress piracy and the slave trade on the high seas. In our own century, in the decade following World War I, the League of Nations pioneered both the military form and political function of modern peacekeeping.

After fifty years of experiment, promise, and disappointment, today's United Nations peacekeepers are—perhaps—on the verge of at last embodying the significant independent military role granted the Security Council by the United Nations Charter of 1945. This potential revolution in military affairs begs a question: What is the historical background to U.N. peacekeeping, beyond the past fifty years' experience? In fact, what can be called a "prehistory" of peacekeeping exists in at least two areas. First, the entire U.N. idea, including international military cooperation very like what we now call peacekeeping, can be traced surprisingly far back, even as far as the middle ages. Second, the U.N. predecessor, the ill-starred League of Nations, born of hope and fear at the end of World War I, inaugurated twentieth-century peacekeeping in both theory and practice, if not in name.

The lessons of this prehistory, like almost all aspects of peacekeeping, past and present, are ambiguous. On the one hand, the compelling idea of the great powers abandoning their petty antagonisms and small-minded conflicts to act in concert, in the name of the world, to enact a vision of peace has attracted optimistic Western intellectuals for centuries. And, when one of those intellectuals—namely Woodrow Wilson of Princeton—achieved both power and opportunity, that vision could be made concrete: the League of Nations. On the other hand, peacekeeping operations seem naturally fraught with a host of frustrating difficulties, from the diplomatic to

11

the practical, making it easy to draw pessimistic parallels between league and U.N. experiences. Also, though peacekeeping in the name of world security may appear to be an unambiguous goal, with hindsight past projects (such as various Christian crusading schemes against the Turks) suggest that a just world peace may not be an absolute. While the triumph of Christendom is no longer the goal of the globe's most powerful nations (at least, not from the perspective of the West—many in the Muslim world doubtless suspect otherwise), defining what constitutes a genuinely equitable peace—a necessary precondition to enforcing that peace—remains a core problem confronting all modern peacekeeping operations. The prehistory of peacekeeping warns us that all too often the best of intentions are not enough, and what once seemed the acme of progressive, responsible international military cooperation (like the international force that suppressed the Chinese Boxer rebellion in 1900) today appears a blatant example of national and cultural aggression.

How old is the idea of peacekeeping? Over-enthusiastic historians have traced the U.N. ideal back as far as the fifth-century B.C. Delian League, an alliance of Greek states under Athenian leadership dedicated to evicting the Persian king from the Aegean. But the Delian League was an exclusively Greek association deliberately antagonistic to the Persian "barbarians," and it quickly passed from a mutual defense pact to an Athenian imperial racket as oppressive as any Persian overlordship. Other early examples of interstate associations similarly reveal themselves, on closer examination, to be standard alliances of no great ethical purpose or dedication to peace.

Probably the first powerful supranational institution to attempt to define and even enforce anything like a universal peace was—in its better moments—the medieval Catholic church. Through the Peace of God and Truce of God, first preached in the late tenth century, the church tried to limit the feudal nobility's insatiable appetite for war by specifying given days (from dusk on Wednesday to dawn on Monday) and certain holy places (churches and cemeteries) off-limits. To enforce these radical ideas, churchmen could threaten recalcitrant nobles with anathema and excommunication. As well as being spiritually devastating, such declarations cut the formal bonds tying lord to vassal, allowing—even encouraging—a noble lord's feudal underlings to rebel. Cooperative nobles often swore their compliance over the bones or other relic of a saint. This was no light pledge, but a formal, sacred vow. Though not as transforming as the preachers had hoped, the peace and truce edicts were not entirely without success, and in France some villages seem to have formed around the protection offered by the sanctuary of church and churchyard.

The attempt to control feudal violence sometimes brought the church into military confrontation with nobles. In 1038 the French bishop of Bourges formed a militia, the so-called "Peace League of Bourges," made up of armed and righteous peasants sworn to defend the Peace of God. These militia members might even be considered the first peacekeepers, as they seem to have had no political agenda beyond preventing the endemic low-level warfare that convulsed their countryside. At first the Bourges peace league successfully cowed the local baronry, but, perhaps inevitably, in an open battle the trained knights of a powerful local warlord massacred the peasant militiamen, ending the movement. Besides the Peace of God and Truce of God, the medieval church also experimented with arms control, banning crossbows in wars between Christians at the Second Lateran Council of 1139. Selling arms to the infidel would later be one of those grave sins (burning churches was another) that needed absolution directly from Rome. Naturally, despite these theoretical legal obstacles, weapons did cross the boundaries of Christendom and, of course, this traffic went both ways: The West coveted Damascus steel for sword blades, and the trebuchet, the most powerful and sophisticated medieval siege catapult, was originally an Arab invention.

The well-intentioned peace initiatives of the medieval church were not entirely pacific. A major goal was to redirect Christian knights toward crusades against the infidel. Though the church did succeed in exporting many of Christian Europe's most violently ambitious nobles to the Holy Land and the other religious frontiers (Spain and the Baltic), their exodus little dulled the stay-at-home's appetite for war. Whatever its effect on warfare within Europe, the idea of the crusade remained for centuries the Christian ideal of principled military cooperation—even past the middle ages (many twentieth-century recruiting posters and television advertisements have featured a knight in shining armor). In 1453, at the very end of the medieval era, the Turkish seizure of Constantinople inspired various schemes for a pan-European Christian alliance. From the late fifteenth century a succession of holy leagues pledged united action against the Turk, though most never actually got around to launching a crusade—there being so many nearer, Christian foes to deal with first. An exception was the alliance of Spain, Venice, and the Pope that smashed the Turkish fleet at the epic galley battle of Lepanto in 1571. This victory fell short of making the Mediterranean a Christian lake, but for generations its success remained, for Europeans, the model of military collaboration.

Not all Europeans found Lepanto edifying. In 1623 a young Frenchman, Emeric Crucé, published an appeal for peace and cooperation that, quite

The league was the dream of President Woodrow Wilson. But he could not convince the American congress or public of its value, and the U.S. did not join.

exceptionally for the time, embraced the non-European as well as Christian worlds. Crucé proposed that all the world's princes, including the Indian, Chinese, West Indian, Ethiopian, and Turkish monarchs, be content with their existing territories, and that international disputes be mediated by representatives at a world council held at a central, neutral site. He suggested Venice. Though the trip from China would undoubtedly be a long one, Crucé pointed out that the arts of navigation were always improving, and that a goal as great as world peace was worth the effort. If any prince played the renegade and defied world opinion (as expressed by majority vote in the council) coercive action could be taken, though Crucé piously believed such situations would be few. Individual men who preferred war to peace would be exiled as savages to live with cannibal tribesmen. The whole treatise is breathtakingly modern, not only for its universality and respect for democratic process, but for its insistence that increased world trade would bring interdependence and thus reduce the appeal of war. Crucé's polemic was the first in a long line of proposals finding the key to "perpetual peace" (the eighteenth-century Enlightenment formula) in the establishment of permanent international representative bodies.

From the seventeenth to the nineteenth centuries these proposals proliferated, growing in number and gaining in confidence—and at the same time becoming, in general, more avowedly moral and less pragmatic. This trend culminated in pacifist tracts such as the American William Ladd's 1840 proposal for a congress of nations and an international court entirely actuated by moral suasion. For the treatise writers, the problem of making and enforcing peace was less satisfying than the speculative project of devising a perfect world harmony.

While the theorists theorized, hard-nosed European diplomats created a parallel tradition of practical cooperation. The great peace treaty congresses of early modern Europe—Westphalia, 1648; Utrecht, 1713; Paris, 1763—gave the European states experience and faith in the power of negotiated settlement as the foundation of international law. After the final collapse of Napoleon in 1815 the remaining European powers—Great Britain, Austria, Prussia, Russia, and a restored monarchical France—established a formal system, the Concert of Europe, for the management of European affairs via international conferences. Though this system amounted to a heavy-handed territorial division of Europe (with each power free to impose its will within its own sphere), it also allowed international military collaboration to keep the larger peace. However, these European powers' collective values were not unconnected with the ideals of the pre-Enlightenment past, including a certain dose of Christian triumphalism.

In 1827 France, Great Britain, and Russia banded together and demanded that Turkey grant an armistice in the ongoing Greek Christian revolt. From the Turkish perspective, this was unacceptable meddling in an internal affair; from the European perspective, it was a question of what today would be called "human rights." When the sultan refused to grant the stipulated armistice, an allied naval force cornered and destroyed a Turkish fleet in the bay of Navarino in the Peloponnese. The encounter was a virtual replay of Lepanto, in sentiment as well as in geographic location, and though professedly an ethical intervention, from the Turkish point of view the allied fleet had in fact enforced a European, Christian vision of peace.

Though the Concert of Europe system eventually lapsed in the face of national interest, the nineteenth-century powers continued to cooperate militarily in certain areas—especially those that involved little compromise or sacrifice by Europeans. Besides settling the fate of post-Napoleonic Europe, the 1815 Vienna peace-makers had agreed to abolish the international slave trade. Four years later a flotilla of British and French ships made port calls at Algiers, Tripoli, and Tunis—the principal lairs of the infamous Barbary pirates—to make the new policy clear. The European and the U.S. navies, with the British Royal Navy leading the way, eventually kept squadrons off the West African coast to intercept "blackbirders" illegally

15

transporting slaves to the Americas. The slavers rakish vessels were small, swift, and well-armed, purpose-built both to evade naval scrutiny and to get their valuable living cargo to market as quickly as possible: The notorious, grim mortality of the "middle passage" was, from the slaver's point of view, more a threat to profits than a wastage of human lives.

From the 1860s, with the Atlantic trade well suppressed, attention shifted to the Arab slavers of the Indian Ocean. Anti-slavery work was intermittent, but like the related task of piracy suppression, it did require unanimity of purpose and international cooperation at the level of consuls and ship captains. It certainly assumed a shared, international—and European— vision of peace. Perhaps tellingly, one area of Western moral concern and world policing today, the drug trade, occasioned no great call for action in the nineteenth century. To the contrary, after the British used force to preserve access to the huge Chinese market in the 1840–42 Opium War, British merchants made handsome profits, paid in silver bullion, shipping chests of the narcotic to the addicts of China.

In the second half of the nineteenth century, while other areas of European colonial ambition—notably Africa—smoldered with confrontations between the imperial powers, international agreements peacefully (from the European perspective) divided China into "spheres of influence." Maintaining those spheres of influence required collaboration. International military expeditions in 1860 and 1870 ensured that treaties between the colonial powers and the faltering Chinese imperial court reflected a Western interpretation of China's best interests. When in 1900 the Boxers (an anti-colonial secret society, its members known as "Boxers" for their martial arts exercises) rebelled against the increasingly powerful foreign presence in China, the great-power response remained collegial. The "international relief force" that marched to lift the Boxers' siege of the embattled foreign diplomatic community in Peking was an impressive act of great-power collective action. An American marine eyewitness described the force's colorful ranks: "French Zouaves in red and blue, blond Germans in pointed helmets, Italian Bersaglieri with tossing plumes, Bengal cavalry on Arabian stallions, turbaned Sikhs, Japanese, Russians, and English." This polyglot, multinational host's line of march was that of the Anglo–French expedition of 1860. The world powers had trod this route before, literally as well as figuratively. Though many today would consider the relief force a shameless instrument of exploitative imperialism, at the turn of the century most in the Western world cheered it on as a shining example of principled international action in the face of unacceptable barbarities. Had the expression existed, the Western press might well have labeled the expedition to relieve

The league assembly (above, at its opening session in Geneva, November 1920) pioneered peacekeeping, but was never able to create an effective international force.

Peking a "peacekeeping force."

The horror and destruction of World War I (1914–18) shattered any confidence in the existing international system. It also hinted that barbarism was not a monopoly of the less-civilized non-European peoples. Morally as well as materially shaken by this wartime experience, the victorious Allied powers (France, Great Britain, and the United States) resolved, at the Paris peace talks following the war, to create a permanent international diplomatic association to ensure European and world peace. This association, the League of Nations, was the dream of President Woodrow Wilson, viewed by many in a devastated Europe as their "deliverer" and even their "god of peace." Inspired and emboldened by his own idealism, Wilson imagined the league as "a living thing" almost mystically guaranteeing future amity and cooperation, and his equally idealistic supporters imagined that Wilson stood upon "an unprecedented pinnacle of splendour." However, Wilson's more pessimistic—and perhaps more war-hardened— British and French diplomatic colleagues distrusted the American president's motives and resented what they called his "intellectual and moral arrogance." From its conception, then, there were those who saw the League of Nations as a suspect enterprise.

Even pessimists, however, embraced the league as a vehicle for their own political goals. At the Paris talks, French representatives, concerned that Germany might rise again to wage a war of revenge, presented plans for an international force, under League of Nations auspices, to execute military sanctions against aggressor nations and generally enforce league decisions. American and British objections to this international force meant that the league, as defined by its constitutional covenant, had only economic sanctions and "reason and good will" at its disposal to keep the peace. Despite this compromise, President Wilson, gravely ill after suffering a paralytic stroke, was unable to convince the Senate or the American public that the league would maintain the security that the Allies had fought so hard to win. Therefore, even though the league was the pet project of the American president, the United States did not join the organization, and this refusal was a "body blow" from which the league never fully recovered.

America's absence forced league members to keep one eye on Washington at all times in an attempt to guess Washington's reaction to league decisions. Without an international armed force at its disposal, and without American membership, the league nevertheless boldly acted to bolster the post-war peace. In so doing, the league found itself policing local disputes, supervising plebiscites, and imposing economic sanctions. Some of these actions necessitated the introduction of small bodies of disinterested, nonaggressive military personnel—in character and purpose exactly what are today thought of as peacekeeping forces. Here, as in many other areas, the league pioneered the practices later developed by its post–World War II successor, the United Nations.

Despite its difficult birth, the infant league sailed through its first challenges with apparent ease. First on the agenda was Upper Silesia. When Germany objected to the cession of Upper Silesia to Poland, France supported Poland's claims in hopes of securing a valuable ally, while Britain and Italy favored Germany. In truth, both Poland and Germany had cause to claim the region: The workers were mainly of Polish descent, while the middle class (the "capital, brains, and energy," according to the London *Times*) were German. The Allies decided that a plebiscite should decide the matter, and in March 1921 British and Italian troops occupied the region to ensure the vote took place without incident. These troops set the precedent for later league plebiscite-monitoring peacekeepers. As it turned out, the polling results in Upper Silesia were a clear victory for union with Germany, but the Allies decided that, due to a significant minority vote, parts of the main industrial triangle would be awarded to Poland after all.

The German government reacted with outrage, as in the months leading up to the vote both German officials and the German people had come to see any loss of Upper Silesian territory as "a tyrannical violation of the laws of both God and man." In August 1921, still unable to draw the German–Polish frontier through Upper Silesia, the Allies passed the whole business to the League of Nations—a move that reduced journalists in Geneva to incredulous fits of laughter. No one expected the league to find a solution to this thorny problem. Nine months later, in May 1922, the league passed the fifteen-year Geneva Convention on Upper Silesia. This granted much of the area's mineral wealth and industrial properties to Poland, but promised the promotion of economic unity across the political frontier. The compromise decision prompted the London *Times* to predict that such independent and successful action would tremendously increase league prestige.

A second league success came in the aftermath of the Greco–Bulgarian incident of 1925, the first time two league members actually came to blows. After Greek troops mounted an incursion into a virtually demilitarized Bulgaria, the league instantly demanded that both powers cease fighting. In December the council commission, which consisted of military officers from Britain, France, and Italy, reported that the Bulgarians had murdered a Greek officer despite his waving a white flag; in response, the Greeks "[took] the law into [their] own hands" and invaded Bulgaria, destroying villages and killing both soldiers and civilians. As a settlement, the league ordered Greece to pay an indemnity to Bulgaria, less an amount estimated for the death of the Greek officer. The disputing parties also accepted a league plan to place two neutral officers of the same (third-party) nationality in the area to promote Greco–Bulgarian cooperation, and also to reorganize the frontier guard system. The league had successfully defused a minor but potentially explosive situation.

The supervision of plebiscites in disputed territories remained the organization's most common collective-security function well into the 1930s. Upon the conclusion of the war, both France and Germany had claimed the iron- and coal-rich Saar, the mines of which had been granted to France in compensation for the German destruction of coal mines in northern France during the war. In the pre-league era, it is likely that no nation would have bothered to raise serious objection to French absorption of the territory; however, with the league a potential arbiter, outright French occupation would have provided Germany with "a glaring grievance" easily exploited at league headquarters in Geneva. To avoid such temptations and confrontations, and rather than granting the area outright to either France or Germany, the league instead imposed a temporary government under a five-man council commission to serve for fifteen years. Although the

German residents of Oppelyn, Silesia, greet British cavalry, June 1921, en route to help suppress fighting between German volunteers and Polish insurgents in Upper Silesia.

Saarlanders resented what they considered "second-class" citizenship under this commission, "the territory enjoyed efficient and, for the most part, trouble-free rule during those fifteen years." When the commission expired, a plebiscite was scheduled for January 1935 to determine by popular vote whether the region should return to Germany, become French, or remain a league protectorate. As the polling day approached, pro-German and Nazi propaganda proliferated, and fluttering Swastika flags and German imperial colors decorated the region. To supervise the voting, the league recruited an international force of approximately 3,300 men, including 1,500 British, 1,300 Italians, 250 Swedish, and 250 Dutchmen. Flags, alcohol sales, and fly-overs by aircraft without permits were prohibited. Because the region was very small, the London *Times* concluded that "warlike complications" would be unlikely, with the exception of "political rowdies." The league force patrolled the region for ten weeks throughout the vote, in which ninety percent of the three-quarters of a million Saarlanders voted in favor of reunion with Germany. The soldiers never had to resort to the use of arms.

Another post-war territorial dispute centered on Vilna, today Vilnius. The contending parties were the newly independent Lithuania, which claimed the city as its capital, and a resurrected Poland, to which the majority of the area's inhabitants owed their allegiance. After an early tug of war that even brought in the Red Army, the league intervened in the summer of 1919. The council followed its standard procedure, determining a line of demarcation and preparing to dispatch a military commission to maintain peace until the arrangement of a plebiscite; however, before the agreement could go into effect, the Polish claimants took matters into their own hands. Supposedly acting without official approval, a Polish commander, a General Zeligowski, crossed the line of demarcation and occupied Vilna "almost without firing a shot." Despite this alarming development, the league continued to make provisions for a popular vote, including the commitment of a 1,500-man international force. The Polish government, which eventually admitted prior knowledge of Zeligowski's actions, flouted league authority by refusing to order the general to remove his troops (a league condition for a plebiscite), instead arguing that withdrawal would place Vilna in the hands of the Bolsheviks.

Over time, the Poles eventually came to see the "popular consultation" of a plebiscite as the best way of maintaining control of Poland's "rightful territory." Lithuania, on the other hand, argued that a plebiscite, given the prolonged Polish occupation of the region, would only grant an unfair advantage to the Poles. When the Soviet Union announced that the presence of any international force in Vilna would be considered "an unfriendly act," the league eventually abandoned its plans for an international force to monitor a plebiscite. A virtual state of war between Poland and Lithuania lasted until December 1927, long after Poland's occupation of Vilna was approved by a popular vote, a decision by the Conference of Ambassadors, and league concurrence. While the Vilna crisis did not lead to an actual war, the episode did not bode well for the League of Nations. Its critics contended that the league's actions were consistently too slow, and they complained that Poland had received inadequate disciplinary action for her illegal occupation. Nevertheless, it is very likely that Poland and Lithuania would have gone to war had the league not intervened in some form.

None of the league's interventions of the 1930s resulted in the creation of an international force or similar peacekeeping body. Rather, league influence and importance steadily weakened during the decade. After a league commission of inquiry reported that Japan's 1931 attack on Chinese garrisons near the south Manchurian railway zone was a blatant act of aggression, not self-defense, the Japanese delegation left Geneva and never returned. Mussolini's attack on a poorly armed Ethiopia in 1935 did result in league-imposed sanctions; however, these toothless sanctions left Italy's vital petroleum imports untouched. They therefore failed to bring

Mussolini to heel. After Haile Selassie, the Ethiopian emperor, fled his capital and Italy declared its sovereignty over the region, the league quickly voted to lift the sanctions: Fascist Italy had painlessly survived, even snubbed, the worst the league could do. For Haile Selassie, trust in the league amounted to the sacrifice of Ethiopian independence on the "altar of the Covenant." As a final example of league failure in the 1930s, in late summer 1936 the French government proposed a formal international agreement obligating parties not to intervene in the Spanish Civil War (1936–39), then just beginning. Although twenty-seven European countries eventually agreed to participate in the nonintervention agreement, there were gross violations by the supporters of both sides, with entire divisions of the Italian regular army assisting General Franco's Nationalists and over 40,000 men serving in the International Brigades on the Republican side. While many countries were members of both the nonintervention committee and the league, the latter remained officially aloof from this European dispute. Failure to play a role or take a stand further suggested the league's growing irrelevance.

By the last years of the decade, the role of the League of Nations as guardian of the peace was diminishing, and in 1937 many assembly delegates announced that their nations no longer considered themselves bound by the league's covenant pledging members to honor a collective league response to aggression. China's representative, Dr. Wellington Koo, criticized this attitude, insisting that "[o]ne [did] not amputate one's hand merely because it [was] not always used when needed." In the opinion of outspoken Soviet delegate Maxim Litvinov, league members ironically desired to abandon "collective methods of combatting aggression" only now that aggression had become a reality. He compared their actions to a community that formed a fire brigade "in the innocent hope that, by some lucky chance, there would be no fires." Now, however, fires had broken out, and the community wanted to disband the brigade—not forever, but just until the danger of fire had disappeared.

In summary, international peacekeeping forces did help the league contain and control a few small-scale crises in the first post–World War I decade, and therefore perhaps helped the league delay a general European war, but the league clearly proved itself incapable of addressing the international crises of the next decade, the 1930s. Realistically, the league's modest peacekeeping experience, like the league in general, could not be adapted to confront the more serious crises of the second interwar decade. The league possessed neither the resources, nor the statute authority, nor the collective will of its membership to face events like the Italian invasion of Ethiopia or the Spanish Civil War. As a result, the League of Nations, as a concept as much as a structure for diplomatic activity, practically collapsed.

The league was perhaps doomed from the start to being judged by the idealism and lofty goals of its founding spirit; an idealism that was not matched by its own member nations' commitment. Major states preferred traditional "diplomatic exchanges" and "hasty political conferences" to an open forum for discussion, and smaller powers followed suit in the belief that the submission of disputes for international arbitration was undignified. The league's existence was not, however, in vain, because in many cases its experienced and competent personnel carried over after World War II to propel the U.N. to a flying start. After that second world war, the surviving and victorious powers—as in 1815, as in 1919—dedicated themselves to the project of collective security. Though discredited by the events of the 1930s, the promise of the league concept had not been forgotten: The U.N. therefore arose, phoenix-like, from the ashes of the league. Peacekeeping, a striking feature of the league's few successes in the 1920s, subsequently became a standard policy of the its successor.

Thomas F. Arnold is an assistant professor of history at Yale University. He is the author of The Geometry of Power, *an analysis of the influence of geometry on the theory and practice of early modern warfare (to be published by Harvard University Press).* **Heather R. Ruland** *is Director of the United Nations History Project and a lecturer in history at Yale University.*

A flak-jacketed British soldier with UNPROFOR guards surrendered Bosnian weapons, mainly large mortars, at Tito Barracks, U.N. headquarters on the outskirts of Sarajevo, February 1994.

A Short History of United Nations Peacekeeping

by Paul Lewis

For nearly five decades, the Blue Helmets have carved out an impressive, and often overlooked, role for themselves monitoring cease-fire agreements, disarming irregulars, and preserving order in troubled lands. As U.N. operations become more and more "hybridized" with the end of the Cold War, their importance to world security may only increase—if the money doesn't run out.

IFOR. Those big black letters, an acronym for Implementation Force, painted on the sides of heavily camouflaged armored vehicles prowling through the Bosnian snows, symbolized the recent sudden turn for the worse in the United Nations' fortunes as a peacekeeper. No white armored cars with a big black U.N. on the side. No blue berets. No blue steel helmets. No blue flak jackets. Instead, everywhere the dark khaki camouflage of NATO's carefully oiled war-machine, carrying out its first real military operation since the alliance was created to defend Western democracy after World War II. When after years of bickering President Bill Clinton and his European counterparts finally agreed on a peace plan for ending the war in the former Yugoslavia (and forced it down the gullets of the protagonists at the Dayton air-base talks), they also agreed that an international military force should be sent to make sure the parties kept to the deal they had signed.

But there was no disposition to entrust that task to the United Nations Protection Force (UNPROFOR), the 30,000-strong U.N. peacekeeping mission that had been trying to hold the ring in Bosnia and Croatia since the early days of the former Yugoslavia's bloody disintegration. This had been the biggest and most ambitious of the "second generation" peacekeeping operations that the U.N. had undertaken in the late 1980s and early 1990s, and that had brought a spectacular explosion in the size, cost, and complexity of these missions.

In 1988 there were five peacekeeping operations costing $230 million a

An Irish UNIFIL soldier, above, serving in southern Lebanon, does look-out duty at a check-post close to headquarters at Tibnin, May–June 1980. Below, members of a Swedish infantry battalion attached to UNFICYP participate in a military exercise along the coast near Larnaca, Cyprus. Among them are the first women to join the force, autumn 1979.

year monitoring trouble spots like Lebanon and Cyprus. In 1995, there were seventeen operations under way, employing at their peak some 80,000 soldiers, police, and civilian administrators at an annual cost of $3.5 billion. U.N. forces were deployed all over the globe in war-ravaged countries ranging from the Far East to Africa to Central America, and increasingly involved in such complex "peacemaking" tasks as disarming rebels and organizing elections. Many of them were successful. Namibia moved peacefully out of South Africa's grip to become an independent nation. Civil wars were extinguished in El Salvador, Mozambique, and Cambodia, and new governments were freely and fairly elected.

But now the shine is coming off peacekeeping. The "can-do" optimism of the U.N.'s big post–Cold War push into second-generation peacekeeping is fading fast under the impact of perceived failures in Bosnia, Somalia, and Rwanda. And the growing unwillingness of countries to pay their U.N. dues has left the organization close to bankruptcy. Today's world leaders have little appetite for new and costly U.N. initiatives. As the *New York Times* editorialized, "Rethinking and retrenchment are in order . . . . There should be a shift back towards more limited objectives like policing ceasefires. U.N. peacekeeping does what it can do very well. It makes no sense to continue eroding its credibility by asking it to do what it cannot."

UNPROFOR was not up to the task of enforcing the fragile Dayton peace agreement on bitterly divided factions armed with modern weapons. For four years it helped get relief supplies through to suffering people, looked after refugees, and provided some slight break in the war-mongering instincts of Serbs, Muslims, and Croats.

What it had never been able to do, however, was enforce discipline on those unwilling to accept it. Its troops were too lightly armed, its command structure too rickety and riven with conflicts and jealousy. And American efforts to strengthen its muscle through the addition of NATO air power only robbed the force of its impartiality in the eyes of the Serbs, and exposed UNPROFOR forces on the ground to reprisals. The result was a long string of humiliations. Peacekeepers were pushed aside and taken hostage as Serbs overran the "safe areas" the Security Council had declared in Srebrenica and Zepa. Croat forces seized the so-called "protected areas" in the Serbian- inhabited Krajina area of southern Croatia. Aid agencies saw their relief convoys blocked by the warring parties while U.N. soldiers helplessly stood by. For three years the U.N. was powerless to stop the murderous bombardment of Sarajevo. And all the time the world was watching this shame on television. As General Rupert Smith, a British commander in Sarajevo, once put it, "You don't fight wars in white-armored cars."

So with the U.S. planning to provide a third of the 60,000 troops needed to impose the Dayton accords and American public opinion in no mood to see its forces sent on so dangerous a mission under inexperienced, ineffective U.N. command, the Security Council "contracted out" the task to NATO's war-machine, just as it had contracted out the task of liberating Kuwait from Saddam Hussein's brutal grip to the Bush administration and its Desert Storm allies. U.N. Secretary-General Boutros Boutros-Ghali accepted this with as good grace as possible, admitting that his organization lacked both the strength to impose a peace settlement on the former Yugoslavia's politicians and the military resolve to enforce it. "In Bosnia the United Nations was sent as peacekeepers into an ongoing wartime situation. This had never been done before," he said in a speech late in 1995. "In war situations, the international community should authorize the combat forces needed to deal with it. Where a cease-fire is in place and where the consent and cooperation of the parties is reliable, peacekeepers should be deployed."

But Bosnia is not the only setback U.N. peacekeeping has suffered of late. No less humiliating was the unsuccessful attempt to bring law and order to Somalia and avert tribal massacres in Rwanda, both searing experiences that sharply dented the organization's self-confidence and the willingness of members to entrust it with new missions. While the worst of the starvation has been eliminated in Somalia and harrowing pictures of hungry children no longer flicker across Western television screens, neither the U.N. nor the powerful humanitarian force the U.S. sent in (first under separate American command) was able to end the anarchy and chaos.

The downing of two U.S. helicopters on October 3, 1993, and the loss of eighteen American lives in subsequent fighting, culminating with the half-naked body of an American soldier being dragged through the streets of Mogadishu, sealed the fate of that American intervention. Within six months U.S. forces were gone and the dream of "peace-building" had faded. Eventually, the U.N. packed its bags, too, blaming "lack of tangible progress in national political reconciliation for which the responsibility must be borne by the Somali leaders and people."

The bloody nose America suffered in Mogadishu that October 3 was to have far-reaching consequences. As genocide broke out in Rwanda, the Security Council bickered for eight months before sending even a modest force to the capital of Kigali, although the killing was nationwide. "We could have saved hundreds of thousands of lives," said Canadian Major-General Romeo Dallaire, the force commander who had pleaded for far more troops than he was ever given. Meanwhile, the Clinton administra-

A detachment of Pakistani peacekeepers assigned to UNTEA disembarks from an American air transport in West New Guinea (now West Irian), September 1962.

tion, which had come to office espousing "assertive multi-lateralism," changed tack and set tough new criteria for U.S. participation in and support for new peacekeeping operations.

Finally, as it regularly does at the U.N., the money ran out. At the end of 1995, members' accumulated debts to the U.N. reached $2.3 billion, equal to roughly half that year's due contributions to the regular and peacekeeping budgets combined. Of that figure the U.S. owed more than $1.2 billion. The U.N. met its payroll in 1996 only by spending money that should have been reimbursed to member states for peacekeeping expenses.

The U.N. still runs peacekeeping missions all over the world, showing the continued utility of the concept to the international community. But the total number of peacekeepers is down and will fall further as operations are reduced. As Secretary-General Boutros Boutros-Ghali has warned, "The number of U.N. operations, the scale of the operations and the money spent on operations cannot keep growing indefinitely. The limits are being reached." And Shashi Tharoor, special assistant to the under-secretary-general for peacekeeping, wrote in the Winter 1995–96 issue of *Survival*, the journal of the International Institute for Strategic Studies in London, "It is clear it will be a long time before the Security Council again authorizes one of the hybrid operations whose ever-mounting scope spiraled seemingly out of control in a flurry of Council resolutions in 1992 and 1993."

An Uruguayan observer with UNMOGIP, on his way to investigate an incident, steps out of his jeep to ask passersby for directions to the cease-fire line, Kashmir, 1955.

Peacekeeping is found nowhere in the U.N. Charter. Its invention is credited to the former Canadian prime minister Lester Pearson and Secretary-General Dag Hammarskjöld. The latter jokingly called it "Chapter Six and a Half," meaning that it fell between Chapter VI of the charter, which calls for the peaceful resolution of disputes, and Chapter VII, which empowers the Security Council to reverse aggression by calling on the armed forces of member states—as it did to drive North Korea out of South Korea in 1950 and Iraq out of Kuwait in 1991. But while the U.N. founding fathers concentrated on creating a mechanism that would enable them to put their armed forces at the disposition of the Security Council to enforce peace, Cold War rivalries quickly ensured that this plan for a team of "world policemen," as Franklin D. Roosevelt called them, would be stillborn. Nevertheless, the U.N. was quickly drawn into a series of small disputes that laid the basis for peacekeeping, despite frequent criticism from the Soviet Union, which felt these operations favored the West by helping resolve conflicts it might otherwise have exploited.

In 1947, the United Nations sent military officers to investigate communist infiltration of Greece from the neighboring Balkans. But Soviet suspicions forced the U.S. to get authorization not from the Security Council, where Moscow had a veto, but from the General Assembly, which in those early days was dominated by America's allies. A similar maneuver was needed to authorize the Korean War. And throughout the Cold War, successive secretaries-general entrusted peacekeeping operations first to an American, Ralph Bunche, and then to two senior British officials, Brian Urquhart and Marrack Goulding, keeping the Soviet Union at arm's length. Also in 1947, the United Nations created a good-offices committee assisted by military observers to end fighting after Indonesia tried to claim independence from the Netherlands.

The largest of these early U.N. observer missions—and the first true peacekeeping mission under the control of the secretary-general—was the United Nations Truce Supervision Organization (UNTSO), which oversaw the truce that followed the end of the first Arab–Israeli war in 1948 and established the U.N. in the business of monitoring cease-fires. The Suez crisis of 1956 saw the opening of a new, more assertive phase of U.N. peacekeeping, with the mounting of major operations in the Middle East, the Congo, and Cyprus. What had started with small, unarmed observer missions was now evolving into much larger operations involving thousands of men to serve as buffers between contending forces, patrol boarders, maintain law and order, and manage day-to-day developments.

By the fall of 1956, it was clear that the U.N. efforts to maintain the armistice between Israel and its Arab neighbors were collapsing. Violence flared along Israel's borders with Egypt, Syria, and Jordan. In July, Egypt had nationalized the Suez Canal, after the West canceled financing for the Aswan High Dam. On October 29, following a number of armed clashes, Israel invaded Egypt through the Sinai with the avowed intention of cleaning out Palestinian guerrilla bases. Two days later, working to a prearranged plan, Britain and France started bombing Egyptian airfields after demanding that Egypt and Israel withdraw ten miles from their respective sides of the canal so that an invasion force could take back control of it.

But this force was still five days' sailing from Suez, giving opponents of their scheme time to organize a massive campaign of diplomatic resistance. The idea of sending in a U.N. force had been raised by then Secretary-General Dag Hammarskjöld, at the very start of the crisis. And by November 3, as the strength of the opposition to their action became clear, even Britain and France were suggesting that their forces should join such a U.N. operation when they reached the canal.

Seventeen years later U.N. peacekeepers were to pull the world back from a nuclear confrontation between the superpowers in this very same region. But this time the U.N. job was to provide a face-saving cover behind which Britain, France, and Israel could retreat from the Suez fiasco. On November 4, the General Assembly formally asked Hammarskjöld to negotiate a cease-fire and explore the novel idea of deploying a nonviolent U.N. military force not just to monitor a cease-fire but to ensure the withdrawal of the invading British, French, and Israeli forces and preserve peace. For the West, this would remove any pretext for a rumored Soviet incursion into the region.

Speed and improvisation were needed. Curious problems arose that required imaginative solutions. With three foreign armies fighting on Egyptian soil, the U.N. troops needed clear identification, particularly as the peacekeeping contingent Canada offered would be wearing British battle dress. Berets of the same light shade of blue as the U.N. flag was the agreed solution—until it was discovered that these would take months to manufacture. So the United States quickly spray-painted thousands of army helmet liners the right shade of blue and shipped them to Suez. The "Blue Helmet," or "Casque Bleu," was born.

With no logistical pipeline to the area, the United Nations solved its supply problems by buying food and equipment on ships blocked in the canal by the fighting. This first 6,000-strong United Nations Emergency Force (UNEF I) maintained a buffer zone in the Gaza strip and Sinai between the Egyptian and Israeli forces. But in what was later to seem a costly mistake, Israel confined deployment to Egyptian soil and did not allow the Blue Helmets into territory it controlled.

Its size and complexity, as well as the speed with which it went in, made

Austrians with UNDOF, on the Golan Heights, Syria, December 1975, use skis to patrol the buffer zone, which ran from Mt. Hermon in the north to the Jordanian border in the south.

At left, a relief convoy, escorted by UNDOF, delivers water to the villagers of Hadar, Syria, 1974. Below, U.N. observers (carrying a white flag) and Palestinians make their way toward the Jordan/Israel border, 1954, to investigate a complaint. The U.N. vehicle above was flattened in the 1969 shelling of Israeli-occupied Sinai.

UNEF I the model for several subsequent operations. And its success—it kept the peace in the area for ten years and guaranteed freedom of movement through the Suez Canal—encouraged Hammarskjöld to take a deeply pragmatic approach to peacekeeping, even rejecting a call from Secretary of State John Foster Dulles for a standing force because he feared this might "freeze a pattern of action." The United Nations had improvised once; it wanted to be able to do so again. Above all, the U.N. involvement in the Suez crisis showed for the first time that even though countries might fear becoming involved in another Korean war, they were prepared to deploy substantial forces under the U.N. flag to keep the peace in troubled areas with the consent of the parties to the crisis.

But this first emergency force in the Middle East ended its mission in controversy and, many would say, failure when on May 16, 1967, President Gamal Abdel Nasser of Egypt abruptly demanded its withdrawal from Egyptian territory, confronting the new secretary-general, U Thant, with an agonizing dilemma. All the signs suggested Nasser wanted the force out because he planned to send his soldiers to help Syria stage a new confrontation with Israel.

Many have said U Thant should have refused to withdraw and summoned the General Assembly or Security Council into emergency session to discuss what was clearly a threat to peace. Whether either body would have been able to agree on concrete action to avert war in the climate of Cold War paralysis affecting the United Nations in those days remains questionable. But if Israel had allowed the force to be deployed in its territory earlier, the secretary-general would have found it easier to play for time and resist Nasser's demand.

In the end, after first warning Egypt in bellicose language that the force had a right to remain on its soil, Canada abruptly withdrew its contingent when Nasser said he could no longer guarantee their safety. Left without logistic support or aircraft, U Thant had no option but to withdraw his remaining peacekeepers. Israel responded promptly with the massive pre-emptive strike that started the Six-Day War.

In 1958, within two years of UNEF's formation, the United Nations began its long peacekeeping association with Lebanon when it dispatched the 600-strong United Nations Observer Group in Lebanon (UNOGIL) to investigate complaints that Egypt and Syria (both then known as the United Arab Republic) were infiltrating guerrillas into that troubled country. By the end of the year, the internal situation in Lebanon appeared stable and UNOGIL was disbanded.

The largest, costliest, and most controversial peacekeeping operation by the standards of its time came in 1960, when the U.N. virtually took over the administration of the Congo (now Zaire) after Belgium granted it independence and the country collapsed into chaos and civil war. Cold War tensions marred the undertaking, with Moscow furious at the overthrow of the Soviet-oriented prime minister Patrice Lumumba, while the West was lukewarm about suppressing the secession of the province of Katanga.

But peacekeeping survived, with small new operations in West New Guinea, Yemen, the Dominican Republic, and Kashmir between 1962 and 1965. And in 1964, the U.N. launched an altogether more sophisticated and controversial exercise with the creation of the United Nations Peacekeeping Force in Cyprus (UNFICYP), which is still in place today. Originally charged with restoring law and order after intercommunal violence between the island's Greek and Turkish inhabitants, UNFICYP took on the new task of monitoring an armed truce between the two sides after Turkey invaded in 1974 and effectively divided the island into separate ethnic areas. The Cyprus operation was the first financed by voluntary contributions, since the Soviet Union had no interest in paying for a mission that staved off war between two NATO allies. And today, more than thirty years later, the United Nations is often accused of having perpetuated the conflict by keeping the two communities divided for more than a generation.

In 1978, the United Nations further augmented its peacekeeping presence in the Middle East with the creation of the United Nations Interim Force in Lebanon (UNIFIL), which was to confirm the withdrawal of Israel and its Christian militia allies from the south and help the Lebanese government re-establish its authority. But the force, which still exists today, has never enjoyed the cooperation of either Israeli or Palestinian factions in the troubled border region and has proved ineffective in stopping violence.

The United Nations launched no further peacekeeping operations for a decade. But these were still eventful years for the peacekeeping concept because they witnessed the ending of the Cold War and a radical shift in Soviet policy that paved the way for the resurgence of peacekeeping in the late 1980s and early 1990s. As East–West tensions eased, the Soviet Union under Mikhail S. Gorbachev came to see the United Nations as the cornerstone of its new foreign policy and realized the organization could help extricate it from conflicts around the globe it no longer wished to exploit.

By 1988, the United Nations was sending a fifty-officer team to monitor the Red Army's pullout from its Afghan adventure, opening the door for a flood of new peacekeeping operations in subsequent years. With the Soviet Union and the United States now working together in the Security Council to resolve conflicts around the globe, the United Nations' peacekeeping role

A genocidal civil war broke out in Rwanda in 1994, causing 2 million people to flee over the border. Relief workers in squalid camps like this one outside Goma, Zaire, were over-whelmed by an unprecedented flow of refugees and troubled by the dilemma of aiding perpetrators along with the innocent.

UNIKOM soldiers from the U.S. and U.K. play with refugee children in the demilitarized zone, Abdali, Kuwait, May 1991.

began to change. Increasingly these operations became complex exercises in political reconciliation, with the U.N. sending in civilian administrators and policemen as well as soldiers to oversee peace plans agreed to by the parties to a conflict who now wished to resolve their differences through the ballot box. Of the thirteen peacekeeping operations set up before Cold War tension began to fade, all but one were of the traditional Cyprus type, in which the Blue Helmets monitored a truce between warring sides while mediators sought a political solution to the underlying conflict.

But most of those launched afterward were "second-generation" operations, as they have come to be known, set up to implement a political settlement already accepted by the parties to a dispute. This means that in addition to traditional peacekeeping duties, the U.N. finds itself engaged in such other activities as organizing elections, disarming guerrilla forces, restoring law and order, resettling refugees, and providing humanitarian relief. Typically, the present-day conflicts such operations are designed to deal with are no longer wars between countries but those fought within a single state, involving irregular forces. Civilians tend to be the main victims, while the institutions of government are often destroyed in the fighting.

The record of these second-generation operations is mixed, with the United Nations scoring undoubted successes in El Salvador and Nicaragua, Namibia, Mozambique, and Cambodia, where civil wars were shut down and democratic governments brought to power. Yet these missions succeeded because there was a sufficient measure of agreement between the factions for the peacekeepers to be able to operate with their consent.

At Jabal Hamrayn, Iraq, August 1991, a group of UNSCOM inspectors stands at the base of Iraq's 300-millimeter long-range "supergun."

In Bosnia, Somalia, and Rwanda, on the other hand, that consent was lacking. But the international community still demanded the U.N. "do something," even though Security Council members were not prepared to authorize a full-scale war to stamp out these crises. The result was a series of peacekeeping operations flawed by the contradictory mandates given the peacekeepers, who, without the weapons or troop strength necessary for the job, were expected to enforce "safe areas," "exclusion zones," and "no-fly areas," hunt down Somali warlords, and stop Hutus and Tutsis massacring each other—all the while trying to act impartially. Even their role escorting humanitarian-aid convoys was often perceived as help for the enemy by those hoping to use hunger and suffering to achieve their political aims.

A major lesson the U.N. drew from these setbacks as it celebrated its fiftieth birthday in 1995 is that peacekeeping is not the same as peace-enforcement. In his report to members marking that occasion, Secretary-General Boutros Boutros-Ghali emphasized that U.N. intervention tends to fail where it lacks the true consent of all the parties to a dispute and where the Blue Helmets lack impartiality and resort to force. That is why NATO and not the U.N. went into Bosnia with all the military might necessary to enforce the Dayton accords. "Nothing is more dangerous for a peacekeeping operation than to ask it to use force when its composition, armament, logistical support, and deployment deny it the capacity to do so," the secretary-general wrote.

Another lesson has been the difficulty of securing peacekeeping troops and equipment quickly enough. Although the U.N. now has a significant number of experienced officers as well as a "situation room" manned round the clock in New York, wired to its operations all over the world, the secretary-general likes to recall how not one of the nineteen countries which at that time had pledged 31,000 troops for future U.N. peacekeeping operations was prepared to send a single soldier to Rwanda. And the handful of African countries that finally offered troops had to hire American armored cars because they had nothing suitable themselves.

In an attempt to draw an obvious lesson from the Rwanda fiasco, Boutros-Ghali stepped up his campaign for some kind of a U.N. "rapid-reaction force" that could be rushed into a crisis area at short notice. But the great powers turned a deaf ear to his pleas, showing themselves determined to maintain control over what the U.N. does and does not do and avoid giving any hostages to fortune.

Increasingly, therefore, as the United Nations finds it cannot mobilize the men, equipment, and money needed to cope with all the ethnic turbulence brewing up around the world, it is being forced to share responsibility with, in the secretary-general's words, "other [entities], such as groups of states, regional organizations, or regional arrangements." Sometimes the dangerous opening stage of an operation is undertaken by such a group acting under Security Council mandate. Thus, in Somalia a U.S.-led force went in first in December 1992, then handed off to the U.N. in May 1993. A similar approach was successful in Haiti in 1994.

In other cases the U.N. makes a "division of labor" between its own presence in a crisis area and that of a regional organization. U.N. observers provide a fig leaf of respectability for the Russian peacekeeping forces in Georgia and other parts of the "near abroad" as well as for the West African force trying to bring peace to Liberia.

With peacekeeping resources in such short supply, the United Nations is also putting more emphasis on what is known as "preventive diplomacy," or expanding the secretary-general's "good offices." This means that instead of sending in Blue Helmets to clean up the mess after a fight has begun, the secretary-general will try to keep the belligerents from coming to blows in the first place. Boutros-Ghali also made a virtue out of necessity at the United Nations' fiftieth anniversary celebrations when he introduced the novel idea of using the threat of U.N. withdrawal as a way of coaxing belligerents towards peace. Withdrawal from a peacekeeping operation "must not be considered a failure," he argued. On the contrary, it could represent "a new approach" to a trouble spot that highlights the fact that "unless there is the political will among the protagonists of a dispute to solve it by themselves, the U.N. cannot impose a solution."

Tunisian, Pakistani, and U.S. soldiers (left to right) attend a ceremony in Mogadishu, Somalia, May 1993, transferring command from a U.S.-led task force to a U.N. peacekeeping mission.

This is precisely what happened in Angola, where the U.N. withdrew its observer force in 1992 after the results of an election it had certified as fair were rejected by the losing side. War started up again, and in the ensuing two years more people were killed in Angola than in all the regions where the U.N. maintained peacekeeping operations. This proved a salutary lesson for the Angolan parties, who were finally coaxed into a new peace agreement. With difficulty, the secretary-general persuaded the Security Council to send in a new 7,000-strong peacekeeping force in 1995 to help the parties implement it.

Peacekeeping is still alive, then, even if it is not very well.

Paul Lewis *was the United Nations correspondent for the* New York Times *for eight years, during which he received the 1990 Korn/Ferry International Journalism Award for Excellence in U.N. Reporting. He now covers international economic affairs for the* Times.

Brian Urquhart (center) meets with his bosses Ralph Bunche (left) and Dag Hammarskjöld in Léopoldville, August 1960, to discuss the use of 10,000 U.N. troops in the Congo.

An Interview: The Man in the Middle

by Lance Morrow

No person has done more to shape the nature of peacekeeping than Brian Urquhart, the former under-secretary-general of the United Nations for special political affairs. Always outspoken about the "essential idiocy " of war, in this interview Urquhart ruminates on the new (and sometimes age-old) peacekeeping problems that have arisen from the rearrangement of the world.

Once in 1974, when Brian Urquhart was negotiating a truce to pry Greek and Turkish Cypriots from one another's throats, he sought a moment's relief by reading P.G. Wodehouse, and came upon this exchange between Gussie Fink-Nottle and Bertie Wooster:

"During the courting season the male newt is brilliantly colored. It helps him a lot . . . ."
"But if you were a male newt, Madeline Bassett wouldn't look at you. Not with the eye of love, I mean."
"She would, if she were a female newt."
"But she isn't a female newt."
"No, but suppose she was."
"Well, if she was, you wouldn't be in love with her."
"Yes, I would, if I were a male newt."
A slight throbbing about the temples told me that this discussion had reached saturation point.

The mutual incomprehensions in Sir Brian Urquhart's line of work are as complex but never as benign or charming as those in Wodehouse. Sir Brian retired in 1986 as undersecretary-general of the United Nations for special political affairs. In his forty years at the U.N., he helped to invent the forms and techniques of peacekeeping on a global scale. Urquhart, who left Oxford in 1939 to join the British army's airborne, was part of a commando force that, advancing across Germany ahead of the front lines in 1945, stumbled onto the horrors of the Bergen–Belsen concentration camp.

43

Within a month of leaving the army, Urquhart found what he called "the vocation I had always aspired to." He became private secretary to Sir Gladwyn Jebb, the executive secretary of the Preparatory Commission of the United Nations. Urquhart was present at the U.N.'s creation.

He wrote in his memoir, *A Life in Peace and War:*

> Although I had started the war with a dread and hatred of military life, I had soon become accustomed to it and quite good at it, but I never lost my revulsion at violence and destruction or my fear of bombs, bullets, and death. As the war continued this revulsion had increased, reaching a peak at the sight of the atrocities, the misery, and the ruin of Europe, and the incomprehensible monstrosity of the concentration camps.

He embarked on his life's work with a sharp sense of "the pointlessness and essential idiocy of war." In the following years, Urquhart applied himself to what were often the frustrations of U.N. peacekeeping in the Congo (now Zaire), in the aftermath of Prime Minister Patrice Lumumba's assassination, as well as in Cyprus, in Kashmir, and through the cycle of four Arab–Israeli wars in the Middle East.

Now in his seventies, Urquhart is a compact man with an air of cheerful urbanity. He is very funny, an international connoisseur of the ridiculous. His countenance may focus and darken to indignation if he confronts something he thinks is especially stupid or barbarous. His dominant trait is a sort of civilized sanity and common sense—a diplomat's equilibrium and alertness backed by resources of patience and conviction. Urquhart has called himself "a rational, international Whig." He worried sometimes about his boss Dag Hammarskjöld's mystical or evangelical turns of mind: "I was sometimes uneasy at the possibility that [he] might be beginning to hear voices."

One of Urquhart's assets has been a shrewd eye for character, a gift for appraising the actors and judging how far they can be led, and which way they will break in crisis. In 1962 Urquhart wrote of Patrice Lumumba: "The world would not let Lumumba alone, and he had none of the inherited resistance to flattery and self-delusion which is so essential for a public man. He was naive, however intelligent, and when power and celebrity came to him his naivete turned to mania."

"My mother's favorite word was 'worthwhile,'" Urquhart has written. "It was a moral criterion [that] weighed pleasure against moral worth, and invariably came down on the side of moral worth . . . . To this day, I sometimes have difficulty in enjoying unalloyed the pleasure of the moment. It certainly gave one a sense of purpose." His father's family originally came from the Scottish Highlands. One ancestor of accomplished eccentricity was Sir Thomas Urquhart, who "invented a universal language, wrote the tale of the Admirable Crichton, and traced his pedigree back to Adam and Eve. Sappho was, it seemed, a Miss Urquhart. Pamprosodos Urquhart was the husband of Princess Termuth, who found Moses in the Bullrushes." And so on.

I once suggested to Urquhart that he might be the prototype of a new kind of hero in the world—the accomplished, effective peacekeeper to replace the warrior-hero who has dominated the world's myths for millennia. "I'm going to turn you into a hero," I joked.

Urquhart snorted. "I wouldn't do that if I were you."

Peacemaking sometimes requires, among other things, the cunning of Odysseus. Often it is a matter of coaxing idiots and wild animals back to some ground of common humanity and compromise. Hammarskjöld once told Urquhart that the efforts the two were making on behalf of the United Nations to bring peace to the Congo were "like trying to give first aid to a rattlesnake." Urquhart is patient and unillusioned about the peacemaker's exercise: "Reason, justice, and compassion are small cards to play in the world of politics, whether international, national, or trivial, but someone has to go on playing them."

A friend of mine who is a neurosurgeon once laughed at my idea that his was an infinitely delicate art. On the contrary, he said, neurosurgery is usually a crude, primitive business. Urquhart also resists any interpretation that would romanticize the peacemaking profession, or make it seem high, dazzling artistry. His similes are basic: "A peacekeeping force is like a family friend who has moved into a household stricken by disaster. It must conciliate, console, and discreetly run the household without ever appearing to dominate or usurp the natural rights of those it is helping. There have been times when the peacekeeping function was more like that of an attendant in a lunatic asylum, and the soldiers had to accept abuse and harassment without getting into physical conflict or emotional involvement with the inmates."

Often, of course, the inmates are dangerous. One November night in Katanga in 1961, Urquhart's car was approached by "a squad of evidently stimulated Katangese 'paracommandos,'" who accused Urquhart and friends of trying to assassinate their general. The soldiers then followed Urquhart's group to a dinner party and savagely beat them. One of the soldiers grabbed Urquhart by the collar and smashed his head into Urquhart's face, breaking the peacemaker's nose. Pounded unconscious by rifle butts, Urquhart regained consciousness to find himself lying on the floor of a truck between two benches, with soldiers kicking and stomping him from time to time. "The situation seemed unpromising." But Urquhart talked his way out of being killed, persuading the Katangese that he was the only man who could protect them from the wrath of the U.N. Gurkha troops, who were legendary: They were thought to have thrown people off the roof of the Elisabethville post office and hacked off limbs with their kukris as the victims fell through the air. Urquhart's captors became apprehensive. "Si les Gurkhas arrivent . . ." they muttered. After several tense hours, he was released.

Urquhart still travels widely and lectures on the urgencies of international peace. He was interviewed in his office at the Ford Foundation in New York, where he is a scholar-in-residence in the international affairs program.

In 1993, you advocated that the United Nations form a small, highly trained volunteer military force to be deployed in the early stages of international crises. Do you see any prospect for such a force in the near future?

Unfortunately, there is an enormous number of people now who are nervous about anything that makes the United Nations look stronger, as if it were the short way to world government. In Washington the idea has been attacked in the most outlandish terms. Much of the American public, and in fact the rest of the world, believes in the U.N., but the right-wing American caricature of the U.N. attacking in black helicopters and so on has been very effective. Strangely, the sorts of objections raised to the U.N. force are exactly the same as those raised when Robert Peel suggested a national police force in England.

Also, it is certainly true that Bosnia served to damage the United Nations' credibility. I would like to see the United Nations operate on a much more systematic basis. Up to now, it's been a kind of sheriff's posse: Something terrible happens and the U.N., with a little luck, gets together a group of chaps that'll go off and do their best just to put a stop to it. But the ideal thing would be to prevent it from happening in the first place. That should be possible in a number of places if it were known that there is an intervention force ready to go if something really goes out of control.

Compare the level of development of the United Nations to the development of nation-states within the last 300 years. nation-states came into being because conditions were so bad that institutions had to be established to cope with them. Now, in the world, we come close to some kind of world society, whether we like it or not. Therefore, you have got to develop the essential institutions to stop that society from killing itself, and to take care of peace and security and some degree of order, to watch over the environment, to address the extreme contrasts between wealth and poverty, to control natural resources. In fact, we have got the beginnings of a system of law, a police department, a sanitation department, and a fire department. Peacekeeping is the equivalent on an international scale of what the civil police are on the national.

That's fine, as long as everyone cooperates. In a nation-state, if the police can't manage, they call in the national guard. I think something along the lines of an international guard—like armed police acting on a large scale— has got to be introduced into the world society.

Maybe the U.N. should just mobilize a flying squad of Gurkhas to terrify everyone into behaving.

It's funny: A great number of the British have this sentimental attachment to the Gurkhas. I am always receiving proposals, especially from old generals who had some service in India and say, "They are hereditary soldiers and there is no real place for them in the modern world. Why not use them as a U.N. rapid-deployment force?" It's an interesting idea, though the force would have to be much more representative of other nations. But the Gurkhas are pretty impressive. I know. I had two battalions of Gurkhas in Katanga in 1961. After the first experience of them, we had only to breathe the word *Gurkhas* and everybody would calm down and go about their business without any more nonsense.

In what sort of situation does peacekeeping work best? When, do you think, is it really ineffective?

It works best as a buffer between two conflicting governments that wish to have peace between them. A perfect example was the disengagement on the Golan Heights that Kissinger arranged in 1974 between Syria and Israel. It was greatly to the advantage of both countries—a classic situation. And not more than fifty miles away in Lebanon you see a totally imperfect situation: within the boundaries of one country, no government authority, but a mishmash of irregular bands of soldiers, so that there is no authority with which a peacekeeping force can come to agreement. This tends to produce civil wars, tribal wars, general anarchy. A nightmare.

How does the U.N. inject itself into messy, legally ambiguous conflicts?

Often, as in Yugoslavia, you are dealing with hatreds and feuds that are very deep-seated and very, very brutal. In Somalia, it was different. There was no authority. There was just a shoot-out between kids using any weapons—unfortunately including the artillery supplied by the Soviet Union and the United States. There has to be same means of breaking the cycles of violence by external interventions. The difficulty is that the U.N. Charter says the U.N. should not interfere in internal affairs of member states. But if you have a world where national sovereignties are unraveling rather fast, does the world stand by and watch it on television, or does the world have some kind of obligation to try to do something about it?

What would you consider a classic piece of negotiating?

I think of Ralph Bunche negotiating the Middle Eastern peace in January of 1949. Bunche was trained as a social anthropologist, and he was a very good one . . . . He settled both sides down in the Hotel des Roses on the island of Rhodes. You never want to negotiate in a luxury resort. You should have conditions that make everyone want to leave as soon as possible. At the Hotel des Roses, everyone was miserable. The weather was wet and cold; the food was terrible. The place was isolated. Bunche was indefatigable. He would listen to their disagreements all day, and then at two in the morning, after everyone else had gone to sleep, he would draft a new proposal fitting all the elements together for a new agreement. He was the best draftsman I have ever seen. Both sides trusted him, because he had no vested interests. He knew more about the situation than they did. And in the morning, they would find new proposals, complete with maps.

Does the U.N. have authority to enforce peace?

The Gulf War certainly enhanced the feeling that the U.N. is not just a paper tiger. One of the great weaknesses of the U.N. has been that its decisions have not been enforced. But it has a long way to go. If international law is adopted, it has to be monitored, and, if necessary, enforced. After all, nobody would think anything of laws of a nation-state that weren't enforced. We need a system like this: A convention exists on tankers not being allowed to clean their tanks at sea. So tank cleaning should be monitored, and once you've caught a tanker doing it at sea, and issued a couple of warnings, somebody goes out and drops a very small bomb down a funnel: "That's it, boys, you've had two warnings to stop it. The next time, down you go." The moment that one tanker, after three warnings are ignored, goes to the bottom, I don't think there will be any more tanks being cleaned at sea.

How do you walk in and get people to stop shooting?

It depends on whether they want to stop shooting or not. You can get people to stop for a short time, but it almost always breaks down because some ass fires at a shadow at night or a chicken runs across the cease-fire line. If one person fires a burst, you can be damn sure that everybody will start up. They always do. So, what you have to do very quickly is either put observers in to hold everybody down when somebody fires by mistake, or, if you have a big situation as we had in the Sinai in 1973, you have to put in an interposing force. Once you start to move people back as the Israelis were doing, you need to have a U.N. group as a buffer in the middle.

Would it make sense to found an international peacekeeping academy, a sort of West Point or Sandhurst turned in a peaceful direction?

I have been interested in trying to get a U.N. staff college going, civilian and military, which would train people in the kinds of things that U.N. people are now asked to do, everything from humanitarian relief to supervising elections, peacekeeping, and maybe conducting police actions. After all, you didn't develop nation-states without developing this kind of institution, without staff colleges and military training institutions and so on. So if we are heading for a world society (which we are, like it or not), we'd better damn well develop the institutions to manage the parts of that society that need to be managed.

Lance Morrow, senior writer and essayist for Time *(and a winner of the National Magazine Award), is a professor of English literature and communications at Boston University.*

Iranian members of UNIFIL monitor traffic at Akiya Bridge, one of three main crossing points into southern Lebanon, April 1978.

U.N. Peacekeeping Tactics: The Impartial Buffer

by Rod Paschall

Peacekeeping, as much as war making, has its tactical rules—the most important of which is never to let a critical incident develop into a full-blown crisis. This rule was well demonstrated by one of the world's most experienced peacekeepers, Ghana's Emmanuel Erskine, during a potentially disastrous event in Lebanon.

Blue Beret soldiers serve such a wide variety of functions that it is impossible to identify a typical U.N. peacekeeping mission. The last half century has seen the world body's banner over unarmed truce observers, cease-fire supervisors, active-combat pacification operations involving ground and air attacks, officers monitoring negotiated troop withdrawals or conducting humanitarian efforts, and armed, battalion-sized units taking part in interposition operations. If there is a "worst" or "toughest" case for the U.N. soldier, it is probably the latter, placing a lightly armed organization from some neutral country squarely between two still-bloody and maybe vengeful belligerents, parties that the United Nations hopes have agreed to try peace—at least for a while.

Whether a U.N. interposition operation is successful or not depends mostly on how well a U.N. mandate is understood and observed, but also partly on the peacekeeper's tactics. The first tactic for creating an impartial buffer between two belligerents is to establish and maintain a firm presence. That is simple enough in theory, particularly when you consider that U.N. peacekeeping procedures include a prerequisite that contending sides must agree to an interposition of neutral forces before they are deployed.

But, as in other military affairs, tactical theory does not always correspond to tactical practice. For example, when the United Nations Emergency Force (UNEF I) set up a headquarters in the city of Gaza after the 1956 Arab–Israeli War, it was immediately subjected to mob violence. Danish and Norwegian peacekeepers were ordered to fire over the heads of the rioters, but unfortunately, one of the stone throwers was killed. In 1976, a clearly marked U.N. hilltop observation outpost along the Lebanese and Israeli border, at Khiam, became the focal point for seventeen days of bombardment and heavy fighting. The observers, an American and a French officer, survived only due to their careful preparations—a shellproof underground bunker stocked with a month's supply of rations and water. Two years after that, in the same region, a Fijian battalion operating with the U.N. Interim Force in Lebanon (UNIFIL) stood off a concerted, eight-hour-long attack on one of its long-established roadside checkpoints. Aided by a U.N. mobile reserve force of Dutch- and Senegalese-manned armored vehicles mounting heavy machine guns, the Blue Berets steadfastly maintained their presence and authority.

A second tactical principle of interposition is to have continuous, multilevel, multiparty communications. Especially in dangerous, fluid, and unpredictable environments, accurate information is vital to the lives of the peacekeepers and to the mission itself. A relentless dialogue must be maintained with residents, local police authorities, and potentially belligerent units to prevent resumption of hostilities. Further, U.N. field commanders and the secretary-general's representatives often must make midnight telephone calls to ask for immediate corrective action.

What peacekeepers can do usually depends on what they can see—or what they can determine after the fact. U.N. observation posts are normally sited on ground that has a commanding view of the countryside and its tactical approaches. Ideally, the posts should be mutually supporting. For instance, an entire demarcation line might be under the observation of a string of posts, the ground that is masked from one spot being within the clear view of another. That situation is not always possible, however, so peacekeepers must often resort to foot or vehicle patrols. All of this must be carefully explained to, and well understood by, the contending parties.

Peacekeeping is best done openly. U.N. patrols normally are not conducted at night. There is no advantage for U.N. forces to surprise an infiltrator, and there is always the chance of mistaken identity. This tactical handicap can be partially compensated for by using ground-surveillance radar, night-vision devices, and searchlight sweeps from an observation post. Peacekeepers should also operate "in the clear" electronically. Contending parties are sure to monitor a U.N. outpost's radio report of an incursion. Since this type of broadcast can alert a defender, anticipation of such a call is therefore apt to deter a potential transgressor.

A fourth tactical principle, gaining and maintaining credibility, has more to do with moving minds than with maneuvering forces. If the peacekeeper's conduct is impeccable, his observation thorough, his reporting accurate and timely, and his patrolling continuous, he is likely to gain the confidence of local adversaries. Potential belligerents may then begin to register a written or verbal protest about a violation with the Blue Berets rather than make their point with bullets or shells fired on an enemy.

To maintain the peacekeeper's credibility, each allegation has to be investigated quickly and impartially, and the U.N. command might offer its good offices to mediate a dispute. The United Nations has sometimes augmented its military forces with contingents of third-party civilian police. The latter are far more skilled in investigative techniques than are soldiers, and far more likely to gain the trust of civilian victims who have the misfortune to live on a battleground. U.N. civilian police have served successfully in the Congo operation, Irian Barat (formerly Dutch New Guinea), and Cyprus—and more recently in Namibia, Cambodia, and Haiti. Terrain, maneuver, and weapons aside, credibility is an essential component in establishing an effective buffer.

Finally, the peacekeeper should have as much or even more tactical mobility than the local warriors possess. That principle was well illustrated by a potentially disastrous Lebanese event during 1979. A U.N. Truce Supervision Organization (UNTSO) outpost spotted a battalion-sized Israeli unit moving into a demilitarized zone and promptly reported the incident to an Irish UNIFIL contingent in the path of the approaching battalion. The incursion was in response to a two-man raid the evening before,

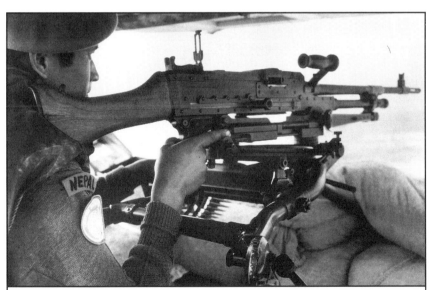

Part of the original UNIFIL mandate in March 1978 was to confirm the withdrawal of Israeli forces from southern Lebanon. A Nepalese soldier stands guard at a strongpoint.

By summer 1980, U.N. commander General Emmanuel A. Erskine of Ghana had total troop strength of nearly 6,000. This checkpost is manned by Irish soldiers.

and the invading battalion commander was intent on finding the pair of raiders and exacting revenge. However, he entered a U.N.-designated zone under the control of one of the world's most experienced peacekeepers, Ghana's lieutenant-general Emmanuel A. Erskine. The general immediately ordered his mobile reserve of Dutch, Nigerian, and Senegalese soldiers to mount their armored personnel carriers and reinforce the Irish troops, who would soon have been heavily outnumbered.

When the pursuing battalion arrived at the Irish army's roadblock, it did not face what it undoubtedly had expected, a lightly manned checkpoint that could be easily pushed aside or bypassed. Instead it faced a well-deployed, substantial United Nations force armed with antitank guided missiles and heavy machine guns. And, if need be, the determined Blue Berets could call on the support of a battery of 120mm mortars. Since U.N. ground rules prohibited armed troops from passing the checkpoint, the battalion was halted in its tracks. At the same time, General Erskine's rapid reports about the unfolding situation had already put U.N. diplomats in motion. His protests and warnings were being lodged in several capital cities and in the halls of U.N. headquarters. An uneasy standoff developed at the Irish army's position.

Erskine then seized the upper hand. In order to gain time so that the diplomatic process could work its way, he refused the pursuing battalion commander's request for a parley. The U.N. general insisted on speaking to the battalion commander's superiors. Meanwhile, Erskine's subordinates at the roadblock began working toward a solution. The raid of the night before could not be ignored. There was every reason to believe that the two terrorists had infiltrated through the U.N. zone. And it was equally evident that the battalion would not simply turn around and go home without some sort of face-saving gesture.

Eventually the peacekeepers learned that the battalion commander's intelligence pointed to two particular houses where the raiders were thought to be hiding. The Irish soldiers refused to allow the battalion commander to search the houses. But as a compromise, they offered to do it themselves. A bargain was struck. When U.N. soldiers made the inspection, the battalion commander's intelligence proved inaccurate; no terrorists were found. Meanwhile, no further blood was shed that day. The pursuit came to an end. Peace was restored.

In the hands of a master such as General Emmanuel Erskine, peacekeeping is not passive. Rather it is tactically proactive: A critical incident is never allowed to develop into a crisis. In handling the incident at the Irish roadblock, Erskine acted to establish a firm, unyielding presence. He used multilevel, simultaneous communications to bring speedy diplomatic action to bear and find an on-the-spot, face-saving solution. He operated openly, reducing the chance of creating suspicion or misunderstanding. By standing his ground, being fair, and conducting an impartial investigation, Erskine gained credibility for his small but competent band of peacekeepers. And his previous wisdom in constituting a substantial, highly mobile reserve force paid off. General Erskine proved to be a skilled peacekeeper—and a sound tactician.

In essence, tactics is the method of applying power. In peacekeeping, that power can be the threat or even the use of an offensive combat operation. Or it may entail only a single observer armed with little more than the dubious force of world opinion. Often the United Nations applies power by placing a neutral force in harm's way. It will likely be an armed force, but one that will only defend itself—and then reluctantly. In these cases, peacekeepers rely on defensive tactics. However, the true military experts in this field—troops from Ghana, Senegal, Fiji, Ireland, Austria, Canada, Norway, Sweden, and a few other nations—will tell you their defensive tactics are neither stationary nor passive. These soldiers know their forces must be well placed, well informed, well connected, active, responsive, and, above all, a step ahead of the troublemaker. All of that makes for a sound impartial buffer.

Rod Paschall, *the former head of the Military History Institute, drafted the first peacekeeping doctrine for the U.S. armed forces.*

The Persian Gulf War took place with U.N. advice and approval, but no blue flag on the battlefield. Afterwards, as one of the conditions for the truce, a Soviet UNIKOM observer surveys the demilitarized zone on the Iraq–Kuwait border, May 1991.

Solving the Command-and-Control Problem

by Rod Paschall

United Nations peacekeeping operations are often complicated by the reluctance of some member states to place their troops under unified command and control. Nonetheless, the best moments in peacekeeping have come when there has been a single responsible officer in charge.

In an editorial in the *New York Times,* published on October 30, 1994, Secretary-General of the United Nations Boutros Boutros-Ghali wrote, "Today's first major challenge is command and coordination." His words might have indicated that he was facing an intractable problem, but in fact the secretary-general was sounding confident and optimistic. He did lament the overcautiousness of member states about placing their forces under U.N. command, and—a perceptive reader could not fail to notice—he did use the word "coordination," rather than "control," a more assertive term that usually peppers any discussion of military command. However, the secretary-general's main point was that the world community is on its way to finally achieving what had been a mere dream fifty years before: a workable and peaceful international system.

Solving the U.N. command-and-control problem is every bit as vital as Boutros-Ghali suggested: It is the U.N.'s top challenge, and it always has been. Some have seriously recommended that the world body have its own international peacekeeping army, and that may eventually come to pass. But for the present it appears likely that every peacekeeping or peace-enforcement operation the U.N. undertakes will have its own particular command-and-control arrangement. A quick review of the past will show clearly why that is so, and consideration of the U.N.'s experience may also confirm why the secretary-general is confident of a better tomorrow for us all.

At its very core, the United Nations is a multinational military command-and-control arrangement. It is patterned after, takes its name from, and currently reflects the character of the World War II international organization that fought and defeated Imperial Japan, Nazi Germany, and Fascist Italy. The Allies designed their 1940s-era structure to formulate agreed-upon war policies, create military strategies to realize those policies, assemble the resources needed to carry out selected strategies, and appoint commanders who would employ those resources. For the most part, they adhered to an important tenet of military professionalism: the principle of unity of command. Allied leaders often appointed a single commander to direct multinational forces in a well-defined geographic theater of war. There were exceptions to this model in World War II, and there have been exceptions since, but the modern-day U.N. has largely succeeded by following the pattern set by its World War II predecessor. The exceptions, both during World War II and since, have been of American origin—and not all of these exceptions have had a happy end.

Although there are lengthy, legalistic military definitions of the word "command" that vary from country to country, the meaning normally includes not only the authority to direct the combat employment of a unit, but the responsibility to organize, equip, supply, and train that force. Additionally, command can carry the responsibility for morale, health, and discipline of subordinate units. Therefore, a true commander can remove, replace, or court-martial a subordinate.

"Control," on the other hand, denotes far less authority. Typically, control might mean that a headquarters can govern only the tactical employment of designated units. In this case, that headquarters is said to have "operational control." Or it might have only administrative responsibilities for a subordinate organization.

There is usually not much command and only some control vested in any multinational or joint-service (i.e., ground, air, sea) headquarters. Typically, a multinational or joint "commander" governs only subordinate units of his own national service and is limited to exercising tactical, or operational, control of organizations from another nation or service. For example, one of NATO's British army commanders might command some of his assigned British army units, but he is likely to have only operational control over German and U.S. army organizations or perhaps even the Royal Air Force units in his charge. So while the press may speak of a "U.N. commander," that officer will at best carry a mixed bag of authority—some command and some control. Incidentally, military lexicographers prefer to use the term "combined" in describing a multinational force. (Although life was much simpler for Napoleon, who commanded everything and everybody on his side of a battlefield, eventually he did lose—to a multinational, combined, force.)

In Nicosia, Cyprus, a Canadian soldier with UNFICYP patrols an abandoned street on the Green Line. This mission has been in continuous existence since 1964, with a maximum troop strength of 7,000.

Representatives of the multinational force that would win World War II first met in Washington, D.C., on New Year's Day, 1942. Men from twenty-six countries pledged to adhere to the Atlantic Charter; to combine their military, naval, and industrial resources; and to make no separate peace with the Axis powers. They called their corporate entity the "United Nations." Besides winning the war, this alliance established a global food program that ended an enormous, conflict-induced famine; created a supranational judicial system to define war crimes and bring war criminals to justice; and laid the groundwork for a permanent post-war replica of itself. But its very reason for being was to marshal scarce military and naval resources in a great and violent global campaign aimed at coercing or bludgeoning its enemies into submission. This first United Nations was very much an organization of military purpose.

During the three-plus years of its existence, the World War II United Nations produced and implemented fundamental, practical procedures essential to the formulation and execution of a winning military strategy. There was little that can be described as democratic or fair about these procedures. The fate of the membership's blood and treasure was entrusted to a small group of elderly males, at first called the Big Four. This group, an American, a Briton (actually British–American), a Chinese, and a Russian (actually Georgian), bickered about the next move, determined who would command the forces dedicated to that move's success, supervised the execution of plans, and argued over the hoped-for spoils of victory. In effect, a few old men made clandestine life-or-death choices for hundreds of thousands of young airmen, soldiers, and sailors. They also made decisions resulting in the deaths of hundreds of thousands of innocents. Perhaps the only excuses for this elitist, autocratic system were that it achieved unity of effort—and it worked.

It worked because it involved only a few powerful decision-makers and because it ensured that those few were committed to employing enough resources to get the job done. This last factor, reserving choice to the most capable powers, conformed to the pragmatist's golden rule: "He who hath the gold maketh the rule." To ensure that those who provided the most power for any particular endeavor would have the right to direct its employment, the field commander for a specific campaign was almost invariably chosen from the country developing, delivering, and expending the majority of resources involved. This commander directed all allied forces—land, sea, and air—in a particular geographic area and conformed his operations to the wishes of his political master, or in some cases, masters: one or more of the Big Four.

The concept of harmonizing policies and strategies and entrusting their execution to a single commander came easily to the coalition's British and American officers. These men had been taught an almost identical set of principles of war from the 1920s on, and among them was the tenet of unity of command: They all understood that each mission required for its achievement unity of effort under one responsible commander.

While the Big Four decided policy, strategy, and command arrangements, other war-related issues were subjected to an entirely different decision process. Indeed, it was essential for all twenty-six governments to agree on certain matters. The huge effort the Allies expended during the war would have been for naught if the conditions after World War II had been the same as before. Therefore, naked aggression was to be discouraged in the future by the wartime creation of defined war crimes and a deliberate system to indict, try, and punish war criminals. After the guns had fallen silent, after hostilities had ceased, there would be a public retribution that was certain to result in the execution of some of the war's participants. Had only the Big Four decided this matter, they might well have been vulnerable to some of the same charges. After all, both sides had bombed cities, killed civilians, and mistreated prisoners. By putting the war-crimes issue, an undeniable peacetime intrusion of sovereignty, before all the Allied governments, responsibility for the forthcoming and deadly judicial acts could be spread among the many.

The Big Four could not force their allies to join another post-war attempt at a global political organization, but they well understood that the last try, the League of Nations, had failed, in part because its membership was not universal. As a start, they needed to persuade all twenty-six allies to join—and they did. So, while month-to-month conduct of the war was determined by a select group who deliberated in private, some of the most important war aims were decided by all members of this diverse group. In contrast to the Big Four, the larger body debated their issues with as much publicity and openness as possible.

The Allied command-and-control organizational formula was thus bicameral from its beginning. On the one hand, an elite group of the most powerful deliberated the immediate, pressing problems. The Big Four could act quickly and in secret. The longer range, perhaps more profound issues were usually handled by the "committee of the whole." But nothing precluded all members convening in conference to decide any issue. There were two routes to creating policy and strategy, each offering inherent advantages and disadvantages.

The military and naval forces that carried out the war aims of the Big Four and the conference of Allied representatives were mostly multinational forces commanded by an officer who exercised only limited authority over the combat contingents given him. There were exceptions. For example, the Soviets and the U.S. Navy, the latter during the early phases in the Central Pacific campaign, fought as single, unalloyed national entities. But most of the power wielded by this first United Nations was borne by joint and combined organizations—complex dissimilar forces of mixed nationality operating under the direction of a single commander. General Dwight D. Eisenhower, who was possibly the most successful of these Allied theater commanders, described his leadership experience in this way:

> In that capacity I had seen many nations work out a fixed unity of purpose despite all the divergences in aim and outlook and way of life that characterized them as individuals and independent states. The combat direction of their military power and commitment of their armies to battle— the most jealously guarded tokens of national sovereignty—they delegated to single authority. While they retained administrative control of their military forces, from the appointment of commanders to the establishment of troop rations, the Allied command was a single engine in its battle mission—the winning of war. Direction by committee, in which unanimity had to be achieved before unified action could be taken, was abandoned in favor of a single commander representing all the nations engaged.

A departure from this commitment to unity of command occurred during the last part of the war when the final campaign was being planned. Operation DOWNFALL, the invasion of Japan, envisioned the use of

American, British, and French forces under an awkward command-and-control arrangement. An American admiral would command all naval forces, an American general would direct the operations of all land forces, and the U.S. Joint Chiefs of Staff in Washington would have authority over the strategic air forces. No single person would be in charge, and there was not even a committee to decide issues that were certain to create heated dispute. Fortunately, the surrender of Japan precluded putting this unwieldy, potentially dangerous arrangement into play. However, this would not be the last ill-conceived, American-sponsored, command-and-control scheme.

The second United Nations, formed in 1945, included the best facets of the first organization, among them the winning command-and-control formula. Today, as in 1942–45, there are two available routes to a decision: The Big Four lives in the form of the Security Council; and the representative conference of the twenty-six allied nations is reflected in the General Assembly. Member states normally see that a single commander is appointed to direct the operations of the military forces. Often, that commander is from the nation supplying the most resources to a particular campaign. And, to ensure that the agreed-upon policy and strategy are served, there is usually a steady stream of reports, directives, inspections, and advisory messages between the commander and his political masters.

The first major test of the new organization came within hours of North Korea's invasion of South Korea in June 1950. Effective U.N. action in this instance hinged on the chance absence of the Soviet delegate to the Security Council. The Security Council could not act without him, but there was nothing to prevent the General Assembly from doing so, and at that time the U.S. and its allies wielded considerable influence within the larger body. Despite the eventual return of the Soviet delegate, who of course objected to U.N. involvement in Korea, the first war for peace-enforcement was, in the main, successful, its command-and-control arrangements handled much like a World War II multinational Allied campaign.

The U.N.'s goal in 1950 was to defend South Korea. Like many World War II examples, a government was authorized to execute the coalition strategy on the battlefield, and U.N. member states were asked to rally forces around the blue-and-white flag. The U.S. took the lead and added U.N. military control in Korea to General Douglas MacArthur's Far East command responsibilities. MacArthur's jurisdiction over his command was essentially the same as Eisenhower's had been only a few years before. He chose neither the allied participants nor their organizations, weapons, or commanders. His control was limited to making battle dispositions and issuing employment directions to the forces within his command. Since

In summer 1974, the Cyprus mission was nearly overrun when the country's national guard staged a coup and Turkish troops landed. Observation post "Roslyn" near the Nicosia airport was manned at that time by Canadians, who stood firm.

some of the allied contingents were small, perhaps only battalion size, the U.N. command placed these units within larger U.S. formations. This procedure was hardly novel. The same system had been practiced in World War II. (The Allies' Italian campaign was possibly the best-known, most complex example of dissimilar-sized, multinational units merging into an effective fighting force.)

The remarkable feature of the Korean War experience was the resilience of U.N. command in the face of extremely trying conditions. The war's first year was characterized by wide-ranging attacks and withdrawals up and down the Korean peninsula ending in a World War I–type stalemate roughly midway between north and south. At this point, July 1951, communist and U.N. sides agreed on a negotiated solution. The U.N. side was represented at the table by members of the U.S. military chosen by the U.N. command. The general shape of the agreement, save one facet, was gained relatively early. The sticking point involved repatriation of prisoners. The U.N. command, knowing that tens of thousands of the Chinese and North Korean prisoners it held did not want to return home, insisted on voluntary repatriation. The communists demanded a forced prisoner exchange following a cease-fire. The U.N. side stubbornly clung to its position and for fifteen months fought for the ability of 50,000 ex-Chinese and North Korean soldiers to reject Marxist rule. Their position cost the U.N. side some 125,000 casualties.

Despite agony over the consequences of this choice and constant reminders of legendary Oriental patience, the U.N. command never wavered from its principle. It remained unified, exhibited its own brand of patience, and in the end, prevailed over its communist adversaries. The aggressors were severely punished, lost more land than they had gained, and suffered the public humiliation of watching tens of thousands of Asian soldiers desert the communist cause.

The other major war with U.N. involvement, the Gulf War of 1990–91, operated with Security Council assistance, guidance, and approval, but no U.N. flag on the battlefield. Once again the U.S. was the major actor in reversing an attempted territorial conquest. Washington worked through and with the U.N. Security Council. The council formulated diplomatic initiatives aimed at a peaceful resolution, put its imprimatur on the deployment of forces to Saudi Arabia, threatened and then finally authorized the use of force to oust Iraqi invaders from Kuwait. In the aftermath of allied success, the council dictated a lengthy list of intrusions into Iraq's sovereignty aimed at maintaining as much peace as possible in the volatile region. In short, the U.N. provided the ground rules for the international community's response to aggression and established the methods to secure the fruits of victory.

But the Security Council did not establish the terribly fragile military command apparatus that opposed Iraq. That apparatus was of U.S. origin. The Saudi lieutenant-general, Khalid bin Sultan, commanded all Saudi and Arab forces. The American general, Norman Schwarzkopf, commanded or controlled all U.S. forces and had operational control of the remaining allied contingents. During the short war, Schwarzkopf and Khalid bin Sultan coordinated their plans and acted in cooperation. Thanks to weak opposition, this dubious, twin-headed, forty-nation military effort was never severely tested.

While the two large-scale military episodes, the Korean War and the Gulf War, involved taking sides, the fifty-year U.N. experience in conventional peacekeeping has been a neutral endeavor. A command-and-control arrangement usually begins with a decision by the Security Council. However, as early as 1947, when it dispatched military personnel to Greece to investigate border violations, as well as on several other occasions, the General Assembly has sometimes acted in lieu of the Security Council.

The need for neutrality in U.N. peacekeeping operations has greatly enlarged the importance, prestige, and authority of the organization's Secretariat, headed by the secretary-general. The most obvious cause of this phenomenon has been that since every country has selfish interests, no single nation can be entrusted with a U.N. peacekeeping mandate. So, almost by definition, U.N. peacekeeping is a multinational affair. The secretary-general, an essentially stateless person subject to the control of many masters, is often given broad powers to produce a negotiated solution, one that may obviate the need for outside intervention. Failing that, the secretary-general attempts to gain approval from the contending parties to deploy disinterested, military peacekeeping contingents. To free himself from constantly monitoring these tense, attention-absorbing situations, the secretary-general normally appoints a personal civilian representative to carry out essential political negotiations and to receive reports from the U.N. military field headquarters.

There is one U.N. military commander for each of these peacekeeping operations, and usually many tasks. The commander, whose nationality is least likely to raise the ire of a potential belligerent, may be responsible for guarding ballot boxes, protecting humanitarian efforts, facilitating the operation of other U.N. agencies and the work of nongovernmental assistance organizations, reporting agreement violations, or resolving local disputes. Something identical to this chain of authority, or close to it, exists in more than a dozen potential war zones throughout the world. Largely, it works.

While the notion of a single commander is by now embedded in the U.N. peacekeeping psyche, standard military operational and organizational norms are not. Many peacekeeping operations are extremely passive. Shashi Tharoor, special assistant to the under-secretary-general for peacekeeping operations, says that while the typical military task is appropriate to the adage "Don't just stand there, do something," a peacekeeping task sometimes calls for "Don't do something, just stand there." This can create a proclivity toward stationary, placid, and unusual structures.

For example, in 1992, the United Nations Transitional Authority in Cambodia (UNTAC) consisted of twelve infantry battalions, all reporting directly to the U.N. commander, Australian lieutenant-general John Sanderson. This arrangement would have been unthinkable in most military circles since the professional rule of thumb is that one headquarters should control only three to five subordinate units. This experienced-based "span-of-control" norm is derived from the optimum number of actors a commander can effectively control during an attack or a fast-paced defense against an attack. But in Cambodia Sanderson did not put an intervening headquarters between himself and the twelve battalion commanders. Because of the low tempo of operations, his method worked, demonstrating that command and control of peacekeeping operations can be quite different from other military operations.

Thus far, traditional U.N. peacekeeping command-and-control arrangements have been applied to the more active, sometimes offensive operations that the world body has undertaken in the 1990s. Some experienced peacekeepers, however, have pointed to the differences between past U.N. peacekeeping and the ongoing efforts in Somalia, Bosnia, and other post–Cold War hot spots. Many have proclaimed the emergence of a new, unprecedented era and have emphasized newly coined terminology, substituting "peace-enforcement" for "peacekeeping." They point to a watershed event, the 1991 creation of the U.N. Iraq–Kuwait Observation Mission (UNIKOM) and the demilitarized zone it is expected to monitor. Without question, this was the first U.N.-supervised border founded without consent of both parties. A new era and new missions may demand new command-and-control procedures.

Yet a good case for prior U.N. experience and success can be made. The 1978 deployment of the U.N. Interim Force in Lebanon (UNIFIL) into a lawless battle zone introduced peacekeepers in the midst of ongoing fighting. Previous agreement between the contending parties on UNIFIL's deployment was of little consequence. Blue Helmets were manning armored vehicles, mortars, and heavy machine guns. But some eighteen years before this event, the U.N. had been deeply enmeshed in a shooting-type peace operation.

In modern day Zaire, then the Congo, a peacekeeping mission evolved into a small war. The Security Council dis-

patched peacekeepers to replace departing Belgian troops amid horrifying scenes of slaughter and rape. The command-and-control system involved the usual arrangement for peacekeeping. There was the secretary-general, his political representative, a U.N. military commander, and upwards of thirty different armed national contingents. The U.N. force reached almost 20,000 before the operation was over. In 1962–63, it fought against the attempted secession of Katanga province and successfully drove out intruding white mercenaries. At the cost of 195 peace-enforcers killed, the U.N.

Peacekeepers, in an armored vehicle with a 106-millimeter anti-tank gun, patrol the U.N.-controlled Nicosia airport, September 1974. On the runway is a destroyed Cyprus Airways plane.

force delivered a whole, relatively peaceful and independent country before its departure.

Although the 1990s may call for a wholly new approach to providing the U.N. with adequate resources to meet its vastly enlarged military responsibilities, events in the decade have yet to point out the need for new principles. Certainly, peacekeeping is different from peace-enforcement, but it is not especially new. The world body demonstrated a credible performance in the Congo during the 1960s. While that operation did not bear the label, it was a clear-cut example of effective peace-enforcement. What the 1990s have demonstrated is that departures from established command-and-control principles have not been successful.

A novel American command-and-control arrangement was used in Somalia during 1992–93 and contributed to what may prove to be the U.N.'s most disastrous military endeavor. In late 1992, the U.S. government placed its soldiers in Somalia alongside U.N. troops in order to conduct an effective and badly needed humanitarian effort to relieve the starvation of a desperate population. While Washington arranged for the U.N. to receive reports of its activities, it refused to either command all U.N. forces in the country or subject its own troops to U.N. command. The result was a common effort but no unity of command.

By mid-1993, as U.S. troops withdrew, they began offensive operations against warlord general Mohammed Farah Aideed, whose forces had been responsible for the deaths of several of the peacekeepers. The U.N. commander, Turkish lieutenant-general Cevik Bir, did not control the Americans in these raids. The American element designated to carry out the raids, the U.S. Quick Reaction Force, was responsible to General Bir's deputy, an American officer who, for the offensive portion of the operation, reported to the U.S. Central Command in Florida.

There is no indication that the Turkish U.N. commander was even aware of the dramatic and ill-fated American raid of October 3. When a U.S. helicopter was downed and a small band of soldiers was surrounded, the U.N. force had no ready reserve and no rescue plan. The Americans were defeated and killed. The news of eighteen combat deaths in a peace operation, as well as the shock of seeing the desecrated bodies of American soldiers dragged through the streets, was enough to force Washington officials to react. After a brief, face-saving reinforcement, U.S. forces withdrew from Somalia.

There was shock and something more at the U.N. Until the disaster in Somalia, United Nations military commanders had a reputation for successfully achieving the goals set out for them. Their tasks may have been relatively simple—only to observe a demilitarized zone or to provided a buffer. U.N. commanders have not been expected to resolve age-old ethnic disputes. But operations like Korea and the Congo aside, the vast majority of successes enjoyed by U.N. military contingents had been their inexorable presence in a potentially volatile situation. While observer posts had been ignored and bypassed on several occasions in the Middle East, peacekeeping units had never been defeated and run out of a country. The tragic events in Somalia on October 3, 1993, raised that possibility. Speaking of the debacle, a U.N. peacekeeping official stated, "The impression has been created that the easiest way to disrupt a peacekeeping operation is to kill Americans."

In contrast to the disjointed U.N. command scheme in the Somalia debacle, unity of command produced one of the most brilliant peace-enforcement actions in United Nations history. It came about in the mid-1970s when a small Blue Beret force managed to act in a way that, in the opinion of at least one world leader, prevented a war between Britain and Turkey. In his memoirs, *Final Term—The Labour Government, 1974–1976*, former British prime minister Harold Wilson recalled a turbulent and dangerous week on Cyprus.

Turkish forces landed on the island on July 20, 1974, five days after the military dictatorship in Greece took power away from the Cypriot president, Archbishop Makarios III. The Turks were fearful for their countrymen's safety on the island and were determined to send in a strong, protective military presence. But the invaders also threatened the small U.N. Force in Cyprus (UNFICYP) and the ensuing events, according to Mr. Wilson, brought Britain "within an hour" of war with Turkey. Fortunately, a bold move by then Secretary-General Kurt Waldheim and resolute efforts by the UNFICYP commander, General Prem Chand of India, produced peace and an all-round face-saving victory for the United Nations.

On Turkey's intervention, the Security Council met and called upon the three guarantor powers—Britain, Turkey, and Greece—to negotiate a solution. U.N. headquarters in New York advised General Prem Chand to "play it by ear," limit violence, and protect civilians. Prime Minister Bulent Ecevit of Turkey accepted a call for a cease-fire that was to take effect at 4 PM on July 22. But Ecevit was ill-informed by his generals, who were indicating that Turkish troops were in possession of far more of the island than was actually the case. Ecevit was under the impression that Turkey's objectives would be realized by the time the shooting stopped. At the time of the cease-fire and for a considerable period afterward, Turkish troops were battling their way toward the only international air point-of-entry on Cyprus, Nicosia Airport.

This airport was important for a number of reasons. When Archbishop Makarios was removed from office, the Greek Cypriot national guard seized the facility and began bringing in reinforcements from Greece. Securing the airport was, obviously, one of Turkey's primary goals. Whatever happened there would be extremely crucial for both sides. But parts of Nicosia Airport were vital for the United Nations peacekeepers as well. Although there were not many U.N. troops there—just some supply personnel, medics, staff clerks and communications specialists—the airport served as the site for the UNFICYP headquarters, its medical center, a U.N.–secured arms storehouse, and the logistics base for the organization's Canadian contingent.

A hint of UNFICYP's plight came when Turkish planes attacked the airport forty-five minutes after the cease-fire. Fortunately, only one British soldier was injured. However, when Turkish troops continued their advance the next morning, U.N. officers believed that there was a distinct message in the bombing and the advance—that the Turks were determined to seize the airport, cease-fire or no. For the Blue Berets, this meant that not only their own ability to receive reinforcements would be jeopardized, but their ability to bring about peace on the island—and possibly even to survive in

A convoy of armored personnel carriers patrols near Nicosia, August 1974. A dangerous situation had just been narrowly averted by placing all U.N. troops under one command.

the midst of a renewed civil war—would be put at risk. The U.N. commander sent word to both sides, the advancing Turks and the defending Greek national guard, to come to a peaceful agreement. The appeal failed. The Turks marched on and when they were within range of the airport, the national guard began firing. Renewed U.N. negotiations produced an uneasy noontime truce.

General Prem Chand took advantage of the lull to enact a crucial decision. After receiving approval for his scheme at U.N. headquarters in New York, he announced to both sides that the airport was a U.N.–protected area. In effect, if either the Greeks or the Turks attempted to gain or retain control of Nicosia Airport, they would be fighting the U.N. Both sides were informed that they could not have troops within 500 meters of the airport. By early evening on July 23, a small force of about 150 U.N. troops had expelled the Greek National Guard and were in possession of the airport.

It appeared that a dangerous situation had been averted. But before dark, Prem Chand's solution unraveled. The local Turkish commander informed the peacekeepers that he did not regard U.N. control of the airport as legitimate. The Turkish advance would continue. There was no mistake of intent. If need be, Turks would fight to win control of the facility.

The next morning, July 24, Secretary-General Waldheim, without consulting the Security Council, took it upon himself to order General Prem Chand not to yield the airport. There would be no U.N. withdrawal. Simultaneously, the commander of the British contingent with UNFICYP contacted British forces on Cyprus and explained the worsening situation at the airport. London had issued no instructions to these national forces, which consisted of several well-equipped ground and air units. During the day, U.N. officers gleaned from Radio Ankara that Prime Minister Ecevit was under the mistaken belief that the airport was in Turkish hands. This relevant tidbit was hurriedly relayed to New York. At nightfall, Turkish troops and tanks were spotted moving into positions around the airport, well within the forbidden 500-meter perimeter.

The next few hours were spent in hurried phone calls to the Turkish prime minister. Secretary-General Waldheim managed to convince Prime Minister Ecevit that the U.N., not the Turkish army, held the airport. British prime minister Wilson told the Turkish leader that Britain would not stand by while its own and Canadian forces in UNFICYP were being shelled or bombed. Ecevit merely remarked that his troops knew where the British forces were and would not allow them to be bombed. In New York and London, it appeared the Turks would not be deterred from their purpose. A dawn showdown was grimly anticipated.

At 8 AM on July 25, eight British Phantom jets arrived at a Royal Air Force base in Cyprus; four more came in a bit later. After quickly arming and refueling their planes, British air crews stood by. Units of the 16th British Lancers and 7th Dragoon Guards, armored reconnaissance units, and infantrymen from the Coldstream Guards rushed by road toward the airport. It was a sobering thought: Britain was making ready to fight its NATO ally if the Turkish army moved on Nicosia Airport. Prime Minister Wilson thought he had no other choice.

However, General Prem Chand had made a suggestion the previous day, and it was being rapidly moved up the decision chain in London. His idea was based on two fundamental military precepts. Prem Chand knew where the Turks were and his officers on the ground knew how best to defend the airport. It would make for a better defense if he, not a British commander, made the sector assignments when the British ground units arrived. Then, there was the principle of unity of command. To have two commanders at Nicosia Airport would invite confusion—and possibly failure.

But it was the international policy and psychological aspects of the U.N. general's idea that brought about its hurried realization. If Britain and Turkey confronted each other over the possession of Nicosia Airport, two sovereign nations would be attempting to assert their own, competing interests—a well-trod path to disgrace or honor, defeat or victory. On the other hand, if the incoming British troops were suddenly transformed into U.N. peacekeepers, the confrontation would be between a country asserting the right to protect its own nationals and a world body that had the same aim. It was all a matter of command and control. If there were a British defense, war would be likely. If there were a U.N. defense, peace had a chance. The word was flashed from London—Lancers, Dragoons, and the Coldstream Guards would join U.N. forces under Prem Chand's command.

At a midnight Security Council meeting (the morning of July 25, Cyprus time), the secretary-general presented a communication from the Turkish government. Without conceding the legality of the U.N.'s possession of Nicosia Airport, Ankara assured the secretary-general that Turkey would not attempt to seize the facility by force or the threat of force. There would be no war.

The United Nations has ably conducted many military operations. When it has had to either display or use armed force, its best moments have come when it has placed a unified effort under a single responsible officer who exercised command and control. There is every reason to believe that principle will continue to work well into the twenty-first century. Secretary-General Boutros Boutros-Ghali is right to regret the reluctance of some U.N. member states to place their troops under United Nations command. But he undoubtedly knows that under duress, when it is to their advantage to do so, they can often be persuaded. Perhaps that fact alone is reason enough for optimism and confidence in our future.

Rod Paschall, the former head of the Military History Institute, drafted the first peacekeeping doctrine for the U.S. armed forces.

From a perch in the doorway of an observer aircraft, the author photographed troop concentrations and artillery fire.

Assignment: Cyprus

by Basil Zarov

The U.N. Department of Public Information employs photographers to document the organization's work, including its peacekeeping operations. One Canadian photographer, ordered in haste to a troubled spot, soon found himself embroiled in negotiating a cease-fire. He also produced the memorable pictures of the Cyprus mission that illustrate this essay.

My first assignment for the United Nations was to cover the 1960s crisis in the former Belgian Congo (now Zaire). The Katanga mercenaries were shooting at the U.N. forces; the Blue Helmets were returning their fire; and I was shooting it all with a camera. I became conditioned to the sound of gunfire: Whenever I heard high-pitched spitting sounds close by—the flight of bullets—I hit the dirt. I came out of this conflict thankful to be alive, but one of the cameras slung from my shoulder got hit by a mercenary's bullet.

My next task in 1964 was to photograph the peaceful operations of the U.N. agencies UNESCO, FAO, and WHO in the West African countries, a gem of an assignment. Then I got a terse cablegram from the U.N. Secretariat: "Go Cyprus soonest," it read, and I muttered, "Go back to hell, you mean." Greek and Turkish Cypriots were in the midst of hostilities, with the added threat of Greece and Turkey intervening.

I flew from Abidjan to Beirut, then on to Cyprus. When I landed at the almost forsaken airport in Nicosia, I heard shots in the vicinity. A battle-scarred helicopter with one landing wheel and twisted rotor blades stood on the tarmac like an eccentric sculpture. I stood by the battered control tower and waited to be picked up. A blue Land Rover soon screeched to a stop beside me, and its ruddy-faced British driver called out, "Hop in, mate. We'll drive through the Green Line to the U.N. headquarters." I asked if the Green Line was painted green. He smiled and told me that an officer had drawn a line with a green marker on their operational map, making that narrow area a buffer zone.

As we drove, I counted seven bullet-riddled cars and vans abandoned on both sides of the roadway. We rode through a checkpoint; I saw armed Greeks and armed Turks standing behind sandbag enclosures facing each other, grimly defiant, waiting for someone to make a move. Everyone was armed: Women carried small rifles along with their shopping bags and flowers; children played war with makeshift wooden guns.

When we got to the U.N. headquarters, the mission chief gave me a road

The first picture Zarov took upon arrival in Cyprus, March 1964, was of sandbags being installed outside the Ledra Palace Hotel, the headquarters in Nicosia.

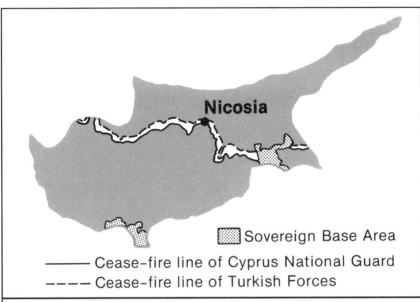

This map shows the division of Cyprus as of 1974. The two sovereign base areas are British. Between the two cease-fire lines is the Green Line, the buffer zone.

map and briefed me on the locations of various national forces. "You're on your own now; take whatever photographs you wish," he said, then cautioned, "but don't ever get involved in military matters."

The following morning, I got an unmarked jeep and, as a precaution against snipers, tied a six-foot U.N. flag onto a short pole and attached it to the tailgate. I made arrangements to cover the Irish patrols in the Famagusta sector, loaded my equipment—consisting of two Nikons, a battery of lenses, and twenty-five rolls of film—and drove off with the huge flag behind me flapping in the breeze.

The countryside was redolent with orange blossoms, broom shrubs, and wild rosemary. As I took deep breaths of this fragrant air, I wondered why the fields and hillsides were devoid of both people and livestock. I could hear the bleating of sheep and goats, but I couldn't see them anywhere. Sporadic gunshots echoed in the distance beyond the hills.

I drove about fifteen miles and suddenly came across a barrier of pine limbs spread across the roadway. I stopped. A rifle shot cracked nearby. I knew that it was risky to turn around and go back, so I stopped the motor and put the key in my pocket. Moments later I heard a hissing sound: "Psst—psst." A man in his twenties holding a rifle scurried up to the jeep. He wore a gray sweater covered with bits of thorn and burdock that showed he had been hiding in the bramble thicket beside the road. He looked me over with his dark eyes and greeted me.

"Good morning, sir. My name Dimitri. I live here."

I saw the Greek cross hanging from his neck and answered with a greeting in Greek: "Kalimera sas."

"You speak Greek. Good, me Greek."

"Just a few words. Sorry."

Dimitri laid his rifle down and poked his head into the jeep.

"We see you on the road coming here. Want you stop. Make report. Turkish people on other hill shooting us ten days. No stop. Crazy people. We shooting back. Want shooting business stop. We hide animals. Outside, get killed. Sheep and goats very hungry, need graze, need grass. Tell Turkish stop shooting and we do same. Not shoot—no sir."

I thought about the warning I had had about meddling in military matters. "I'm not a military patrol. This is not my job. I'm the United Nations photographer." I took out a camera. "See, I'm going to Famagusta, so let me pass through. If I meet a patrol, I'll report your problem immediately." Dimitri was perplexed. He pleaded with gesticulating hands.

"I no see no patrol here. Animals die soon—maybe three, four days. Please—go tell them stop shooting. We not shoot."

"Why can't you send a messenger carrying a white flag over there and talk to them?" I asked.

"Never! For sure get shot!" Dimitri tugged at my U.N. flag. "You official. They not shooting you."

"Okay—I'll give the Turks your message that you want a cease-fire truce. I don't know if it will do any good. I cannot force them to stop shooting."

"You come back here with answer?" Dimitri gripped my arm.

"Yes, God willing. For now, hold your fire." The barrier was pushed aside, and the jeep lurched forward toward a side road to a ravine and across a narrow bridge that spanned a shallow creek—the dividing line between the Greeks and Turks. I drove up a hill, which led to a cluster of fieldstone cottages. There was not a person anywhere to be seen. I stopped at the first cottage and tooted the horn. A boy of about twelve appeared at the doorway, holding a rifle as tall as himself. I shouted, "I want to see somebody who speaks English." The boy looked warily at me and pointed his arm to the third cottage.

I drove slowly and stopped at the neat stone-and-plaster cottage. I walked to the gate and called out, "Good morning—anybody home?"

A deep voice boomed out of the dark interior, "Come in!" I entered, and a burly Turk with a thick black mustache and bushy eyebrows appeared, dressed in a white collarless shirt, gray trousers, and high leather boots.

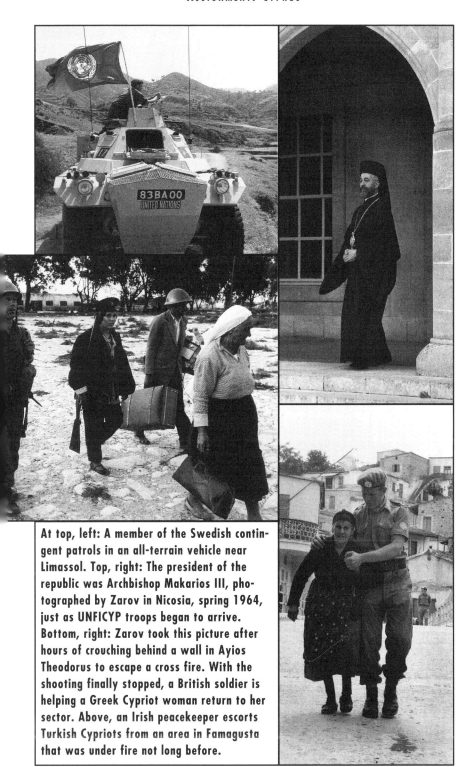

At top, left: A member of the Swedish contingent patrols in an all-terrain vehicle near Limassol. Top, right: The president of the republic was Archbishop Makarios III, photographed by Zarov in Nicosia, spring 1964, just as UNFICYP troops began to arrive. Bottom, right: Zarov took this picture after hours of crouching behind a wall in Ayios Theodorus to escape a cross fire. With the shooting finally stopped, a British soldier is helping a Greek Cypriot woman return to her sector. Above, an Irish peacekeeper escorts Turkish Cypriots from an area in Famagusta that was under fire not long before.

Part of UNFICYP's mandate is helping communities resume normal activities. In a Turkish Cypriot camp near Hamitkoy, a woman collects the family wash. She and others left homeless by the war live in tents and other converted shelters.

"Good morning. You like some coffee, mister?" he asked, holding a *cezve,* a long-handled brass coffeepot.

"Yes, please!" I smiled and thought that he would make a good portrait—but I was not there for pictures.

"Where you come from?" he asked amiably, pouring the sweet Turkish brew into small earthenware cups.

"I came from Africa, but I work as a photographer for the United Nations in America."

"Ah—America! I have uncle in Chicago, sell carpets. He very rich, drive Cadillac. I have cousin, too, in Montreal. Maybe you know him: Nihat—have restaurant business."

I sipped the hot coffee and explained why I was there. "I have a message from your Greek neighbors on the other hill who want this shooting to stop. They want a cease-fire—a truce. They want to put their livestock out to pasture; their animals are starving—"

He interrupted me. "We have same trouble here! Animals here also starving—feed all gone. Very dangerous to put on pasture. Greeks shoot anything that move. Donkey killed here. You want see? Come, I show you."

"You all have the same problem. The shooting must be stopped now.

This matter can be settled, if you all agree to a truce. Then the cease-fire can start immediately."

"Go tell those damn Greeks stop shooting now and we stop."

"Of course, I'll give them your message. How much time will it take to tell your people to hold their fire?"

"One hour, not more, maybe less."

"Good, start immediately. I'll tell them that you are holding fire, I'll return with the cease-fire time."

"But if those devils shoot, we shoot back," he admonished, shaking his finger toward the opposite hill.

As I drove back to the Greek side, I thought that it was foolish wasting time here, that I should be with the Irish taking photos. I came to the road where Dimitri and two rifle-toting companions waited. Dimitri hurriedly opened the jeep door and spoke anxiously. "Good, you come back. What they say? Please come to store. Tell news everybody." I went reluctantly. We entered a house that was also the local general store, with living quarters in the rear. Six men with rifles were assembled, smoking pungent cigarettes. They nodded amiably at me and one of them offered a cigarette, but I declined politely.

"I spoke with the head man and he too wants to stop shooting. Their animals are also starving and need food—same problem. Right now they are holding their fire." Dimitri repeated my message in Greek to the armed men. "How long will it take to tell everyone to cease-fire?"

"'Proximately half hour. Friend here drive autotruck."

"Great, you all agree. Now a cease-fire signal is necessary—a waving white flag that everybody can see. Oh, how about that church bell—does it ring?" I asked, looking at the short church steeple.

"Yes, very loud. Crazy Turkish can hear!" said Dimitri, tapping his ear twice. I glanced at my watch: 10:05.

"Tell everybody now that at eleven o'clock exactly, when the church bell rings out, they must put their guns down—no shooting. Is it understood and agreed?" I asked emphatically.

"Absolutely," affirmed Dimitri. They all nodded.

I hurried over to the Turk's cottage. He was waiting at the doorway. I told him the results of the Greek meeting.

"At eleven o'clock the Greeks will ring their church bell to signal the truce. Will you agree and honor the truce?"

"For sure, mister. When bell rings, we honor. I promise."

"I believe you. I'll tell them it is agreed."

"How long this truce last?" he asked.

"As long as nobody shoots. A U.N. patrol will surely pass this way. If there's a problem, tell them; but please don't say anything about my being here."

"I understand. Good-bye, mister. Come visit sometime. I make good *sis kebab* and we got good strawberry." He gave me a hug and a smack on both cheeks with his big moist mustache.

I met Dimitri again at the barrier. We ran up the footpath to the store, where the men waited for news from me. I caught my breath and told them, "Your Turkish neighbors agree to stop shooting when you ring the church bell at eleven o'clock." I pointed to my watch and spoke louder. "ELEVEN O'CLOCK—NO SHOOTING! The truce lasts as long as nobody shoots. Understand?"

They nodded and mumbled, "Understand." A small mug with ouzo was pushed into my hand. I raised it and toasted, "Irini—peace!" It was 10:35. 1 hopped into my jeep, drove to the bridge between the hills, and parked where I could see both sides.

Eleven o'clock: not a sound. Another minute passed: still no bell. What was the hitch? Three minutes later, just as I was ready to go back to Dimitri, I heard a muted note from the church bell, followed by loud, resonant clanging. As it continued, an old, shaggy black goat appeared on the Greek hillside and began grazing hungrily. Then a white billy with curved horns trotted downhill from the Turkish side. Two more goats ran briskly

The "Green Line" got its name from the color of the marker used to draw it on the original map. Above, soldiers near the buffer zone await reinforcements. At right, a solitary sentinel outside Kato Pyrgos symbolizes the continuing U.N. presence on Cyprus.

down the Greek hill and three sheep from the Turkish hill. A skinny brown donkey followed from the Greek side, and then a flock of Turkish sheep jostled each other in their eagerness to reach the pasture. The bell kept clanging, and soon both hills were dotted with hungry animals munching ravenously. Several sheep and goats wore bells that made a soft counterpoint to the peals of the church bell.

"What a picture!" I thought. I took out a Nikon and viewed it—but it didn't look right, just an ordinary stock shot of animals grazing. Who would understand? How do you photograph peace?

Basil Zarov, *a Toronto magazine photographer, worked for the United Nations from 1961 to 1964—primarily in the Congo and on Cyprus. He now specializes in art and portrait photography.*

A friendly gesture can go far in easing a volatile situation, or in getting supplies through to an isolated community. Here, a Swedish member of UNEF I talks with a resident of El'Arish, Egypt, 1957.

The Essential Art of Empathy

by Keith Elliot Greenberg

For more than five decades, the Blue Helmets have carved out an impressive, and often overlooked, role for themselves monitoring cease-fire agreements, disarming irregulars, and preserving order in troubled lands. In their training they must unlearn much of what they know about conventional warfare.

In 1989, Canadian major Geordie Elms was standing in a remote pocket of northern Pakistan, attempting to explain the United Nations mandate in the troubled region to a bedraggled refugee from Afghanistan.

"I told him that we were inspecting his refugee camp," recalled Elms, a participant in the United Nations Good Offices Mission in Afghanistan and Pakistan (UNGOMAP), formed to assist the Soviet pull-out from the area. "I specifically outlined what the Geneva accords were. And I told him how much we hoped to get him back to his country soon."

The refugee listened and nodded frequently before finally remarking, "Alright, but can I get another water truck? The one I have is broken."

For Elms, feeling empowered with the nobility of the U.N., there was a moral to the exchange: Peacekeeping training entails much more than unarmed combat exercises, marksmanship, and obstacle courses; on the ground, the most important talent may be walking in the shoes of the native population.

"You can't automatically transfer your values to people in other places and expect them to understand," Elms elaborated. "The man thought all this talk was fine, but he was more concerned with just getting water. And, if I was going to be successful on this mission, I had to remember what *his* priorities were. The quality you need most in United Nations peacekeeping is empathy."

It is an attribute that cannot be attained in a classroom or training facility because—although peacekeepers may spend months preparing for a mission—the real lessons come when interacting with those unfortunate enough to be living in a war zone.

"There's really no technique to doing this stuff," said Elms, whose U.N. assignments have also included the Middle East and Cyprus. "You have to watch and learn."

Before becoming a student of the new environment, certain military skills must be developed at home. While instruction varies from country to country, the average U.N. soldier has gone through fundamental military training and learned a craft useful in the no-frills world of the conflict area: dentistry, plumbing, etc. U.N. officers are known to comment that it is easier to train an electrician or carpenter to become a good peacekeeper than the other way around.

These skills are even more in demand as the United Nations makes the transition from traditional peacekeeping to peace-building—enhancing conditions in a war-torn country by improving the residents' quality of life and the nation's infrastructure. Administering medical care in Rwanda, monitoring elections in Nicaragua, even repainting a temple in Cambodia—all are examples of peacemaking.

As the Cold War ended, long-simmering animosities—fueled by ethnic, religious and tribal differences—erupted everywhere, forcing the U.N. to change the way it dealt with conflict. "Suddenly, we are involved in civil war—Somalia, Mozambique, Angola," said Secretary-General Boutros Boutros-Ghali. The combatants, he added, "are not military armies, but gangs."

With such widespread chaos, the entire foundation of a society must be rebuilt in order to prevent the turmoil from escalating. "We are involved in the return of refugees," said Boutros-Ghali. "We are involved in the reconstruction of the country. We are involved in the creation of new police . . . so here, it is not only a peacekeeping operation, it is a peace-keeping operation, plus a relief operation, plus a rehabilitation, a reconstruction operation."

What type of person is equipped to take on such a daunting task? In the Scandinavian countries, the peacekeepers are frequently reservists who come into the military with a variety of vocations. In Canada and Ireland, they tend to be career soldiers. Either way, a certain groundwork is needed before an individual takes part in history's only "army of peace."

The most comprehensive U.N. training facility is in Niinisalo, Finland, established in 1969 to prepare peacekeepers from Finland, Denmark, Sweden and Norway for missions, often under simulated conditions. It usually takes about five weeks to train officers, four weeks for soldiers. In addition to the Nordic countries, monitors from Poland, Switzerland, Austria and the United States have studied at Niinisalo.

Like all soldiers on alert, peacekeepers try to stay fit. Norwegian members of UNEF I do morning exercises around their camp at Port Said, Egypt, December 1956.

Here, student observers leap into foxholes to avoid mortar fire in a facsimile of the Golan Heights, where two mock armies—"Grayland" and "Blueland"—have agreed to allow the U.N. to create a buffer zone. When an eruption is heard, the peacekeepers must determine whether it came from inside or outside the neutral area and who did the firing.

They are also trained not to overreact. Since one of the points of peacekeeping missions is allowing the people in a war-torn country to live in relative normalcy, mundane occurrences should not be confused with belligerent ones. A construction project explosion should be immediately recognized as just that, as opposed to a grenade detonation or rocket attack.

At a seemingly innocent checkpoint, a gray Land Rover suddenly plunges through the barricade, with the man in the passenger seat firing on the peacekeeper. From the other side of the road, a fellow U.N. soldier grabs a light machine gun and "kills" the driver. As the vehicle crashes into a collection of barrels, the gunman jumps out and races into the woods. Instead of being lured into a firefight beneath the trees, the monitors are expected to get on their radios and report the assault. Then, they inspect the Land Rover—not too closely, though, because the driver was on a suicide mission from "Dangerland," a fanatical militia not involved in the U.N. peacekeeping accord, and is sitting on a hand grenade with the pin removed.

Their Scandinavian background notwithstanding, the soldiers communicate with each other and file their reports in English, one of two working languages used by U.N. personnel. They also must speak English during their leisure time. Additionally, they are encouraged to perfect their cooking abilities, learning five recipes for preparation in the field.

As rustic as peacekeeping is, many return for more than one six-month tour, either because of the compensation or heartfelt commitment. Yet, even those with previous peacekeeping experience are not always ready for the complexities of the next mission. Therefore, it is critical to absorb as much background information about the combat zone as possible: the history of the region; its religions and taboos; the source of the conflict and how long it is expected to last. There are run-downs on the warring parties in terms of arms, equipment, ideologies, and leaders.

Major Scotty Alexander, one of Canada's training officers, said arrangements for a long-anticipated mission can take up to three months. Other times, peacekeepers have as little as 72 hours to get ready. "The minimum we'll do is brief the person on the mandate of the mission, who the opposing forces are, what the particular problems are and any specific medical information," he said. "And, with that, we launch them off."

What the peacekeepers witness after departure is not always pleasant. In southern Lebanon, for instance, a Muslim family may have their home bulldozed by the Israeli army simply for possessing a photo of a fundamentalist sheik, or an Arab teenager can be killed by his neighbors for chatting with an Israeli soldier. While the monitors are not expected to condone the violence, they should grow to understand the religious, cultural and historical causes behind it.

That becomes all the more difficult when the mediators are caught in the cross fire, a sometimes daily occurrence for the United Nations Interim Force in Lebanon (UNIFIL). With the help of the Israelis, the Christian South Lebanese Army (SLA) has built very secure positions on a hill overlooking an Irish U.N. post. With so many real and perceived threats nearby, the SLA is constantly firing its guns, something not ignored by the multitude of rival militias. As the battles rage, the Irish monitors retreat into underground bunkers, with the knowledge that if they take part in the skirmishes, they become part of the problem they are supposed to quell.

While keeping an eye on the salvos—for reports to be filed later—the peacekeepers radio UNIFIL headquarters in the village of Naqoura. From there, an Israeli liaison officer is conveyed a simple direction: Tell the SLA to stop. At the same time, other U.N. units try to, first, discern who is firing on the Christians and, then, beseech them to end the hostilities. The

Irish also send up red flares, a signal—understood by both sides—that it is they who are under fire. The entire process generally takes three or four minutes and, according to Irish lieutenant-colonel Dermot Earley, "it does work." The fighting ceases—albeit, temporarily—and the U.N. maintains its neutrality.

The routine may seem peculiar but, then, so is the very concept of U.N. peacekeeping. "From a military standpoint, you are trained to close with the enemy and kill him," maintained Fijian colonel Isikia Savua. "In the U.N., an army is sent in for the purpose of peace. That means a soldier has to change his entire state of mind." To achieve this, the peacekeeper— whether he or she is from Jamaica or Indonesia, Australia or Kenya, Nepal or Poland—learns to live by three short words: In Somalia or El Salvador, Western Sahara or Cyprus, Haiti or Macedonia, always be fair, firm and friendly.

The first United Nations Emergency Force (UNEF I), dispatched to Egypt in 1956, established the guidelines for fairness in peacekeeping. The units were stationed on the country's border with Israel not as an occupation force, but with Egypt's consent (in fact, eleven years later, the troops were abruptly withdrawn at the request of President Gamel Abdel Nasser, as he accelerated into the Six-Day War). U.N. soldiers carried light weapons, to be used only in self-defense. Today, at its approximately seventeen missions involving some thirty countries, the U.N. deploys these mildly outfitted peacekeepers or unarmed observers.

The restrictions at U.N. checkpoints make it difficult to initiate strife: Loaded weapons are prohibited. A magazine can be kept on a gun, so long as the chamber is empty. Thus, the peacekeeper is forced to go through the procedure of loading the weapon before attempting to discharge it.

When misunderstandings do occur, officers from different countries involved in the peacekeeping operation are sent to negotiate with warring factions. The U.N. representatives may each take a stern stance or play "good cop, bad cop," but there is rarely the perception that the purpose of the mission is pursuing one nation's agenda.

Then, there's the talent of masking anger. "You have to develop a psyche where you will accept a situation that normally would have been fightin' words," said Canadian colonel John Gardam. "You let your eyes smile— even if you're boiling angry inside—and you try to talk around the situation."

More than once, peacekeepers have been bullied because of their non-aggressive stance. In February 1992, U.N. representatives desperately tried to block Israeli forces sweeping into the Lebanese villages of Yater

Before going on night patrol, members of an Indian parachute battalion attached to UNEF I are briefed by one of their officers, who points out their objective on a sand model.

and Kafra ostensibly to flush out Hezbollah guerrillas—first with words and then, several times, with fists—but Israel only departed when its commanders decided it was time. Ten years earlier, during Israel's initial invasion of Lebanon—ironically labeled "Operation Peace For Galilee"—Fijian monitors were powerless to halt an intrusion of the UNIFIL area. "We had to put up a semblance of resistance by placing barricades in the roads," Colonel Savua related. "And the Israelis would plow over them with trucks. Then, the only thing we could do was stand back and watch; this was an observer mission, not an enforcement action."

But, occasionally, the moral authority of the U.N.—the "firm" part of the fair, firm, and friendly ethos—proves to be a potent weapon. In the aftermath of the 1973 Yom Kippur War, a Finnish battalion was charged with deterring an Israeli surge down the Cairo/Suez road. The Israeli unit,

Brazilians with UNEF I are instructed on land mines. Long after hostilities are over, peace-keepers have to pass along information about mine fields to civilians still at risk.

which had yet to receive its instructions to cooperate with the U.N., readied itself to smash through the barrier. Suddenly, the Finns put down their guns, lined up in the middle of the road, linked arms, and invited the advancers to barrel through them. The Finns pointed out that, although they were vulnerable, their battalion photographer was in a safe location nearby, and images of the incident would be transmitted around the globe. Grasping this logic, the Israelis backed off.

Finnish lieutenant-colonel Juhani LoSkkanen considers the episode one of his nation's crowning moments in U.N. peacekeeping: "The attitude of the Finns is not to grab our weapons in a temperamental manner, but show our forcefulness in a calm way. Our national characteristics are very suitable to the emotions of the Middle East."

Again, understanding those emotions—and the beliefs behind them—is the most vital asset. In 1960–61, Colonel Gardam's Canadian unit was posted in the no-man's-land between Egypt and Israel. For centuries, Bedouin tribes had lived on the frontier, leading their herds wherever vegetation could be found. Now, the U.N. had arrived, drawing a line in the sand, limiting the foraging. The Bedouins were hardly persuaded by this change in policy, and the Canadians had to devise a solution. A less than attractive possibility was bringing the uncooperative Bedouins to the nearby town of Rafah and turning them over to the Egyptian police, who treated them miserably. Then, a Palestinian interpreter informed the peacekeepers that the Bedouins feared having their pictures taken. "They believed their souls were now in the black box," Gardam said. "The first group of teenagers we found crossing the border, we lined up and photographed. Then, to show that we really meant no harm, we brought them to the mess hall and gave them whatever they wanted to eat." This method, while not perfect, was generally effective.

When dealing with the actual armies involved in the conflict, the demeanor must be somewhat more professional. "You play the role of the honest broker," stressed Major Alexander of Canada. "There are times when you have to say, 'You're wrong in this particular case,' but you need military training to ensure that you know what you're talking about: What is a threat, what is an escalation of the problem, and what is a normal day-to-day routine with no offensive intention whatsoever. You have to be able to tell the difference between a battalion of tanks packed for repairs and a battalion of tanks dug in with overhead cover, prepared to do battle. A politician might not know the difference, but a military man knows not to make an issue out of something that is not an issue."

Bolstering the peacekeeper's words is the fact that the combatants are aware of the U.N.'s presence and purpose in the trouble spot. When armed individuals would attempt to pass through checkpoints manned by Savua in Lebanon, the Fijian colonel would hold up his hands and implore, "Please, you cannot bring your weapons here. You *know* what the rules of engagement are."

Sometimes, the steadfast approach was convincing. "And sometimes," Savua added, "the guy would go behind a bush and take a shot at you." Since missions began in 1948, more than 1,440 peacekeepers have died on the job.

Somalia ranks as one of the most dangerous operations the U.N. has undertaken. Here, peacekeepers entered a country without a government, split into territories controlled by heavily armed gangs who pillaged relief supplies from the docks before the material could reach the needy. After arriving to much fanfare in December 1992, troops became uncertain over their mandate in the African nation. Were they supposed to neutralize the warlords pirating food, or simply feed the hungry while allowing the bandits to keep their weapons?

Likewise, public opinion in nations contributing peacekeeping soldiers was divided. Many American politicians—after viewing footage of riotous disorganization in the country's capital, Mogadishu, branded the operation a failure. Boutros-Ghali responded that the world wasn't aware of advancements in other parts of the country, where the fighting was contained and the starving were fed.

"We have been able to provide assistance to millions," he said. "We have been able to give vaccinations to thousands of small children. We have created a local police. We have maintained peace in different parts of Somalia—not in the capital, Mogadishu, but in all other cities. So you must not underestimate us."

Jan Eliasson, under-secretary-general for humanitarian affairs, left the country certain that peacemaking was the right decision.

"I was in Somalia in 1992, Baidoa," he remembered. "In that city, 250 people were dying a day. I came to the camp in the morning and saw children who were in bad shape, and I came back at night and saw five paper bags with bodies. And that you can never forget. And after seeing this horror, you ask yourself whether you do not send a strong message that this must end."

In recent years, as civil war tore apart the Balkans, the United Nations Protection Force in the former Yugoslavia (UNPROFOR) came under harsh scrutiny. The lowest point may have been in November 1994, when about 400 U.N. soldiers were taken hostage by Serbian fighters. While politicians and editorial writers in troop-contributing countries were, understandably, dubious about the U.N.'s effectiveness in the region, John Issac, a U.N. staff photographer who has made several trips to the former Yugoslavia, claims that untold numbers of lives have been saved and enriched by the presence of peacekeepers.

In Serb-controlled Knin, Issac witnessed a group of Kenyan soldiers surround an encampment of Muslim families, protecting them from violence, and even running shopping errands for the frightened war victims. In the Bosnian town of Vitez, he watched British troops escort Muslims through Serb-ruled areas to visit relatives. Later in the day, at a prearranged time, the peacekeepers accompanied these people back to their homes—all with the cooperation of the Serb and Bosnian authorities.

"If leaders of the two groups talked to each other openly about this, their own people would grow suspicious," Issac observed. "So the U.N. acted as the go-between, listening to what each side had to say, and attempting to see things from that perspective."

At Abu Beach, Gaza, June 1958, Indian, Danish, and Swedish troops practice disembarking from a landing craft.

Peacekeepers insist that a friendly bearing eases a tour to a volatile region. Locals remember which monitors keep candy in their pockets for the throngs of children who invariably mob the exotic, uniformed visitors. Patience is a virtue when merchants or bazaar shoppers try out their elementary English on a Canadian, Irish, or Australian guest. Carrying an extra water can in the jeep can save a lucky resident a twenty-mile trip into town, and go a long way toward ingratiating the entire peacekeeping unit with both the natives and their leaders.

But what is friendly in the soldier's home country can be provocative abroad. Even when cars are being searched for weapons in Lebanon, peacekeepers must respect the local culture by questioning female passengers only through their husbands. From his experience with Turkish Muslims in Cyprus, Canadian major Alexander came to the United Nations Iran-Iraq Military Observer Group (UNIIMOG) believing that the family was an unobjectionable subject for generic conversation. Iraqis, however, tend to grow suspicious when strangers ask about their families. Said Alexander, "It's prying into an Arab Muslim's affairs, and perhaps prejudging whether he has two wives or three wives."

Hospitality is a tenet of Islam, and outsiders have remained at Arab homes for two or three days, mistaking the host's obligation to ask them to "just stay a little while longer" as a sincere sentiment. Although it is acceptable to make a innocent excuse to depart after a meal, a visitor is supposed to, at the very least, have coffee or tea. Questions should be kept to a minimum, and the host permitted to choose the conversation topics. The purpose for the peacekeeper is not gaining immediate answers to pressing concerns but building a trust that can be utilized over time.

"Food is always a problem," Alexander said. "You either can't eat the food because of the local bacteria, or what they eat isn't your own Western

idea of what is good to eat."

Yet, even when the peacekeeper is comfortable with what is going into his mouth, he must be cautious about what comes out of it. A seemingly harmless opinion about the social or political status of the country can blow up quickly, compromising the U.N.'s impartiality. Often, a monitor is handed a piece of paper with the name of an imprisoned resident of the area, and asked to investigate the person's predicament. "You don't take it," stated Canadian lieutenant-colonel David Leslie. "You don't want to raise expectations that can't be realized and you *never* get involved in the internal affairs of the country or the people."

A dependable mode of indoctrinating a first-time U.N. soldier to this and other truths is practiced by the Canadians. They pair a veteran with a newcomer to acquaint him, formally and informally, to the nuances of peacekeeping. It is useful to learn to sit on your flak jacket in the Golan Heights, as protection from the mines washing down into the roads from Mount Hermon in the spring. In Lebanon, when city streets suddenly

Members of a Swedish unit learn how to descend from a helicopter by rope, Cyprus, 1964.

empty, it is wise to follow the crowd: From years of living amidst the tur-moil, they've acquired a sixth sense about impending danger. When dis-cussing troop formations with one of the warring parties, one must refrain from answering questions about the other side's movements—and becom-ing an unwitting courier of secret information.

Experience is the best teacher, as the Fijian peacekeepers were unfortu-nate to discover during their first Lebanon mission in 1970. Unaware that the Middle Eastern country endured harsh winters, the Fijians arrived in the hail and snow with nothing warmer than sweatshirts. Their World War II–era Enfield bolt-action rifles only fired one round at a time, and were eventually traded in for semiautomatic weapons provided by India and Australia. And the Lebanese rule requiring drivers to operate their vehicles on the left side of the road was something of a culture shock. "Our first accident was in the car park," Savua said. "The tow truck was deployed before we even started."

The troubles didn't end there. A recent round of shelling had knocked out plumbing facilities, and the Fijians, forced to rely on rustic methods of obtaining drinking water, were soon afflicted with a form of diarrhea other peacekeepers had branded the "UNIFIL quick step."

The assimilation that takes place between various U.N. armies should consist of more than just this collective infirmity. According to Canadian colonel Gardam, a little bit of generosity helps drive home the point that the countries are together for a mutual purpose. "When I was in the Middle East, we were better paid than most of the other armies. We had a better canteen. We had movies. We made it a point to share."

For six weeks, Canadian major Elms occupied an observation post in Hayradan, Afghanistan, with three other soldiers from Ghana, Denmark, and Nepal. "You go through every topic," Elms said, "your training, the type of benefits you get, how you feel procedures should be conducted. Every country has its own stereotype in peacekeeping missions: Americans think it's their way or the wrong way. Canadians say that our way is the best way. And the Irish will listen to any way."

Much of the time was devoted to talking about food. As the peacekeep-ers alternated at cooking duties, each enlightened the others to the delica-cies of his home country. Elms made steak, the Nepalese a traditional bean dish, the Dane smoked herring, and the Ghanian curry.

Of course, in order to comment on the provisions, it is necessary to share a common tongue. While English might be the a working language of U.N. peacekeeping forces, not everyone has mastered it by the time a mission commences. When Fijian colonel Savua was in Lebanon, his soldiers could not converse with Francophone Senegalese and French peace-keepers—until a bilingual Canadian communications battalion arrived. When he was in the Sinai Desert, a Colombian brigade brought along translators. Unfortunately, these were university students who could not comprehend military terms in Spanish, much less translate them into English. In the Sinai Desert, Gardam's Canadian unit reached an important concordance with its Swedish and Danish counterparts. There would be no complicated passwords unpronounceable by a particular army. Rather, all the phrases would be universal and phonetic: whisky, bravo, Zulu, tango, x-ray.

On each mission, there are certain events that can never be anticipated beforehand. Canadian colonel Leslie—trained to one day meet the Soviet Union on the battlefield—discovered some startling sentiments while watching the Russian-speaking invaders depart from Afghanistan. "I found myself looking at them not as a soldier, but as a parent, and there was a great feeling of joy to see them going back, unscathed. I never thought that, after all my training, I was capable of that kind of emotion for the Soviets."

In Egypt, Gardam was stunned when a career private on guard duty didn't check the safety on his machine gun, slammed down the magazine and accidentally blasted 20 rounds into the tents and under the beds of a neighboring Swedish guard company. "He was standing there with his gun smoking and his mouth open, and these Swedes were getting ready to kill him," Gardam remembered. "But, very quickly, an officer from both sides appeared. We apologized profusely, and invited all the Swedes to come in and see our movie that night."

On a snowy afternoon in February, Major Scotty Alexander sat in his office in Ottawa and discussed Canada's plans for the United Nations Advance Mission in Cambodia (UNAMIC). With virtually no infrastructure in place in the Indochina peninsula, the Canadians would bring thirty days' worth of food and sixty days' worth of spare parts. Monitors were to be inoculated for every known disease in the region.

Then, he conceded, "We're going to make mistakes. We'll arrive with too much of one item and not enough of another. A soldier may be fully inoculated, and then he'll forget about our warning against trying the food until he's completely acclimated and fall sick."

A few cubicles away, Lieutenant-Colonel Leslie—who long ago mastered the essential art of empathy—worried about encouraging the hopes of another battered people viewing the U.N. as their salvation. "Unfortunately, so many people in these countries think that the U.N. is going to come in and solve their problems," he lamented. "To the more educated ones, you explain that we're here to facilitate things while the situation is worked out from within. To the others, all you can do is show them sensitivity while you're there."

Keith Elliot Greenberg *wrote the narration for a 1990 PBS documentary on U.N. peacekeeping, "The Blue Helmets," and directed the 1995 TBS documentary "In Search of Peace," about the U.S. relationship with the U.N.*

A U.N. soldier in the Katanga operation takes cover behind an armored vehicle that has broken down under fire, December 1961.

Crisis in Katanga

by Stanley Meisler

Only once have U.N. peacekeepers engaged in conventional warfare, when they managed to suppress an African secession and an army led by white mercenaries. It was a story filled with drama—and one of the strangest mixes of personalities ever to command the international stage. It ended in uproar in the U.N. General Assembly, and with the violent deaths of many, including those of Prime Minister Patrice Lumumba and Secretary-General Dag Hammarskjöld.

Most people suddenly found Africa on their minds when the newly independent Congo erupted in 1960. Before then, hardly anyone but missionaries, big-game hunters, and a handful of obscure diplomats knew anything about the place that Hollywood and other mythmakers called "the dark continent." With the Congo crisis, Africa not only thrust itself upon the world's consciousness in a few quick months, but it did so troubled and shrieking. What followed was the only instance to date in which U.N. peacekeeping forces have engaged in conventional warfare.

The U.N. intervention came during some of the tensest years of the Cold War. Within a few months of the outbreak, Soviet leader Nikita Khrushchev would pound a shoe on his table at the General Assembly to protest the policies of the secretary-general, Dag Hammarskjöld, and the United States. In a little more than two years, Khrushchev and President John F. Kennedy would test each other's mettle in the Cuban missile crisis. But there was far more than an East-versus-West conflict at stake in the Congo.

The chaos there had jarred the mood of optimism about a rapidly emerging Africa—there were more than thirty new nations between 1956 and 1966, about half of them becoming independent in 1960 alone. Many Western intellectuals and political liberals, though they knew little about it, fervently wanted black Africa to succeed and blamed adverse news like the Congo chaos on the dark hand of colonialism. Thus it was politically correct to support the U.N. intervention and its suppression of Moise Tshombe's mercenary-led army in the province of Katanga, and neocolonial-

In the summer of 1960, many atrocities were reported in the Congo. Here, a Congolese soldier guns down civilians near Stanleyville. The first U.N. troops arrived July 15.

ist to favor the independence of that mineral-rich province. In the eyes of those who sympathized with the Third World, the Katanga lobby was made up of reactionaries who wanted to dismember and thereby weaken black Africa. Differences over the new Africa did not fit the East–West conflict at all. The British, for example, counted themselves the staunchest ally of the United States in the Cold War but could not fathom Kennedy's anti-Katanga policy during his presidency.

Few colonies came to independence as unprepared as the Congo on June 30, 1960. Belgian colonialism had been harsh and exploitative. Out of a population of 14 million, there were only seventeen black university graduates—not one a doctor, a lawyer, or an engineer. The 100,000 Belgian settlers and bureaucrats ran the commerce and administration and expected to keep on doing so for years after independence. Unlike the British or the French, the Belgians had provided no period of self-rule. Less than a week before independence, a week-old National Assembly elected the new leaders of a coalition government: a fiery, irrational prime minister named Patrice Lumumba, a former post office clerk and beer company salesman whose oratorical skills had won him the leadership of the radical Congolese National Movement; and a stolid, enigmatic president named Joseph Kasavubu, who had studied for the Catholic priesthood but left the seminary in his last year to become a teacher and, later, the head of the Bakongo ethnic group's political association. The independence ceremonies did not foster any good feelings. Lumumba invoked "the insults, the blows that we had to submit to . . . because we were Negroes" and warned the Belgians, "Our wounds are too fresh to forget."

The troubles began just five days later in the Léopoldville (now Kinshasa) barracks of the Congolese army known as the Force Publique. This army of 25,000 men did not have a single African commissioned officer; it was commanded by 1,135 Belgians. Angered by the sight of powerful new black politicians riding around in sleek cars while their own path to prestige was blocked by whites, a group of Congolese soldiers announced they no longer had to obey their Belgian officers. Lieutenant-General Emile Janssens, the Force Publique commander, tried to quash the mutiny with arrogance. In a blatant and now infamous act, Janssens assembled the troops and chalked across a blackboard the admonition "Before Independence = After Independence." But the soldiers started to sack the canteen, and their mutinous mood soon spread to the Thysville garrison less than 100 miles away.

As more rioting shook up garrisons throughout the country, the soldiers directed as much of their fury at Lumumba as at their Belgian officers. The frightened prime minister quickly gave in and dismissed all Belgian officers, appointing his cousin Victor Lundula, a civilian whose only military experience came during a brief stint as medical orderly in the Force Publique, as the new commander, with the rank of major general. Joseph Mobutu, a corporal and former journalist, was promoted to chief of staff, with the rank of colonel.

The instant promotion of hundreds of inexperienced Africans failed to calm the situation, and the undisciplined Force Publique, now known as the Armée Nationale Congolaise (ANC), went on a rampage. Reports spread of the rape and murder of whites throughout the Congo, and thousands of terrified Belgians fled across the borders to Congo-Brazzaville (now the People's Republic of the Congo), Uganda, Angola, and Northern Rhodesia (now Zambia). A Belgian Royal Commission later reported that marauding Congolese troops had raped 291 European women.

On July 10, Belgium, transporting 5,600 troops to join 3,800 already stationed at its Congolese bases of Kitona and Kamina, intervened to restore order within the former colony. But the Belgian intervention was unpalatable to many outsiders in this era of emerging Africa. The disdain for Belgium was exacerbated a day later when the Belgians killed more than a dozen Congolese in the town of Matadi. That same day, Moise

Tshombe—the son of a wealthy black African entrepreneur and, since May, president of the province of Katanga—listened to Belgian advisers from the Union Minière du Haut Katanga and declared the independence of his province, a major source of cobalt, industrial diamonds, copper, and numerous other minerals. The Eisenhower administration rejected all suggestions that U.S. troops replace the Belgian troops and encouraged the Congolese government to turn instead to the United Nations. The appeal to the United Nations from both Prime Minister Lumumba and President Kasavubu came two days after Belgium had ordered its troops into the Congo.

On July 14, barely two weeks after Congolese independence, the U.N. Security Council, called into special session by Hammarskjöld, approved his request to send a U.N. peacekeeping force to the Congo to replace the Belgian troops there and restore order. The vote was eight to zero with three abstentions: Britain and France, the two main colonial powers in Africa, and Nationalist China. Hammarskjöld pledged that the force would include African troops, fire only in self-defense, and keep out of the internal politics of the Congo. After he rushed phone calls to leaders around the world, troops from Ghana and Tunisia (some Tunisians without ammunition) arrived in the Congo aboard American and British transport planes the next day; troops from Ethiopia and Morocco came the day after. A band and an old black goat, the regimental mascot, led the marching Moroccans out of the airport. Hammarskjöld named Major-General Carl Carlsson von Horn of Sweden as commander. Troops from 30 countries continually augmented the U.N. force until it reached peak strength of 19,828 a year later.

From the start, U.N. officials expected maddening difficulties. "This is the craziest operation in history," Hammarskjöld said. "God only knows where it is going to end." He described the U.N. operation as much like giving first aid to a rattlesnake. Politics would circumscribe every military step. "Unfortunately, we were not 'any army,'" von Horn wrote later, "we were a United Nations force in which logic, military principles even common sense—took second place to political factors." The U.N.—or ONU, as it was known in the Congo, from the initials in French for United Nations Organization—puzzled the Congolese, who had heard little about the organization before. "The ONU?" a Congolese official asked Brian Urquhart, an assistant to Hammarskjöld and later the U.N.'s under-secretary-general for special political affairs. "What tribe is that?"

Although Lumumba assumed that the U.N. force would do his bidding, Hammarskjöld soon demonstrated that the Blue Helmets were an interna-

Col. Joseph Mobutu (above, left), announcing the army's takeover of Congo's government, displays a picture of Soviet premier Khrushchev and the words "Hands Off the Congo." Mobutu's soldiers later arrested Prime Minister Patrice Lumumba (above, right) and turned him over to Katangese authorities, who murdered him. The Congo—now Zaire—is a land of immense distances. The map below shows its major cities and the province of Katanga.

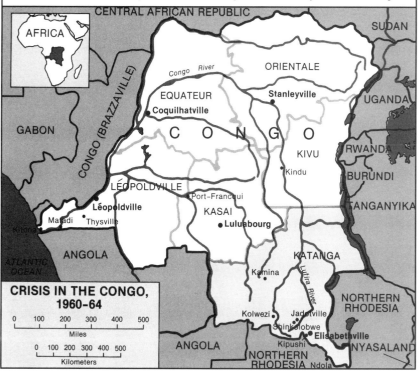

105

tional army with its own mandate, taking orders only from the secretary-general. U.N. troops quickly replaced Belgian soldiers at airports, radio stations, and highways and fanned out to provincial towns like Stanleyville (now Kisangani), Thysville, Matadi, Luluabourg (now Kananga), and Coquilhatville (now Mbandaka) to impose order. By July 23, a little more than a week after the first contingents arrived, the United Nations had replaced Belgian troops everywhere except in Katanga and the two Belgian bases.

But the U.N. force was beset with problems. Each country's contingent had different weapons, vehicles, radio systems, and even eating preferences. Confusion could not be avoided. Major-General Henry Templar Alexander, the British officer who served as chief of Ghana's defense staff and led the first Ghanaian troops into the Congo, subsequently wrote:

> There seemed to be no form of military planning cell in the United Nations Secretariat which could plan and produce the type of military force required to bring peace to a country which had been reduced to chaos overnight . . . . Troops arrived, officers arrived, commanders arrived, and nobody knew quite what they were supposed to do.

The U.N.'s relations with the Armée Nationale Congolaise were nettlesome. With astounding bluffness, General Alexander told Ralph Bunche, the black American who served as Hammarskjöld's undersecretary-general and special representative to the Congo, "The nigger in the woodpile is the ANC." In his memoirs, Alexander made the same point with more tact: "The United Nations military forces went into the Congo to 'assist' the central government in Léopoldville to maintain law and order," he wrote, "but unfortunately the major law-breakers were the Congolese army."

Rajeshwar Dayal of India, one of Bunche's successors in the Congo, described the ANC as "armed rabble." Anyone who had dealings with the Congolese army during the 1960s knows what Dayal meant. For many years, Congolese troops wore their feelings of inferiority on their sleeves. An arrested white always knew that survival depended on calming the frantic fears of the handful of soldiers arresting him. Whenever they felt threatened or defeated, the Congolese soldiers would assuage their humiliation by storming into an undefended village or town, pillaging, and raping and murdering civilians, both white and black. In January 1961, a Stanleyville unit of the ANC murdered twenty-two European missionaries and an unknown number of Africans. The Congolese soldiers would engage an enemy military force only if it was small enough to overrun. When a column of mercenary soldiers approached, some ANC troops would undress, leave their uniforms behind, and flee in their underwear.

General Alexander tried to disarm units of the ANC but was prevented by Bunche and other U.N. officials who insisted they had no authority to do so. The fear of disarming, however, may have contributed to later incidents of ANC assaults on small units of U.N. troops. Congolese troops mercilessly clubbed eight Canadian soldiers at the Léopoldville airport and eight U.S. airmen who had ferried U.N. supplies into the Stanleyville airport, in each case until others came to the soldiers' rescue. More than a year later, Congolese troops murdered forty-four Ghanaian soldiers in Port-Francqui (now Ilebu) and thirteen Italian airmen in Kindu. For a while, Moroccan troops tried to retrain Congolese soldiers, but this stopped after Colonel Mobutu deposed the Lumumba government in a coup on September 14. By then, chaotic events had drawn the United Nations into internal Congolese politics.

In early September 1960, a little more than two months after independence, President Kasavubu and Prime Minister Lumumba attempted to oust each other. Pleading the need for calm and order, Andrew Cordier, the American who succeeded Bunche in the Congo, sent U.N. troops to occupy the radio station in Léopoldville, which shut off Lumumba's main channel for rousing the capital's Africans to his side. Cordier also closed all major airports in the Congo; as a result, a dozen Soviet transport planes were unable to ferry Congolese troops to Léopoldville to help Lumumba. In the midst of this confusion, Mobutu staged his coup and turned the government over to a committee composed of young, educated, nonpolitical Congolese.

By this time, the United States had decided that the Congo would have no peace unless the erratic, demagogic Lumumba was eliminated. Even though confined to his house and surrounded by a protective cordon of Moroccan U.N. troops, Lumumba, according to the Americans, still had enough charisma to inflame the masses. The CIA dispatched an agent with poison to assassinate him. But before the agent could do his job, the Congolese took care of the matter themselves. In an attempt to reach his base in Stanleyville, Lumumba slipped past the U.N. guards but was soon captured by Congolese troops. In January 1961, Mobutu turned Lumumba over to his secessionist enemies in Katanga, where not long afterward he was severely beaten and shot to death in the presence of two Katangan ministers.

U.N. soldiers had watched Lumumba arrive in the Katangan capital of Elisabethville (now Lubumbashi) but had done nothing because of their mandate to stay out of Congolese politics. The murder provoked world-

A white mercenary stops to strip the dead lying in the dust of a country road. He was allowed to keep money and other valuables but was required to turn in any documents.

wide shock and fury, and the United Nations was castigated for failing to protect Lumumba and prevent his transfer to Katanga. Khrushchev denounced Hammarskjöld as Lumumba's "chief assassin."

There was more political turmoil. Antoine Gizenga had set up a Lumumbaist regime in Stanleyville, and Khrushchev, whose flamboyant visit to the U.N. in the fall had included a call for the replacement of Hammarskjöld by a troika, recognized Gizenga as the legitimate leader of the Congo. Several countries, including Morocco and Egypt, announced they would withdraw their troops from the U.N. force in protest against Hammarskjöld's failure to save Lumumba.

Hammarskjöld, who had personally led Swedish U.N. troops into Katanga in October, called on the Security Council for more authority. Although continually criticized by the Soviet Union, the old European colonial powers, and radical African states, Hammarskjöld had the support of most nascent African countries and of John F. Kennedy, the new U.S. president. The Security Council gave Hammarskjöld what he wanted.

On February 21, 1961, a little more than seven months after independence, the Security Council voted nine to zero, with the Soviet Union and France abstaining, for a resolution authorizing the U.N. peacekeepers to use force, if necessary, to prevent civil war in the Congo. The council had never granted such authority before, and has not done so since. The resolution also urged the United Nations to bring the various ANC units under its discipline and control and to remove all mercenaries and Belgian officers from Katanga.

By then, five armies were watching each other in the Congo: the U.N. force of now almost 20,000, posted in small detachments throughout the country; ANC units of 7,000 troops in the Léopoldville area, loyal to Mobutu, who was now a general; ANC units of 5,500 troops in the Stanleyville area, loyal to Gizenga and the memory of Lumumba; ANC units of 3,000 troops in southern Kasai Province, loyal to the secessionist movement of the Baluba chief Albert Kalonji; and Katanga's Gendarmerie of 6,000 troops, under Belgian and mercenary officers loyal to Tshombe. The United Nations, trying to ease tribal and racial conflicts, set up areas of refuge and neutral zones for civilians and spent a good deal of time rescuing European settlers under siege. While the Blue Helmets were never able to whip the ANC units into order, political maneuvering, especially by American diplomats, managed to fashion a fragile unity of all political factions and regions of the Congo except Katanga by the end of the summer of 1961. It was now time for the United Nations to end the secession of Katanga.

The first assault on Katanga—Operation Morthor—began at 4 AM on September 13, 1961, dissipated in recriminations and a humiliating stalemate, and indirectly led to the death of Hammarskjöld in a plane crash, on his way to arrange a cease-fire. For weeks Conor Cruise O'Brien, the Irish diplomat in charge of U.N. operations in Katanga, had been trying to round up the 208 Belgian officers and 302 mercenaries in the Katangese Gendarmerie and deport them from the Congo. Both Tshombe and the Belgian consul had promised to cooperate, but by the time of the assault, 104 foreign soldiers were still listed as "missing." O'Brien suspected that they and perhaps many more unknown mercenaries were in hiding, waiting to fight alongside the Gendarmerie.

Tshombe, intent on preventing his Gendarmerie from turning into a rabble like the ANC, quietly hired mercenaries to replace Belgian soldiers whenever U.N. pressure forced him to let some of them go. "In these matters," he told Major Guy Weber, his Belgian military adviser, "I trust only whites." Tshombe's crew of mercenaries drew on many sources, including French paratroopers fresh from defeat in Algeria, South African and Rhodesian adventurers, Belgian settlers, Italian fascists, and German veterans of World War II. Most were racists who seemed to enjoy shooting down blacks for pay, but there were also idealists who believed in some kind of multiracial Africa. The mercenaries were often known as *les affreux* (the frightful ones) because of their ferocious attacks on Baluba tribesmen in northern Katanga who opposed Tshombe and his secession.

U.N. officials looked on Tshombe with contempt. He had an infuriating way of acquiescing in attempts to bring Katanga back into the Congo and then reneging, of promising to rid his army of foreigners yet somehow never managing to follow through. "Neither statements of fact nor written engagements could be relied on," O'Brien wrote later. "No contradiction, no detected lie, caused Mr. Tshombe the slightest embarrassment. If caught out in some piece of duplicity—on political prisoners, refugees, mercenaries, or anything else—he would show absent-mindedness, tinged, I sometimes imagined, with a paternal compassion for the naivete of anyone who supposed he would tell the truth, if he could derive the slightest advantage from telling anything else." Yet Tshombe also struck many outsiders as a far more able administrator and adroit politician than anyone else in the Congo.

According to O'Brien's version of the events in September, he and Brigadier K.A.S. Raja, the Indian commander of the military forces in Katanga, received their orders from Mahmoud Khiary of Tunisia, the senior U.N. officer in Léopoldville, only a few hours before the battle. Under Operation Morthor, U.N. officials and their troops (one Swedish battalion, one Irish battalion, and two Indian battalions of Gurkhas and Dogras) would surround the presidential palace of Tshombe, arrest four of his key cabinet members, occupy the key centers of communication (the post office, with its telephone and telegraph exchanges, and the radio station), raid the files of the offices of Katanga Security and the ministry of information, run up the Congolese flag on all public buildings in Elisabethville, and persuade Tshombe, under this pressure, to give up his secession. As Khiary left the Villa des Roches, the U.N. headquarters in Elisabethville, he told O'Brien, "Above all, no half measures." O'Brien assumed the plan had been approved by Hammarskjöld.

As heavy firing broke out in Elisabethville, a panicky Tshombe phoned O'Brien twice. O'Brien recounted his U.N. orders and, while guaranteeing Tshombe's safety, asked the Katangan president to make a radio broadcast declaring the secession of Katanga at an end and ordering his soldiers to stop firing. Tshombe agreed, and an ebullient O'Brien told journalists at 6:30 AM, September 13, "The secession of Katanga has ended. It now is a Congolese province run by the central government." The pronouncement was premature.

No U.N. troops had circled Tshombe's palace. O'Brien attributed this to a breakdown in communication between the Indians and Swedes. English,

Above, Moise Tshombe, the president of Katanga, waves to a crowd demonstrating against the presence of U.N. troops, September 2, 1961. The next day, U.N. peacekeepers would fire on Katangese troops and white mercenaries in Elisabethville. The result was a stalemate. Below, soldiers of Tshombe's army beat prisoners before shooting them.

the lingua franca of the U.N. troops, was a second language to both, and many did not speak it as well as they thought. There were political and military disagreements between the two groups as well. "Such are the troubles of an international force," O'Brien said. Instead of making his broadcast ending secession, Tshombe left the palace, hid in the home of the British consul, and then fled to Northern Rhodesia.

Indian soldiers armed with rifles of 1918 vintage tried to take over the post office peacefully by persuading the Katangese gendarmes that they would not be disarmed if they let in the U.N. troops. But a sniper on top of the nearby Belgian consulate building shot and killed an Indian soldier, setting off firing by both sides. "After heavy stiff hand to hand fighting," according to official U.N. dispatches, the Indians overcame the Katangese within an hour, both at the post office and at the radio station. Katanga's new Mercedes armored cars, handled "mostly by Belgians in civilian clothes" and cheered by crowds of whites, tried to retake the post office and radio station. The Blue Helmets, in their 1940-model Irish armored cars and Swedish armed personnel carriers, repulsed this counterattack, but fire from Katangese mortars and Belgian-made FN automatic rifles demolished the studio beyond repair. Automatic-rifle fire continued in Elisabethville throughout the day. The U.N. troops had managed to arrest only one of the hunted cabinet members, and the Congolese flags did not go up on government buildings.

The Katangese counterattack, bolstered by more white civilians who had taken up arms, intensified the next day. Although they failed to dislodge the U.N. soldiers from downtown Elisabethville, the Katangese heavily damaged the occupied buildings. The Katangese also surrounded 158 Irish troops at their garrison in the nearby mining town of Jadotville (now Likasi) and the 500 Irish and Swedish troops at the old Belgian base of Kamina in northern Katanga. A French-made Fouga Magister jet fighter, piloted for the Katangese by a mercenary, bombed and strafed both U.N. headquarters in Elisabethville and the Irish company at Jadotville during the night. The United Nations had no defense against it. Although the fighting in Elisabethville was stalemated, the U.N. had become the besieged force there, and the Irish troops surrendered at Jadotville five days after the U.N. attack began.

Hammarskjöld, who evidently knew about the plans for Operation Morthor but had not ordered it to go forward, arrived in Léopoldville a few hours after the attack began and soon heard the cries of protest from outraged governments. Lord Landsdowne, a special British envoy to the Congo, warned Hammarskjöld that Prime Minister Harold Macmillan believed only the communists would benefit from the chaos sure to come out of U.N. attacks on Katanga; Tshombe had to be persuaded peacefully to join the Congo. President Kennedy agreed. To reassure his critics, Hammarskjöld issued a statement claiming that the United Nations had not tried to attack Katanga but had only defended itself when fired upon by the Katangese, and insisting that its only goal was to remove foreign officers from the province.

On September 17, Hammarskjöld decided to fly to Ndola, in Northern Rhodesia, to meet with Tshombe and work out a truce. To avoid the Fouga, the chartered airline flew at night on a circuitous route without radio contact. After almost seven hours, the plane reached the Ndola area shortly past midnight, but then it disappeared. A search team found the wreckage in a forest a few miles north of Ndola during the day. All thirteen aboard, including Hammarskjöld, were dead. Despite widespread suspicions at the time, most analysts now believe the crash was an accident.

Mahmoud Khiary, while insisting that the United Nations still stood by its demands that all mercenaries must leave, then worked out the cease-fire with Tshombe. Both sides exchanged prisoners, and the U.N. troops withdrew from the post office and radio station. The U.N. also agreed to let Katangese gendarmes join its troops at the Elisabethville airport. According to the U.N., eleven of its soldiers died in the fighting; the Katangese lost fifty dead. The United Nations had achieved nothing with Operation Morthor.

The second battle for Katanga, far more destructive and bloody, provoking far more rage from U.N. critics, erupted less than two months later. Tshombe had proven as stubborn as ever, dismissing mercenaries publicly, then rehiring them surreptitiously. Bolstered by another Security Council resolution authorizing the use of force, the United Nations reinforced its Katanga units with two Ethiopian battalions (bringing total strength to almost 6,000), new equipment like Ferret armored cars and heavy mortar and 108mm guns, and, most important, an air unit of six Indian Canberra jet bombers, six Swedish Saab jet fighters, and four Ethiopian F-84 jet fighters. American transports ferried most of the new troops and matériel into Katanga. Breaking with the British, the Kennedy administration had finally decided that the forcible suppression of Tshombe was the only hope for averting instability that could lead to a communist takeover in the Congo.

There were many sources of tension. In a show of fury at the United Nations, Katangese paracommandos showed up at a party for Tshombe's most prominent American defender, Senator Thomas Dodd of

Much of the Congo's infrastructure was destroyed by the fighting. Here, U.N. soldiers carry Congolese children across a newly opened provisional bridge over the Karwezi River.

Connecticut, and seized Brian Urquhart, who had just arrived to take O'Brien's place, and his deputy. The pair were clubbed mercilessly. Threatened with a U.N. assault on the presidential palace, Tshombe interceded with the gendarmes to obtain Urquhart's release. "Better beaten than eaten," Urquhart told reporters. Katangese gendarmes also mounted roadblocks throughout Elisabethville, impeding the free movement of U.N. troops. When Tshombe defied repeated calls to remove the roadblocks, the

new secretary-general, U Thant, ordered Brigadier Raja to clear them by force on December 5. That set off the battle, which lasted two weeks.

The U.N. planes took off from Luluabourg and destroyed all four Katanga jet planes on the ground at their base in Kolwezi. They then bombed and strafed targets in Elisabethville at will. Encircling the city, the U.N. ground forces attacked the camps of the Gendarmerie. Many gendarmes withdrew into the white residential neighborhoods, and it became difficult to flush them out without harming civilians and their property. There were U.N. excesses that made headlines throughout the world. Trying to terrify gendarmes from nearby camps, U.N. troops misfired many rounds of mortars into the compound of twenty-nine American Seventh-Day Adventist missionaries and into Prince Leopold Hospital. In another error, the Canberra jets bombed the hospital of a former uranium mine in Shinkolobwe and killed four Africans. Swooping over Elisabethville, the U.N. jets bombed and strafed the Roman Catholic cathedral, the museum, and a beauty parlor. British prime minister Macmillan wrote bitterly in his diary, "Yesterday an Ethiopian soldier shot a Swiss banker in Elisabethville with a bazooka. No one knows why, and no one cares. But even Swiss bankers ought to have some rights."

Urquhart was troubled as well. "The moment a peacekeeping force starts killing people it becomes a part of the conflict it is supposed to be controlling and thus a part of the problem," he wrote. "I loathed the battle in Elisabethville, from which no good came for anyone. Many innocent people were killed or hurt and neither the U.N. nor the mercenaries nor Tshombe came out of it with any credit." Urquhart described the Indian Canberra bombers as "a menace," and after they had demolished the post office, he finally persuaded Brigadier Raja to call them off.

The U.N. force moved at a snail's pace into Elisabethville. Urquhart attributed the military problems to a lack of discipline and cohesion. He described Brigadier Raja as "a weak Indian commander who was not respected by his subordinates." The Swedes resented the Indians, who, "being professionals, tended to be patronizing toward the others." He found the Ethiopians "undisciplined, paranoid and dangerous."

By December 18, the United Nations controlled much of Elisabethville but had still failed to dislodge the gendarmes from all their strongholds. As they closed in on the heart of the city, the Blue Helmets were hampered by sniper fire from white civilians. The U.N. agreed to a cease-fire when Tshombe cabled President Kennedy a promise to meet with Congolese leaders to discuss a pact unifying the Congo. By then, twenty-one U.N. soldiers, 200 Katangese, and six white mercenaries had died in the battling. In a few days, Tshombe signed the agreement. He quickly reneged, however, and the secession continued.

The final battle for Katanga came a year later. U Thant kept trying to ease Tshombe back into the Congo through negotiations, but the secessionist leader always seemed to slip out of a compromise at the last moment. His machinations made the secretary-general lose patience with Tshombe and his ministers. Describing the Katangan president as "a very unstable man," U Thant told a news conference, "I don't know what I can do with such a bunch of clowns." With his revenues from Union Minière, Tshombe hired more mercenaries and bought more jet fighters. Firing between the gendarmes and the Blue Helmets broke out again in late December 1962. Once more pleading self-defense, the United Nations launched an offensive designed to rid the Congo of Tshombe and his secession for good. It was called Operation Grand Slam.

Urquhart had no military complaint this time. He wrote:

We had, at last, a magnificent military command in Katanga. . . . The commander was Major-General Dewan Prem Chand, a soft-spoken, serious-minded Indian officer. . . . His operational deputy was the commander of the Indian Brigade, Brigadier Reggie Noronha, a cavalry officer, fast, stylish, decisive and with a capacity for the grand gesture. I could have told Tshombe that it was very foolish to mess about with two such formidable professionals. However, mess about he did.

The U.N. troops, supported by aerial strafing and bombing, moved swiftly this time. After killing fifty Katangese gendarmes on the outskirts of the city, Noronha and his Indian troops took control of the Gendarmerie headquarters and the downtown area of Elisabethville in a day. Swedish U.N. planes destroyed two British Vampire jets and five converted Harvard trainers on the airfield at Kolwezi, eliminating any threat from the Katangan air force. A day later, Ghanaian and Swedish troops seized the military town of Kamina in the north and Irish troops took over Kipushi, the border town that guarded the flow of traffic from Tshombe's allies in Northern Rhodesia. There was little resistance after that. Within two days, Prem Chand and Noronha led their troops toward the mining towns of Jadotville and Kolwezi across the Lufira River.

The U.N. detractors were furious. Senator Dodd called the offensive "a flagrant, inhuman act of aggression." The British and Belgians warned U Thant that if the U.N. crossed the Lufira River, Tshombe's mercenaries would blow up the great Union Minière facilities in Jadotville and Kolwezi. The mercenaries had already destroyed the two bridges across the river. U Thant promised to delay the U.N. troops, but he later said his message did not reach Prem Chand and Norohna in time. Among U.N. officials in the Congo, there was no talk of slowing down. "We are not going to make the mistake this time of stopping short," said Robert Gardiner of Ghana, the chief of U.N. operations in the Congo. The two Indian generals forded the river on New Year's night, pushing their vehicles across on makeshift rafts. The surprised Katangese soldiers fled, allowing the Indian troops to enter a practically undefended Jadotville, twenty miles north, the next day. The mercenaries had run off without destroying the mines. The United Nations now controlled every important town in Katanga except Tshombe's military stronghold of Kolwezi.

Tshombe, escaping to the south on a Rhodesian air force plane and then making his way from Northern Rhodesia back to Kolwezi, broadcast an appeal for a cease-fire and negotiations to end the secession. But U Thant said it was too late for negotiations; he wanted "actions by Mr. Tshombe and not words, written or oral." Tshombe returned to Elisabethville, where he was placed under house arrest by the U.N. and released only after he promised to end the secession. In Kolwezi on January 15, 1963, Tshombe sent a message to U Thant: "I am ready to proclaim immediately before the world that Katanga's secession is ended." Tshombe and General Prem Chand signed an agreement in Elisabethville on January 17. The United Nations had lost only eleven men in the final battle. A few days later, U.N. troops marched into Kolwezi while Tshombe called on his gendarmes to cooperate with the United Nations. Then, fearing reprisals, he fled, turning up in Paris not long afterward. Two and a half years after independence and the intervention of the United Nations, the secession of Katanga was over.

The U.N. peacekeeping force withdrew from the Congo on June 30, 1964, four years after its arrival. The Congo was hardly an ordered society, but there was little left for the U.N. to do. "The United Nations cannot permanently protect the Congo, or any other country," U Thant said, "from the internal tensions and disturbances created by its own organic growth toward unity and nationhood."

Many ironies trailed the U.N. adventure. A week after the Blue Helmets

A bedraggled Tshombe (below) delivers a final speech to followers assembled in the market square of Kolwezi, January 31, 1963. The U.N. is now in control. Not long after Tshombe's speech, his representatives and U.N. officers (left) go over details of the peaceful takeover of the town.

left, Tshombe, just returned from exile in Europe, was named the new prime minister of the Congo. With avid U.S. support, he hired mercenaries, mainly from South Africa, to lead the Armée Nationale Congolaise against the leftist Lumumbaist rebels in the eastern Congo, especially Orientale Province. When the Nigerian civil war erupted in 1967, many of the same people who railed against Katanga now supported the secession of Biafra. And, in a final irony, General Mobutu, taking over as president in 1965 (and more recently renaming himself Mobutu Sese Seko), eventually succeeded in uniting the Congo—since 1971, the Republic of Zaire—and, while doing so, fashioned one of the most tyrannical, corrupt, and avaricious regimes in Africa. But in those confusing times of the early 1960s, Katanga was a blot on the integrity of Africa, and the United Nations succeeded in wiping it out.

Stanley Meisler, the U.N. correspondent for the Los Angeles Times, *was a foreign correspondent for twenty years and covered Africa in 1967–73. His history of the United Nations,* The U.N: The First Fifty Years, *was published by Atlantic Monthly Press in 1995.*

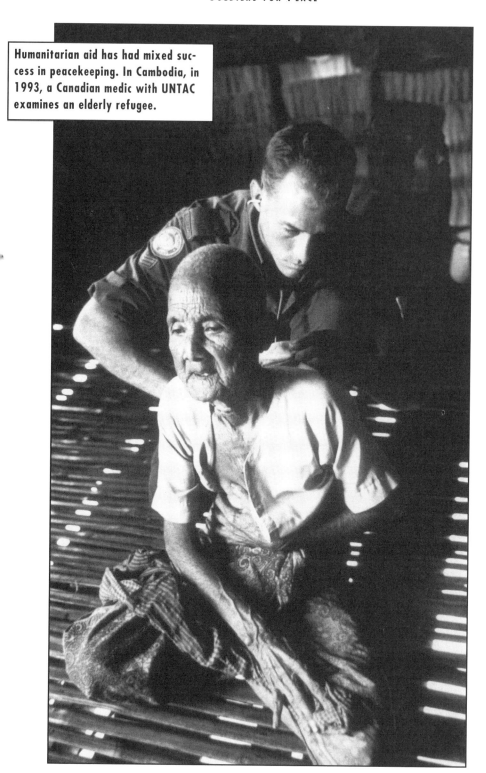

Humanitarian aid has had mixed success in peacekeeping. In Cambodia, in 1993, a Canadian medic with UNTAC examines an elderly refugee.

Peacekeeping and Humanitarian Aid

by Iain Guest

Humanitarian aid has not changed a lot since the end of the Cold War. Relief agencies are still vulnerable to political manipulation. Developing countries are still reluctant to report human-rights violations—for fear they may open the door to unwanted military intervention. And land mines continue to be a deadly, maiming threat to civilian populations long after the wars are over.

In 1981, as a correspondent for the *Guardian* and the *International Herald Tribune*, I accompanied a U.N. food convoy to a small crossing at the border between Thailand and Cambodia. A column of Khmer women emerged from the Cambodian jungle under the watchful eye of Khmer Rouge cadres. Backs bowed, they carried the food back into the jungle to the small settlement of Nong Pru, to be used as military rations by Khmer Rouge soldiers in their war against the government in Phnom Penh.

This was the so-called "land bridge"—one half of a U.N. program that was trying to prevent famine in Cambodia. There was no doubt that emergency food aid was desperately needed in the areas controlled by Phnom Penh as well as in those by the Khmer Rouge. But the U.N. was paying a high price for carrying out this humanitarian mission. Here in Nong Pru, U.N. food was keeping a genocidal movement alive at the insistence of Western governments determined to "bleed" the communist regime in Phnom Penh. The real bleeding was being done by Cambodian women and children. It was the ultimate abuse of the humanitarian mandate.

About ten years later, in June 1992, U.N. Secretary-General Boutros Boutros-Ghali promised an end to this sort of manipulation in his *Agenda for Peace*. The *Agenda*, a statement of purpose by the new secretary-general, sought to redefine peace as development in its broadest sense, and it set out three broad tasks for multilateralism: peace-making; peacekeeping and peace-building.

Such a refinement of tasks implied a dramatic change in the humanitarian mandate. Instead of waiting for a crisis to explode and then rushing in

121

emergency supplies, aid agencies were being urged to anticipate future crises and to direct assistance toward the goal of "peace-building," quite beyond the immediate emergency. This new approach could help prevent conflict and start the process of reconstruction. No longer would humanitarian relief be the sole preserve of agencies; it would engage other players, such as human rights monitors and Blue Berets. Nor would agencies necessarily have to go through the central government in the crisis-struck country. (Previously, emergency aid had been delivered directly to rebels in Afghanistan, Sudan, and Iraq, but these were ad hoc examples.) In a now-famous phrase, the secretary-general insisted that the "time of absolute and exclusive sovereignty has passed." He seemed to be saying that sovereignty now mattered less than saving lives.

This attitude was in keeping with the vision of a new, interventionist United Nations, in reaction to the anarchy that seemed to follow the end of the Cold War. The retreat of communism had removed the glue that held countries like the former Yugoslavia and Somalia together, and produced what some termed a "failed state." Into the void had rushed ambitious warlords, ethnic hatred, and a host of other mischief-makers, creating a new type of emergency, tailor-made for "proactive" humanitarianism.

Gamble in Cambodia

While the secretary-general's blueprint was being written in New York, I was back on the Thai–Cambodian border, watching it played out. On the afternoon of March 29, 1992, pressmen crowded into the U.N. building at Aranyaprathet, Thailand. The following day, the office of the U.N. High Commissioner for Refugees (UNHCR)—for which I was spokesman—was due to repatriate the first of 360,000 Cambodians from the camps in Thailand. It was my task to defend an operation that seemed fraught with risk. The Khmer Rouge still controlled large parts of the north and west of the country, and showed no signs of wanting to stop the war. UNHCR had based its plans on satellite photos, which suggested that there would be plenty of land for returning refugees. This was not to be the case. The photos had been taken when many farmers had sought refuge from fighting in the towns. Now they were returning to the countryside.

Even more important, the photos gave no hint of the extent of land mines, which had been sprinkled with such abandon that 36,000 Cambodians had lost limbs. Not surprisingly, I was asked repeatedly whether it was responsible to return refugees to a country littered with land mines. Maybe not, I replied. But leaving the 360,000 refugees in the camps would be even more irresponsible. Besides which, as we all knew, this was

Disarmament and elections helped to rehabilitate Cambodia. At left and at bottom, Anki soldiers surrender their weapons to UNTAC. Below, special U.N. representative Yasushi Akashi arrives in Takeo province during elections, May 1993.

The UNHCR mandate was to repatriate some 360,000 refugees in Thailand to a country lacking in most resources needed to assimilate them. Here, a Cambodian mother holds her child with one arm, his intravenous bottle with the other.

simply not an option.

Remembering my visit to the border ten years earlier I was convinced that the refugees faced no future in the camps. In addition, the Thai government had made it clear that they would not be allowed to stay. When the four Cambodian factions initialed a peace agreement in Paris in October 1991, their return to Cambodia became inevitable. Yet listening to myself, I realized this was a weak reply, and promised to alert the press to the first mine accident incurred by a returning refugee. We didn't have all the answers, and we might or might not pull it off. But at least we could be honest. It was my first attempt, as a U.N. spokesman, at "proactive" information.

The heat was fierce in the refugee camp at Site 2, the largest of the camps, as the first convoy left on the following morning with 527 Cambodians bound for home. Thirsty well-wishers lined the streets of the Site 2 refugee camp in northwest Thailand, carrying umbrellas and sucking water from recycled plasma bottles through old intravenous tubes. Humanitarian aid still had its uses, it appeared, even after the emergency had passed. The convoy arrived at the Cambodian border, at Poipet, for a short, dignified ceremony. Then it was off down the road to the Cambodian town of Sisophon, past Sarakahom, a small intersection that was known to be heavily mined. I was to travel this road a thousand times, and it was always a relief to escape the vendors at Poipet. The Cambodian sky seemed so huge, the possibilities endless.

The U.N.'s attempt to rebuild Cambodia represented the fullest attempt by the international community to realize the dream of peace-building outlined in the *Agenda for Peace*. It had political backing from the great powers, the U.N. Security Council, the Association of Southeast Asian Nations, and all four Cambodian factions. It also had a generous budget.

The October 1991 Paris peace agreement foresaw an unprecedented role for the United Nations: Over a period of eighteen months, leading up to elections, the U.N. Transitional Authority in Cambodia (UNTAC) would jointly administer the provinces and key government ministries; repatriate the refugees; disarm the Cambodian factions; monitor and enforce human rights; start the process of reconstruction; train Cambodian police; and prepare for and oversee elections. This was intervention on a grand scale—far more ambitious than anything the U.N. had previously attempted.

Cambodia also showed how humanitarianism—in this case the repatriation of refugees—could galvanize peacemaking and peace-building. There was no U.N. presence to speak of in Cambodia at the beginning of 1992, and everyone was nervous at the prospect of repatriation. Even Prince

A Cambodian mimics the image behind him of a man displaying his voter registration card. The billboard was produced by the information arm of UNTAC.

Sihanouk, the Cambodian head of state, got cold feet as the date drew near. But Mrs. Sadako Ogata, U.N. High Commissioner for Refugees, and her special envoy, Sergio Vieira de Mello, dug in their heels and insisted that the process had to start.

Once the first trucks crossed without incident the pace began to pick up. Two engineering battalions from the Thai army, on loan to UNTAC, found themselves with the task of repairing the road to the reception centers; Malaysian army rangers were asked to escort the convoys; U.N. civilian police from Singapore and the Philippines were sent to patrol returnee settlements in the northwest. De-mining experts from the French army set about mapping and marking off minefields that threatened UNHCR's resettlement plan. The first to be selected for de-mining was the field at Sarakahom, on the road to Sisophon.

The repatriation of refugees thus provided a focus to other components of UNTAC that were groping for concrete tasks early in their mission. In time, as repatriation became routine, other parts of the grand plan enjoyed their moment in the sun: human rights, demobilization, civil administration, and finally elections. But the process began with repatriation.

The question was—would it hold? Preoccupied by the challenge at hand, we had little time to speculate on the future, but the seeds of trouble were being sown. The Paris peace agreement not only avoided condemning the Khmer Rouge for their grisly past (referring only to the need to "avoid a return to past practices"), it also ensured their impunity and legitimized

In an effort to reach as many people as possible, an UNTAC civic-education team travels by boat to a Cambodian island to publicize voting procedures.

their role in Cambodia's future. This was an odd way to build peace. It also had a snowball effect. During 1992, UNTAC's human rights component won the agreement of the largest faction, the State of Cambodia (SOC), to the removal of shackles in jail and the release of 100 political prisoners. But the Khmer Rouge—infinitely more violent than the SOC—refused to cooperate with the U.N. There was nothing UNTAC could do, and not surprisingly the SOC took umbrage at being singled out for pressure and criticism. By the end of 1992, U.N. human rights monitors were treated with surly resentment by all sides. This undermined efforts to rebuild the judiciary and to restore respect for law.

Other UNTAC components also had their share of problems as elections approached: Demobilization was largely unsuccessful. Pre-election violence was widespread. The Khmer Rouge areas remained off-limits to the United Nations The U.N.'s civil administrators played administrative hide-and-seek with their Cambodian counterparts as they tried to clean up corruption in the ministries—and lost hands down. Development plans remained largely stillborn.

What we were doing, in essence, was bringing Cambodia in from the cold and restoring its legitimacy. But I remember thinking that Cambodia's isolation in the 1980s had been largely artificial in the first place—a product of the Cold War. What exactly was the U.N. achieving with this massive effort, so severely compromised by having to work with the Khmer Rouge? I was reminded of Nong Pru ten years earlier, when I had seen U.N.

food going to feed war criminals. Was I part of a different kind of humanitarian manipulation?

Crisis in Haiti

I arrived in Port-au-Prince on a steamy evening in late July 1994, on one of the last flights to slip into Haiti before a comprehensive embargo took effect. I was to serve as spokesman for the U.N. humanitarian operation.

Instead of being ushered through with the throng of journalists, I was singled out by three plainclothes policemen and taken to meet an angry Haitian "deputy minister of protocol." He told me that the United Nations had not informed his office of my arrival, which was a grave breach of protocol. He would have sent me back on the next plane if there had been planes running; as it was, he would take pleasure in confiscating my papers and passport. I protested diplomatic immunity and huffed and puffed about how many Haitian lives were being saved by U.N. food aid, drugs, and other assistance. At this, he cocked an eyebrow and reminded me that his country was subjected to the most stringent embargo ever imposed on a member state of the U.N. I handed over my papers.

I had been caught in a routine power play between the beleaguered U.N. humanitarian operation in Haiti and the military-controlled regime. The eight international organizations working in Haiti were under strict instructions not to imply any recognition of the "de facto regime," which had been appointed by the Haitian military earlier in the year. This extended to diplomatic notes. Formally informing the deputy minister of protocol of my arrival could have started an international incident. Yet while the U.N. agencies were struggling to maintain this facade, the "de factos" were doing their best to elicit anything that could imply recognition. It was an ignoble minuet against this larger backdrop.

The emergency in Haiti was caused by a combination of chronic poverty and the effects of nearly three years of military rule. Following the coup which ousted President Aristide on September 29, 1991, development had been frozen; economic sanctions had been tightened; and corruption was so rife that tax revenues fell by 39 percent in 1992. Worst of all, there was the political repression, which singled out Aristide supporters for assassination and destroyed the grass-roots organizations that had formed President Aristide's political base in the countryside. These groups had mobilized to mount vaccination campaigns, remove garbage from slum areas, promote family planning, plant trees, and build wells.

The result was a disaster of epic proportions. Disease, ill-health, and malnutrition stalked Haiti. According to a USAID study of forty health centers, 18 percent of all pre-school children showed severe or moderate mal-nutrition in July 1994 compared to 16 percent in April. Of every 100,000 women in Port-au-Prince, 1,200 were dying in childbirth—one of the highest rates in the world. Tuberculosis had spread rapidly. The level of HIV infection (8 percent to 9 percent) was one of the highest in the hemisphere.

At first sight, the humanitarian agencies were ill-equipped to respond. In the first place, their assistance had to be "emergency" in nature, on the argument that any "development work" would benefit the de facto regime. This meant, absurdly, that the Pan-American Health Organization (PAHO) could provide fuel for the distribution of food aid, but not for the production of bread. The second restriction came from resolutions of the U.N. General Assembly and Organization of American States forbidding any direct collaboration with the Haitian government authorities.

As the de facto regime felt the noose tightening, it became increasingly less inclined to allow the U.N. face-saving devices, and the threats against U.N. officials multiplied. At the same time, the humanitarian operation also faced pressure from some of the constitutional ministers who dared to remain in Haiti. I remember one interview under the jacaranda trees with a minister who would become a power in the subsequent Aristide government. One of his colleagues had been forced into hiding, and I was here to offer him a U.N. radio and access to our security communications system. He replied angrily that U.N. humanitarian aid was dampening popular

Supporters of Reverend Jean-Bertrand Aristide celebrate his election in 1990. Haiti's first peaceful, democratic election was supervised by ONUVEH.

ONUVEH observers drew on earlier U.N. experience with the Namibian elections. At top, they talk to residents in Degard, Haiti; above, they brief people on line to vote.

anger against the regime and so prolonging the crisis. He was perfectly pre-pared to be martyred for the cause.

That, I thought, would certainly have provoked outrage and a murderous response from the regime, which would have plunged the country into an even greater crisis. A plague on all their houses. But I saw his point.

Added to which, there was the pressure of sanctions. In theory, humanitarian aid was exempted, but exemptions had to be sought on a case-by-case basis through a sanctions committee in New York. Once this was obtained, there was the additional problem of getting the materials in: All commercial flights had stopped by the end of July, whereupon the de factos suspended emergency flights. Meanwhile the U.S. Navy was enforcing the naval blockade with such zeal that it was becoming increasingly hard to find shippers willing to deliver a small consignment to Haiti. This—plus the absence of a regular humanitarian flight—held up the arrival of injectable contraceptives, AIDS testing kits, antibiotics, and even food. For most of July and August, Haiti's blood supply could not be tested for AIDS. Inside the country, the transport and distribution of supplies was becoming harder as the roads deteriorated and trucks ran down.

This was a desperately unpromising context for the kind of humanitarianism envisaged in the *Agenda for Peace*—the kind of emergency aid that would help Haiti rebuild even as it was addressing the actual crisis. Gradually, however, I came to realize not only that this was happening, but that it was made easier by the uniquely difficult circumstances in which we were forced to work.

There were several defining characteristics to the U.N. humanitarian operation in Haiti. The number of foreign officials had been reduced to a bare minimum, and they all shared some very real common problems, notably security. This meant that inter-agency coordination—normally the bane of U.N. operations—was not only cordial and concise, but that it dealt with priorities: security arrangements, fuel, drugs, and coordinating food and information. In addition, relations with the U.S. Agency for International Development (USAID) office, and nongovernmental organizations were also close. Quite simply, everyone was in the same leaky boat.

Another feature was that unlike other emergencies, in which the agencies had dealt with military regimes and even war criminals, the U.N. in Haiti was under instructions to deal only with the constitutionally elected government of President Aristide. Led by the U.N. Development Program (UNDP), they tried heroically to respond. In 1993, UNDP had asked the government to help prepare an ambitious economic recovery program. In Haiti itself, Aristide's ministers chaired aid meetings. This allowed them to elaborate a decentralized national health policy as well as the outlines of a new environmental policy. UNDP also put forward money for a new planning unit, headed by the constitutional minister for planning, to back up the ministries most directly concerned with the crash recovery projects.

None of this was easy. Those ministers who were not in hiding would come openly to U.N. meetings—some on bicycles—knowing that they were being watched. It was all predicated on the restoration of constitutional rule. On this, there could be no faltering, even when the cause seemed hopeless. In August 1994, one of UNDP's Haitian partners, Father Vincent, was gunned down outside his church. He was the first churchman to fall to political violence in Haiti, and his funeral was the occasion for an anguished scene as mourners fell into a trance, fainted and clawed at the coffin. We did not know it at the time, but a line had been crossed abroad as well as in Haiti. Father Vincent's death proved to be the final provocation for governments that favored intervention.

A third important feature of the humanitarian operation was that by avoiding contact with the central authorities, the agencies were able to bypass one of the most inefficient and corrupt administrations on earth, and deal directly with local communities and church groups. This allowed them to take initiatives, and find unexpected benefits. By distributing its food aid through schools, the World Food Program was able to double school attendance in the northeast of Haiti. In a country of widespread illiteracy, this was no mean feat.

The challenge of nutrition was tougher because it had as much to do with ignorance and bad practice as with the shortage of food and rising prices. Companies had aggressively marketed infant formula in the 1970s, and breastfeeding had suffered as a result. This made infants more vulnerable to disease. UNICEF had launched a campaign to encourage hospitals to favor breast-feeding, but it was also looking at so-called nutrition clinics, in which mothers with healthy children were trained to pass on the secrets of a cheap and nutritious diet to a small group of their neighbors. This community-based approach to nutrition was particularly realistic for Haiti at the time, because it relied more on changing household habits than raising incomes—something that was simply not practical under the circumstances.

The provision of drugs addressed an obvious need in the emergency, but it also helped to set up a structure that would meet Haiti's drug needs once constitutional rule returned, because like many developing countries Haiti had been bombarded by expensive, sophisticated Western drugs that did little to address the country's real needs. The emergency drugs now delivered by UNICEF and PAHO could form the basis for a list of "essential drugs." Moreover, they were distributed directly and efficiently to 540 separate clinics and hospitals—more than 75 percent of the country's total. Here was the foundation for a rational drug policy.

The specter of AIDS has haunted Haiti since the early 1980s, and a

A U.N. observer monitors an anti-Cedras rally, September 1994. The Cedras government, which had ousted Aristide three years before, was impeding humanitarian efforts in Haiti.

coalition of nongovernmental organizations, with proven specialties, were fighting the pandemic. More remarkable, perhaps, was the involvement of the U.N. Population Fund (UNFPA). The fund was in a particular bind in Haiti, because it was a development agency prohibited from "development" activities. But the health crisis affecting Haitian women made nonsense of such distinctions. More women died in childbirth in Port-au-Prince than in any other city in the hemisphere as a result of inadequate family planning basics, like condoms; back-street abortions in dangerous, unsanitary conditions; poor facilities in hospitals, many of which had no gynecology units; and sexually transmitted diseases, which resulted in dangerous infections.

If the reproductive health crisis was to be checked, UNFPA would have to address each of these subsidiary causes. It engaged Population Services International (PSI) to promote the use of the condom. Working with private advertising companies, PSI launched a hugely effective campaign on television, billboards, and radio. Condoms served the dual purpose of family planning and AIDS prevention. Also, a start was made on the long-term challenge of persuading men not to take multiple sex partners. Surveys even suggested that the increase in AIDS was leveling off in the cities.

The collapse of the public sector was obviously of concern, and in many respects the humanitarian agencies were making this worse by avoiding all contact with the central authorities. At the same time, this was partly offset by their need to involve the local community to as great an extent as possible. In one example, UNICEF helped to recruit and train 120 health agents in cities. Each agent had been chosen by local community leaders and was responsible for covering 300 families in the area where they lived. When they found infants suffering from diarrhea, they taught mothers to administer oral rehydration salts. They also gave out chlorine powder for treating drinking water, condoms, and vitamin and iron tablets for children and women. Serious illnesses were referred to the local medical center. In addition, the health agents organized regular "rally posts" every two weeks at which children were vaccinated and weighed.

But the most important ingredient in Haiti's rebirth would be the determination of Haitians, and this was already present in abundance during the crisis. Shortly before the arrival of American forces in late August in 1994, I sought refuge from invasion fever in Cité Soleil, the big, sprawling shantytown of Port-au-Prince where support for Aristide burned like a slow fuse.

I was struck by the contrast. On the one hand, this was a foul, stinking slum that had trapped 200,000 people. When the rains came, the sewage washed through the shacks. Diarrhea and tuberculosis were rife. Eight percent of the pregnant women were infected with the HIV virus. Half the children were malnourished. On the other hand, there were entrepreneurs at every street corner. Empty fruit cans were pried apart and hammered into water buckets. Discarded sacks that once held U.S. food aid were fashioned into roofing material. Tough, confident women sold small bags of rice that they bought wholesale in the market and repackaged. (One aid group had

Flanked by President Bill Clinton, left, and Secretary-General Boutros Boutros-Ghali, restored Haitian president Aristide waves to supporters in Port-au-Prince, March 1995.

granted loans of forty dollars to over 252 of those tiny businesses at commercial rates of interest. Ninety-two percent eventually repaid all or part of the loan.) This was the spirit that carried the people of Cité Soleil through three terrible years. It would be sorely needed in the months ahead.

Failure in Bosnia

If Cambodia was the high-water mark of U.N. peacemaking, the war in Bosnia was the nadir. Among its many casualties was the notion that humanitarian relief can help to dampen a conflict, and even lead to a settlement. When the war erupted in April 1992, the U.N.'s humanitarian operation was assumed by High Commissioner Ogata. In addition to security and logistical difficulties, UNHCR officials were to encounter three unusual obstacles.

The first was the extraordinary cruelty of the Bosnian Serbs. Early in 1993, while on a fact-finding trip, I visited a UNHCR holding center in the Croatian town of Karlovac, which served as a transit camp for Muslims who had recently been released from Serb detention centers in northwest Bosnia. I remember how one of the inmates wept as he pulled back his shirt and showed me his back. Serb captors had carved an orthodox cross into his skin with bayonets and then rubbed salt in the wound during his captivity. Another awful story was told to me in hushed, embarrassed tones. It concerned a young Muslim who had been forced to mutilate fellow Muslim prisoners with his teeth in a detention center named Omarska. He was so severely disturbed by his ordeal that when he arrived at Karlovac he was given special dispensation to walk the town square at night. Debriefing such refugees was so distressing that camp workers and counselors themselves regularly broke down.

The second unusual feature of the Bosnia conflict was the paralysis of the U.N. Security Council, the U.N.'s arbiter in issues of international peace and security. Bosnia paralyzed the Security Council more comprehensively than any Cold War veto. Britain and Russia felt varying degrees of sympathy for the Serbs; France was wary about having a Muslim government in Europe; the U.S. felt that Serbia had launched a war of aggression against the Muslims and was outraged at the Serb crimes; China opposed any intervention that would strengthen the U.N.'s human-rights capacity.

All five governments could, however, agree on one thing in 1992: There would be no military intervention to stop the killing. This was the thinking behind the meeting that was convened by Britain in August 1992, to launch a humanitarian operation, escorted by a lightly armed U.N. Protection Force (UNPROFOR) and a joint U.N.–European effort to find

An 86-year-old Croat, the oldest inhabitant of the village of Podlug, awaits expulsion in 1993. She had been beaten by a Serb militiaman she had known since he was a child.

a political settlement.

The fact that there would be no intervention ensured that the humanitarian crisis would be immeasurably more damaging. Confident that there would be no military response, the Bosnian Serbs perpetrated some of the worst violations of humanitarian law since World War II. Those on the receiving end, mainly Muslims, had no protection because this task had been left to humanitarian aid officials. At one meeting in Geneva on July 29, 1992, British delegates had argued that the presence of convoys and officials would serve as "confidence-building measures," and conceivably even a form of protection against expulsion. In time this came to be known as "preventive protection."

The U.N. tried to stem the killing by declaring several "safe areas," but its member states failed to provide the means to protect them. By the time NATO finally intervened in July 1995, two safe areas had fallen (Zepa and Srebrenica), another three had been reduced to rubble (Bihac, Gorazde, and Sarajevo), and a sixth (Tuzla) had been repeatedly shelled.

As in Cambodia in 1981, humanitarian aid in Bosnia was undoing with one hand what the other was trying to achieve. Asked to prevent starvation in the Muslim enclaves but denied political and military backing, UNHCR had no option but to deliver food to Croat and Serb forces who were laying siege to Mostar and Sarajevo and occasionally killing UNHCR personnel.

As 1992 gave way to 1993, UNHCR protection officers often found themselves forced to choose between delivering food and protecting human rights. One protection officer in Sarajevo would later recall having visited the Serbian suburb of Grbavica. He had heard that Muslim women were being held in an underground garage and raped, and he was shocked to see elderly Muslims unloading the aid. But, as he told me, he did not intervene with the Serbs for fear that they would suspend food convoys to the besieged Muslim areas of Sarajevo.

Perhaps the hardest choice came when UNHCR officials were faced with a choice between helping civilians flee—in effect, cooperating with the invaders of their communities—or leaving them to die. Early in 1993, I saw this dilemma unfold in the small village of Podlug, which straddled the disputed frontier between eastern Croatia and western Bosnia. Before the war, the population had been mixed. By 1993, the village was under control of Serbs, and the Croats had been reduced to a terrified handful of elderly farmers and their wives. They had been driven from their homes, and grouped together in a safe house, under the protection of the 3rd battalion of the Kenyan army. When I visited, they were about to be "ethnically cleansed."

It was a forlorn, and peculiar, situation. The oldest person in the compound, eighty-six-year-old Jandra Zelic, had bruises on her face. She had been accosted by two young Serb militiamen in the road of her village. One of them, named Dragas Novica Grlic, whom she had known since he was a boy, had knocked her down and kicked her.

Later that night, the Serbs fired mortar shells and tracer bullets low over the roof of the house, and the Kenyan battalion commander decided it was time to leave. The next day, I watched Jandra Zelic shuffle to the UNHCR truck, as a Kenyan soldier loaded her small bag of belongings. Serb militia stood by, flaunting their guns. One of them was Dragas Novica. The old lady lowered her eyes as she passed him. Under strict instructions to act as a fact-finder and not as a journalist, I remained silent. But when I left for Croatia with the convoy, there were no Croats remaining in Podlug and I felt that we had all been accomplices to ethnic cleansing. In the event, everyone lost: The Croatian army recaptured the entire area in the summer of 1995, and the thuggish Dragas Novica was himself forced to flee.

The humanitarian agencies knew that they were being cynically manipulated in the former Yugoslavia. Even the International Committee of the Red Cross broke with its customary discretion, and went public with increasingly doom-laden warnings. In one editorial, a senior Red Cross official wrote: "We are forced to admit that we have all failed—and created a

In spite of cynical manipulation by warring parties in the former Yugoslavia, humanitarian efforts continued. Below, UNPROFOR troops unload supplies at Sarajevo. Right, a British medical battalion evacuates Croatian patients from Serb-held territory. Bottom, a UNHCR convoy carries food and medical supplies to Sarajevo.

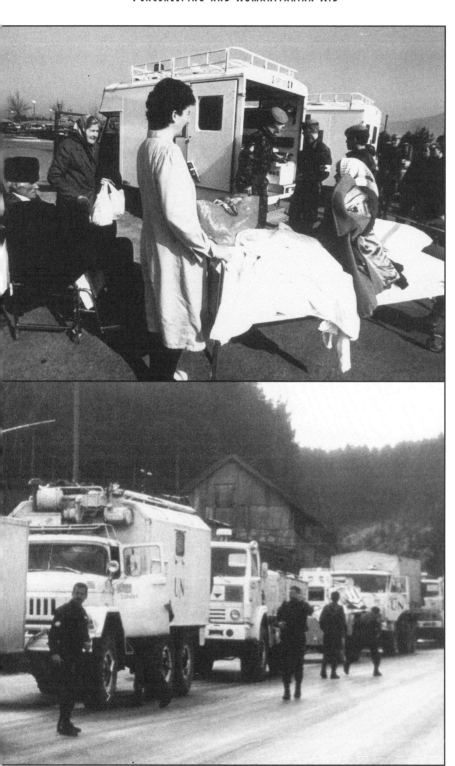

dangerous precedent. Humanitarian organizations should be part of an overall response, not a substitute for policy."

Politics and Humanitarian Aid

Crises like Bosnia suggest that from a humanitarian perspective not a lot has changed since the end of the Cold War. There was a distinct sense of déjà vu when several nongovernmental organizations decided in 1995 that they could no longer work in the Rwandan refugee camps of Zaire, because their relief aid was helping the Hutu militia who had launched the genocide in Rwanda. It mirrored the situation that I had found in Cambodia in 1981, and it prompted one author, David Rieff, to conclude in the winter 1995 issue of *The World Policy Journal* that "the humanitarian enterprise is always going to be a moral failure, as much as it is one of the few moral successes we can boast of."

Morality aside, humanitarian agencies will always have to operate in a tense political context that will lay them open to the risk of manipulation. The question is whether politicians will allow them some space or merely make the problem worse.

This is for political leaders to decide, because it is they who have unleashed the Pandora's box of ethnic conflicts, not the end of the Cold War. The two most deadly conflicts in modern times—Bosnia and Rwanda—were both deliberately fomented by unscrupulous leaders, using all the accoutrements of modern communications and warfare. Before the war, Bosnia was one of Europe's most multicultural societies. It was left to Serbia's calculating president to destroy this in his search for a "Greater Serbia," and turn Serb against Muslim against Croat. As the 1995 report of Human Rights Watch argues: "Without stimulation by opportunistic governmental leaders, communal tensions rarely rise to large-scale violence."

Bosnia and Haiti also showed that any weakness or indecision by the five permanent members of the U.N. Security Council will be ruthlessly exploited. This is particularly true when the U.S. loses its nerve. The death of eighteen U.S. Marines in Somalia in October 1993 prompted a premature withdrawal by U.S. forces, creating a whole new set of problems for the humanitarian agencies that remained. It also unnerved the American public and made it harder for the Clinton administration to take a lead in Bosnia and Haiti. A few days after the confrontation in Somalia, the U.S. troop ship *Harlan County*, which was carrying U.N. police to Haiti, withdrew after a demonstration by paramilitary "attachés" at the harbor. This retreat by the dominant superpower prompted a wave of killings in Haiti, which claimed the life of the constitutional minister of justice and led to the ouster of the U.N./O.A.S. human rights monitors.

Eventually, in the summer of 1995, NATO intervened with force against Serb aggression in Bosnia, but only after thousands of men and boys were massacred at Srebrenica. There is even less stomach for intervening in less "strategic" parts of the world, notably Africa. In 1994, at the height of the killing in Rwanda, the Clinton administration vetoed a request by Secretary-General Boutros-Ghali to dispatch a larger force of peacekeepers. The U.N. force commander later estimated that a few hundred extra U.N. troops in Rwanda in 1994 might have saved many thousands of lives.

This lack of political will dooms any hope that emergencies can be nipped in the bud and prevented from exploding—one of the cherished assumptions of the *Agenda for Peace*. This is not to say that they cannot be spotted in advance. (UNDP presciently warned that conditions in the Mexican state of Chiapas were ripe for conflict before the indigenous revolt in 1994.) But very few governments will admit that their repressive policies may be sowing the seeds of a future conflict, and even fewer will invite the United Nations to come and set up an "early warning system." The U.N.'s Commission for Human Rights has over thirty individual "rapporteurs" and thematic inquiries monitoring consistent violations, which could certainly form the basis for intervention if their conclusions were reviewed by the U.N. Security Council. But this has been resisted by developing countries who fear it could open the way to military intervention.

Political will, however, is also lacking in countries that should know better. For example, many Western governments continue to resist a nongovernmental call to ban the production, trade, and use of land mines—even though their military usefulness is almost negligible. Moreover, while mines are the quintessential contemporary weapon for use against civilians as well as soldiers, they are unlikely to be the last such example. Arms exports to the developing countries from the West have, ironically, increased since the end of the Cold War.

Britain, the United States, and the Netherlands still accept children into their armed forces under the age of eighteen, in violation of the spirit of the Geneva Conventions and the Convention on the Rights of the Child. Many other liberal governments are turning their backs on the 1951 Refugee Convention by detaining, turning away, or otherwise deterring asylum-seekers on the grounds that they are "economic migrants." The U.S. has yet to ratify the two additional protocols that update the Geneva Conventions. As of December 1995, only one of the five permanent members of the U.N. Security Council had made a legal commitment to extradite witnesses and suspects to the international tribunal on war crimes in the former Yugoslavia.

This is a sorry performance by governments that pride themselves on having helped to draft fundamental principles of humanitarian law, and it further weakens the fraying humanitarian safety net. Perhaps, when all is said and done, this should be the starting point for a new approach to humanitarian aid, one more in keeping with these confused times. But if the message is new, the essence of humanitarianism is the same as it has always been—a belief in law and the value of human life.

Iain Guest is the author of Behind the Disappearances: Argentina's Dirty War Against Human Rights and the United Nations *(Philadelphia: University of Pennsylvania Press, 1990). He is currently a senior fellow at the U.S. Institute of Peace, Washington, D.C.*

═══

A Step in the Wrong Direction

On the day before repatriation of Cambodians began, March 29, 1992, as spokesman for the United Nations High Commission for Refugees, I unwittingly made land mines into a kind of yardstick of a safe return, and pledged to report any accidents to the press. Toward the end of my tour of duty, I had to face the consequences.

We were lucky throughout the first five months. Some 82,000 refugees returned, without a single casualty from mines. Then, in July, I received word by radio from Battambang that a twenty-four-year-old former refugee named San Say had stepped on a mine and lost a leg. With a sinking heart, I travelled by U.N. helicopter to Battambang, to find out what had happened.

It was all sadly familiar. San Say had ignored U.N. warnings and gone off into the woods at Tippadey, near Battambang, in search of firewood. The area was near the front line and known to be mined. But San Say had exhausted his $50 repatriation grant, and he needed fuel.

UNTAC had been in Cambodia for over four months by then, but we had made very few inroads against land mines. No one knew how many mines had been laid (the estimate runs to 10 million), but we all knew that mines were still being laid by the factions and even by farmers with grudges to settle against their neighbors. None of the minefields had been mapped; several had been mined and remined several times over. The result was chaotic and lethal.

None of the governments that contributed troops to UNTAC were willing to expose their de-mining experts to the risk involved in actually clearing Cambodian minefields. Instead, the task was assumed by engineers from the Cambodian factions that had laid them: UNTAC's de-miners helped with initial training and, in the case of the French, with supervision at the actual sites.

By the time UNTAC left, in September 1993, Cambodia had its own mine-clearance unit, which was able to field several proficient mine-clearing teams. The problem was that many more mines were being laid than cleared. The same is true the world over. About 84,000 mines were removed in 1995, at huge expense; but at least 2 million new mines were laid.

How can we slow this rush to self-destruction? Since 1992, two separate approaches have been tried. One is to press for a total ban on the production, use, and export of mines. This has spawned an impressive international movement, comprising 400 groups in forty countries. They are supported by all the major humanitarian agencies and nearly forty governments.

The other approach is to revise and update a proposed protocol on land mines appended to a 1980 U.N. convention on weapons deemed excessively injurious, or to have indiscriminate effects. As adopted in 1996, this protocol requires that all antipersonnel mines be clearly marked and mapped. They are to be removed by those who laid them after the end of hostilities. The second major category of mines—those that are "remotely delivered"—are to be built to self-destruct or self-deactivate after a maximum of 120 days. Both categories are to be made detectable to de-miners.

This may seem like a step in the right direction, particularly as the new protocol covers internal (civil) wars, like Cambodia's, in which most mines are used today. But the problem is that it legitimizes a new generation of high-tech "smart" mines, capable of delivering huge numbers of detonations. Instead of trying to appease this implacable foe, say advocates, we should declare the land mine an international pariah, like chemical weapons. The military response is that mines are indispensable to modern warfare—a cheap and painless form of self-defense. The real aim, they argue, is to reduce the threat to civilians.

And yet, twenty-four NATO peacekeepers were killed or wounded by mines during the first two months of their mission in Bosnia, suggesting that the mine is no friend of peacekeepers. At a time when the Western military is being increasingly drawn into humanitarian crises, and

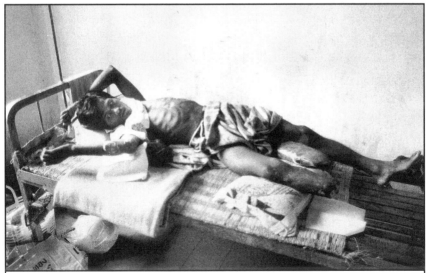

San Say, a 24-year-old former refugee, lost his lower leg to a mine while gathering fuel.

peace-building, is it not time to rethink the military value of land mines? Many think so. At the very least, they feel, military tacticians should start looking for military reasons to scrap mines, instead of automatically arguing for their retention. Then let the politicians decide.

However crucial the arguments for and against a global ban, they seemed barely relevant to the scene that greeted me when I went to visit San Say at the Battambang hospital in 1992. The boy lay on his side, on a checkered scarf made of cheap, thin material, naked from the waist up. They changed the wounds every morning, at 8.00 AM, and the bandages around the stump were already streaming. The stench came back to me immediately, like long-forgotten bad food. As I took out my notebook, I felt suddenly queasy, and a little bit surprised. I thought I'd developed a stronger stomach for this kind of thing.

San Say tried to sit up as a mark of respect and groaned at the effort. I had a sudden flash of what his life must have been like for the last thirteen years—being ordered around by overweening Thai soldiers, U.N. officials, and refugee-camp administrators. Now this. What a homecoming! Struggling to start a conversation, I asked San Say whether it hurt. He nodded and pointed at the foot that was no longer there. He had bandages on his elbows, and shrapnel had peppered the inside of his legs. The wounds blossomed like tiny red flowers. I felt the dizziness come over me and sat down hard on the next bed. I felt something poking at my side, looked down, and saw another bandaged stump.

An old woman, who had been caring for a child in the next ward, came in aggressively. She had stitches in her lower lip, and filthy, matted hair. Inches away from my face, she shouted that San Say and his friend had been forced to use their repatriation grant to pay for the operation, blood, and medicine. I realized that the rest of the ward was watching.

Cambodia alone is thought to have around 10 million undetonated land mines. Here, participants in an UNTAC de-mining course learn to handle trip wires.

A de-mining school in Mozambique displays an assortment of land mines still prevalent in former war zones.

Suddenly I had had enough. "He's obviously very ill. Let's come back tomorrow," I said. My interpreter looked at me inquiringly, and asked whether I was all right. "I'm fine," I lied, determined not to lose face. "But he needs some rest." I gathered up my notebook, and hurried outside to the car, where I sat and watched the drizzle fall until my stomach had settled. "We are failing in Cambodia," I wrote, "if people are forced to risk death in order to find firewood. This country is a wreck . . . ."

I had made a pact with the press, and I immediately notified the wire services. Most of the printed stories noted that one accident in 82,000 refugees was a remarkable record, given that Cambodia was thought to have millions of land mines. But this did not sit well with the UNTAC chiefs, who did not like the idea of U.N. spokesmen volunteering bad news. In retrospect, they should have been grateful. Journalists took us at our word, assumed that we would continue to volunteer information, and ceased to probe for mine stories. Yet, more Cambodians died from land mines in 1995 than in 1992. No less than 164 injuries and deaths were reported from mines in Battambang in March 1995 alone. Each casualty represents a broken family, and another impediment to Cambodia's revival.—I.G.

A young marine, part of the original U.S.-led task force assigned to end the looting of food aid in Somalia, stands guard at a crossroad in Mogadishu, February 1993. In about a month, his unit would be replaced by traditional U.N. peacekeepers.

Redefining "Victory"

by John F. Hillen III

Americans—who are seen by some other U.N. member states as not "culturally attuned" to the military peculiarities of peacekeeping—need to understand that our future involvement in international conflict resolution will most likely not deliver the kind of quick and decisive victory we prefer, but require low-level, protracted commitment. Onerous as that may seem to a public deeply suspicious of open-ended military involvement overseas, it is often far less expensive than its calamitous alternative.

On February 26, 1991, while serving as a cavalry officer in Operation Desert Storm, I was one of the first American soldiers to come into contact with the heavy divisions of the Iraqi Republican Guard. That afternoon, the armored reconnaissance squadron in which I served fought and destroyed a brigade of the Iraqi Tawalkana division in an action now known as the "Battle of the 73 Easting." Army historians later attributed our success in that battle not to superior tactics but to the sheer ferocity of our attack, the offensive mentality of our troopers, and the combat skills they exhibited while under fire. While it was just one fight in a large and complex campaign of war, it was a proud addition to the war-fighting heritage of the U.S. Second Armored Cavalry Regiment. The regiment, on continuous active service since 1836, had also fought with honor in the Mexican-American War, the Civil War, the Spanish-American War, and both world wars. The Wehrmacht nicknamed the cavalrymen of my unit the "ghosts" of Patton's army, for the ease with which they led his forces into their rear and flanks.

Four years later, the regiment was again deployed in the service of the American nation, this time in Haiti. The Haitian mission could not have been more different from the combat missions for which the regiment had trained over its previous 160-some years. Gone were the M1A1 tanks and the Bradley fighting vehicles. Gone were the combat helicopters and the multi-launch rocket artillery. Instead, the U.S. Second Armored Cavalry was deployed as a peacekeeping force, armed with the ubiquitous "humvee" (the jeep of the 1990s) in an operation more suited to billy-clubs than machine-guns. In this mission the troopers of the second cavalry would try not to identify, engage, and destroy an enemy force, but to act as peacekeepers. Alongside these combat-trained soldiers was another proud war-fighting unit, the U.S. 101st Airborne Division. When asked about his assignment to Haiti, one 101st sergeant who had fought in the Gulf War remarked that the experience "just shows how the world is changing, and how we have to change it."

It has often been said that peacekeeping is not a soldier's job, but only a soldier can do it. This irony is reflected in any conceptual attempt to involve the United Nations in the use of military force as a political exercise. After all, the U.N. is not a sovereign government that has access to military forces; there is not now, nor has there ever been, a U.N. army or police force. And yet, in 1993, the U.N. was directing the military activities of almost 80,000 soldiers under its command in eighteen missions around the globe. In addition, since the creation of the U.N. fifty years ago, more than 1,200 soldiers have died in its service.

The supreme irony of U.N. involvement in military operations is that the only types of operations for which the U.N. Charter makes specific provisions are the ones that the U.N. has never attempted. As Sir Brian Urquhart, who was present at the U.N.'s inception, has noted, "The 'United' in United Nations referred to nations united in war, not in peace." Chapter VII of the U.N. Charter was based on an extension of the wartime alliance system, and it specified the mechanisms by which the U.N. could direct international military forces in the pursuit of international peace and security. Chapter VII provisions were intended to foster great-power military cooperation as it had existed in World War II. As is well known, the dynamics of the Cold War ensured, even to this day, that this goal was never realized. Thus, the vehicle through which international soldiers serve the U.N. today is elastically known as "peacekeeping."

Peacekeeping, an improvised and modest military activity that became fairly well defined over the course of thirteen U.N. missions between 1948 and 1978, has now given way to a whole new genre of military operations. Still rooted in the principles of peacekeeping, these are known variously as peace-enforcement, peacemaking, wider peacekeeping, enhanced peace-keeping, second-generation peacekeeping, or even "inducement" operations. The profusion of terms reflects not only the lack of conceptual clarity about their nature, but the much broader range of military challenges they entail. These new missions, especially those in Cambodia, the former Yugoslavia, and Somalia, have been overwhelmingly "peacekeeping" in character. Yet they also have reflected profound changes in their operational environments and dynamics and in their mandates.

Even a cursory glance at statistics reflects the profound change in U.N. military missions since the end of the Cold War. The sheer numbers of troops involved has increased, from less than 10,000 Blue Helmets in 1987 to almost 80,000 in late 1993. The cost of operations has gone up exponentially, from $480 million in 1991 to $3 billion in 1993. However, what should really draw the attention of the professional soldier or military historian is the change in the character of the missions themselves. Since 1988–89, U.N. missions have had operational environments and mandates very different from their predecessors.

Traditional peacekeeping missions took place in an environment of *consent*, in which the belligerents had already agreed to a peace settlement and to the participation of the U.N. peacekeepers. The job was either to act as individual observers, or to occupy a clearly defined linear buffer zone that separated the belligerents. These preconditions were considered a sine qua non for deploying U.N. forces for peacekeeping duty.

Of course, for the individual soldier the environment of these missions was not always so benign. Hundreds of U.N. peacekeepers have been killed in tactical incidents. However, from a strategic or political point of view, the environment was one of consent: The parties involved had agreed to end the armed conflict, to work towards conflict resolution, and to respect the impartial role of the peacekeepers in their efforts to keep small incidents from flaring up and disrupting the reconciliation process. U.N. peacekeepers usually succeeded in limiting armed conflict in these situations, especially if the nation-states involved could be held accountable for their actions. When sub-state actors were involved, efforts to limit armed conflict were less effective, as has been the case in the United Nations Interim Force in Lebanon (UNIFIL).

In contrast, many of the newer missions take place in belligerent environments of chaos and continuing civil war, where consent for the U.N. mission is not assured. The political environment is dominated by sub-state actors—many times irrationally motivated regional, religious, or ethnic groups. The absence of competent civil authority, law and order, and national infrastructure greatly complicates the mission environment.

U.N. peacekeepers have not traditionally operated with a mandate that would include large-scale actions to replace civil authority. On occasion, U.N. forces have assisted national authorities in temporarily maintaining civil order, as in the Port Said area during the first U.N. peacekeeping mission to the Sinai (UNEF I) and in several other traditional missions. However, this particular role has always been temporary and very much a secondary effort for the forces whose priority has been to occupy a sparsely populated buffer zone, observe, and report. As such, U.N. military forces have always counted on the willing and competent cooperation of lawfully minded belligerents in order to accomplish their missions. As one can imagine, the chaos of environments such as Cambodia, and even more so the former Yugoslavia and Somalia, greatly changed the nature of this traditional peacekeeping function.

Given that traditional U.N. peacekeeping missions were deployed with this assumption of cooperation and consent in mind, the mandates of U.N. forces were modest by military standards. U.N. military forces were traditionally sent to help *sustain* an environment of peace and reconciliation. There was never any doubt that the primary responsibility for *creating* that environment rested with the belligerents. It is for this reason that the great majority of U.N. military operations to this day have been observation missions, consisting of individual military observers from U.N. member states, never numbering more than a few hundred unarmed or lightly armed troops. The mandate of these military forces has been to observe and report on the compliance of the belligerents with treaty provisions. The U.N. forces had no mandate to sanction or punish those in violation of the settlement accord.

As mentioned above, in several instances, the U.N. has deployed entire armed units of member states to physically occupy buffer zones that separated the belligerents. However, even in these cases, the U.N. military forces were small and lightly armed, rarely numbering more than a few thousand troops. In occupying these buffer zones, their mandate was to deter any small-scale transgressions of the peace settlement. The legitimacy of the U.N. military forces came not from their power to defeat transgressors, but from their moral authority as an absolutely impartial arbiter. The Blue Helmets represented the moral authority of the international community through the U.N.

As such, the mandate of traditional peacekeepers allowed the use of force only in the self-defense of individual soldiers, or in the defense of the mission against armed attack. The traditional operations of U.N. military forces were passive and defensive, and with the exception of some operations in the Congo in 1961, they never sought to actively compel belligerents to adopt a course of action through the offensive use of military force.

However, the end of Cold War tensions on the Security Council and the success of international cooperation in the Gulf War of 1991 led the council to authorize more ambitious mandates for several missions. These reflected the newfound confidence of the U.N. to influence complex intra-state dilemmas. The new mandates are also evidence of the chaotic and complicated environments of these new security challenges. For the first time since the Congo operation, U.N. forces have been authorized to *create* the conditions that would lead to conflict resolution in areas such as the former Yugoslavia, Somalia, Rwanda, and Haiti.

The combination of these more ambitious mandates and the more belligerent environments of their operations has led to a profound change in the military character of some U.N. peacekeeping missions. Whereas traditional missions were small, lightly armed, and predicated on the use of force only in the passive sense, newer missions have been very different in character. The mission in Cambodia involved almost 16,000 troops, the biggest since the almost 20,000 deployed to the Congo some thirty years prior. The missions in the former Yugoslavia and Somalia were even larger, with over 30,000 heavily armed troops backed by tanks, artillery, combat air support, and a heavy naval presence.

More importantly, in some limited circumstances these new operations authorized troops to use active military means to *force* compliance with U.N. mandates. This was the case in both the former Yugoslavia and Somalia. In the Balkans, the U.N. called on NATO aircraft to actively enforce the "no-fly" zone over Bosnia–Herzegovina and the U.N. protected "safe areas" on the ground. In this role NATO aircraft shot down Serbian planes and bombed targets on the ground. In Somalia, the U.N. authorized an American-led international task force to use military means to provide a secure environment for the delivery of humanitarian aid. The U.N. also later authorized the capture by force of those responsible for the massacre of twenty-four Pakistani peacekeepers in 1993.

Despite the limited enforcement provisions authorized by the U.N. in these missions—and in the Congo, Rwanda, and Haiti—the overwhelming nature of the missions was that of traditional peacekeeping. On the surface, the character of these newer missions seemed to contradict traditional peacekeeping. However, the large, heavily-armed U.N. forces that deployed to the former Yugoslavia and Somalia were still operating on tried-and-true principles: the consent of the belligerents, the impartiality of the U.N. troops, and the use of force only in self-defense. Of course, there was considerable consternation on those occasions when active force was used on missions that purported to be passive in nature. The debate rages on about exactly if or how coercion can be mixed with peacekeeping. Regardless, the

A pile of skulls at the "Killing Fields" memorial in Cambodia testifies to that country's tragic history. The chaos that confronts the U.N. in such places has greatly changed the nature of peacekeeping since the end of the Cold War, as well as the public's expectations of outcome.

more "muscular" approach of U.N. peacekeeping attempted to date in the post-Cold War world is still firmly rooted in consent, impartiality, and the minimum use of force.

Military strategists, both at the U.N. and in member states, have been trying since 1992 to formulate a new doctrine for this latest approach. Thus far it appears to have been a qualified success in Cambodia, but a failure in Somalia and the former Yugoslavia. In 1995, Secretary-General Boutros Boutros-Ghali stated that, in the future, mixing enforcement tasks with peacekeeping operations "must be avoided."

In order to reinforce the impartiality of United Nations peacekeeping forces, the great powers have not usually been represented in traditional U.N. missions. Exceptions to this include British participation in Cyprus (UNFICYP) and French in Lebanon (UNIFIL). However, the requirement for an impartial U.N. force saw the active involvement of the so-called "middle powers" in U.N. peacekeeping, who came to represent military expertise in the field: the Nordic countries, Canada, Ireland, Austria, Fiji, and others. In many of these countries, U.N. peacekeeping became the de facto raison d'être for the national armed forces.

However, the new generation of peacekeeping, with its requirements for large numbers of well-armed and -equipped soldiers, expensive combined-arms force structures, and sophisticated command-and-control systems has necessitated the active engagement of the great powers. As such, Britain and France were heavily committed in the former Yugoslavia, Russia to a much lesser degree. The U.S. had over 20,000 soldiers deployed to Somalia at times, as well as 10,000 to Haiti. For the U.S., whose previous participation in U.N. operations was limited to a few individual observers, this raises the question of criteria concerning when to be involved in a U.N. mission.

In order to judge the critical decision of when to commit American forces, American policymakers to this day tend to use the guidelines of the "Weinberger Doctrine" put forth in 1984 by then secretary of defense Casper Weinberger. This doctrine maintains that American forces should not be deployed abroad on military missions unless three conditions are met: There must be vital national interests at stake; the military must have the active support of Congress and the American people; and all other policy options must have been tried and either rejected or exhausted. Weinberger then posited a further three conditions on the use of this military deployment: The force should be committed only with the clear intent of winning; it should have clearly defined and attainable objectives; and its structure and methods should be continually reassessed in view of its goals.

Not to put too fine a point on it, those criteria greatly restrict the possibility of the U.S. becoming militarily involved in a U.N. peacekeeping operation, especially in the complex and ambitious operations that have taken place in chaotic and belligerent environments such as the former Yugoslavia. The debate over whether American national interests are in accord with the efforts of the United Nations will not be examined here. However, the Weinberger preconditions are predicated on achieving a clear, quick (to ensure public support), relatively inexpensive (ditto), and decisive "victory." This reflects America's continued consternation over the long, inconclusive, costly, attritional, and ultimately self-defeating effort in Vietnam. Similar worries concern the U.S. role in NATO's Bosnia Peace Implementation Force (IFOR). Many critics maintain that there is no way to define victory in such a mission.

The desire to never again repeat the Vietnam experience is reflected on several levels, both among the public and among American military professionals. Public (and congressional) support for prolonged American military interventions is fickle. If the intervention supports vital national interests or is carried out at little cost (especially in terms of casualties), then public support can be sustained. However, the death of eighteen U.S. soldiers in the October 1993 battle in Mogadishu, and the humiliation and anger inspired by the television footage of a soldier's body being dragged through the dusty streets by a mob, is trenchant testimony to how one event can turn the tide. It is safe to say after this event, and the subsequent release of President Bill Clinton's cautious policy on U.N. peace operations, that rallying public support for prolonged participation in U.N. operations in the future will be decidedly more difficult.

The American military came away from Vietnam having learned profound lessons regarding the use of military means to achieve political goals in a limited war. The military establishment was convinced that the incremental use of force, "fine-tuned" by civilian policymakers to send complex and subtle signals to adversaries, was ultimately self-defeating. The American military restructured its doctrine after Vietnam to emphasize achieving clear and overwhelming battlefield victories that could contribute directly to a conclusive political solution: The military should strike at the heart of any aggressor to deliver clear and decisive victory; it should not be expected to fritter away resources in a low-key and prolonged battle at the "capillaries." The Gulf War, which gave the military wide latitude to make a coordinated and overwhelming campaign of battle throughout the depth of Iraq's defenses, appeared to vindicate the new doctrine.

Even to the casual observer of the characteristics of U.N. military operations, this doctrine would seem at extreme variance with the principles of peacekeeping. Naturally, U.N. peacekeeping is not a military operation in the same sense as war-fighting; in fact most U.N. operations are much more political in nature than military. After all, it would seem that the U.N. emphasis on impartiality and the non-use of force could hardly accord with a military doctrine emphasizing the use of force to achieve "victory."

In fact, as a military activity, traditional peacekeeping is more akin to a police doctrine than a war-fighting doctrine. The goal of a policing, or constabulary, action is to enforce the laws to an acceptable level of compliance. A police force would never expect to use overwhelming power to eliminate crime altogether—the expense and level of intrusiveness would disrupt society completely. Similarly, a U.N. peacekeeping force, as just one facet of an overall political, economic, and humanitarian effort—and one in which the main burden of reconciliation is placed on the belligerents—does not seek in any fashion to coerce belligerents into a pattern of behavior. It would appear on the surface that the two doctrines are incompatible at best, or, more accurately, inapplicable to exceptionally different military (or quasi-military) challenges.

The war-fighting attitude of the U.S. military community, greatly respected the world over for its utility and effectiveness in all-out military conflicts, is viewed with considerable apprehension by nations with greater experience in U.N. peacekeeping. The U.S. effort to use conventional force to capture General Aideed in Somalia, as well as congressional calls for more aggressive air strikes in Bosnia throughout the life of the U.N. mission there, reinforce this anxiety among some of America's allies. Indeed, it is not entirely inaccurate to say that some allies view the U.S. approach to military operations as that of a reckless cowboy. Even the most serious observers have noted that the U.S. may not be "culturally attuned" to the unique military challenges of U.N. peacekeeping. In addition, the different attitude of the United States toward U.N. peacekeeping has been exacerbated by the debate over putting U.S. troops under U.N. command.

However, what is not widely known outside professional circles is that the American military establishment recognizes the wholly different nature of peacekeeping operations, and has formulated a thorough and competent doctrine with which to address these types of missions. The U.S. Army doctrine on peace operations notes that "victory" in these sorts of operations comes much more subtly than in war. It lists principles for these operations that contravene war-fighting doctrine but are solidly compatible with peacekeeping: perseverance, restraint, and legitimacy. It also accepts that U.S. troops can operate very effectively while under the operational control

Multinational forces, part of a special commission in Kuwait after the Gulf War, examine an abandoned Iraqi tank. Behind them a blazing oil well lights the sky.

of a U.N. commander of another nationality during a whole range of missions. The doctrine has been lauded by U.N. officials and a recent letter from the U.S. Army Chief of Staff to the British Chief of the U.K. General Staff applauded the compatibility of their doctrines.

In military parlance, the U.S. military establishment can triumphantly say that it is "on board" with the military requirements of peacekeeping. U.N. peacekeeping, predicated on the use of force in a passive sense, has included throughout its history the most incredible panoply of ad hoc passive military measures. While it has been noted that some missions in the past, such as the Congo, and many of the newer missions have limited enforcement provisions, nowhere has the U.N. contemplated using overwhelming aggressive force. Even in the large, heavy, ambitious, and complex peacekeeping missions today, consent, impartiality, and the minimum use of force are the U.N.'s guiding military principles.

Although the American military understands the unique nature of U.N. peacekeeping, and trains its peacekeepers accordingly, there is still consternation at the government level. Americans are ever wary of involvement in operations that will be protracted, inconclusive, expensive, and could result in low-level but persistent casualties. U.N. peacekeeping is not a decisive exercise, as evidenced by long-running missions in Palestine (established in 1948), Kashmir (1949), Cyprus (1964), the Golan Heights (1974), and southern Lebanon (1978). In order for the government to be assured of public and congressional support for participation in these sorts of operations, the unique military nature and limited political value of peacekeeping must be communicated to the public: "Victory" must be redefined.

The new character of U.N. military operations adds to the confusion of this situation, not only for the United States, but for all U.N. member states. It is undoubtedly easier to appreciate the unique dynamics of U.N. peacekeeping when the mission is represented by unarmed observers or a few lightly armed troops in a relatively quiet buffer zone. However, public perceptions are harder to shape when the mission consists of a corps-sized combined-arms force, backed by naval power and combat-air support, under constant threat and pressure in a belligerent environment such as Somalia or Bosnia. In these situations, it is all too easy to understand the dilemma as one that may be more responsive to an application of war-fighting doctrine than to the principles of peacekeeping.

However, even these missions, despite limited enforcement provisions, are solidly "peacekeeping" in nature. As such, several characteristics need to be clearly communicated to the public: the passive nature of the peacekeeper's military operations; the absolute need for impartial behavior on the part of U.N. troops; the obligations of the belligerents to lead the reconciliation process and to cooperate with the U.N. presence; the dominating political imperative of the mission (which relegates the military facet to just one tool in a diplomatic, economic, and humanitarian enterprise); and the prolonged nature of such an effort.

The American military establishment has little U.N. peacekeeping experience, but it explicitly recognizes the rules of this very different sort of engagement. The U.S. political establishment, however, must very clearly communicate to the public its expectations about what American military involvement in U.N. peacekeeping must entail. Low expectations must prevail and peacekeeping missions should not be undertaken in environments of chaos and belligerency. A U.S. military presence is not likely to deliver the kind of quick and decisive "victory" Americans would prefer, but to entail a low-level, protracted commitment.

The U.S. must always ask itself if contributing ground troops to U.N. peacekeeping operations is advantageous for either the U.S. or the U.N. Many observers would rather see experienced U.N. peacekeeping nations managing operations on the ground, with the U.S. contributing intelligence, airlift, and logistical support. However, on occasion the U.S. can contribute ground troops to international crisis management and conflict resolution. Applied to selected situations, U.S. involvement can be far less expensive than any number of calamitous alternatives.

John Hillen, a former U.S. regular army officer who served in Operation Desert Storm, is a defense policy analyst at the Heritage Foundation, Washington, D.C. Widely published on issues of international security, he is currently writing a book on the strategy of U.N. military operations.

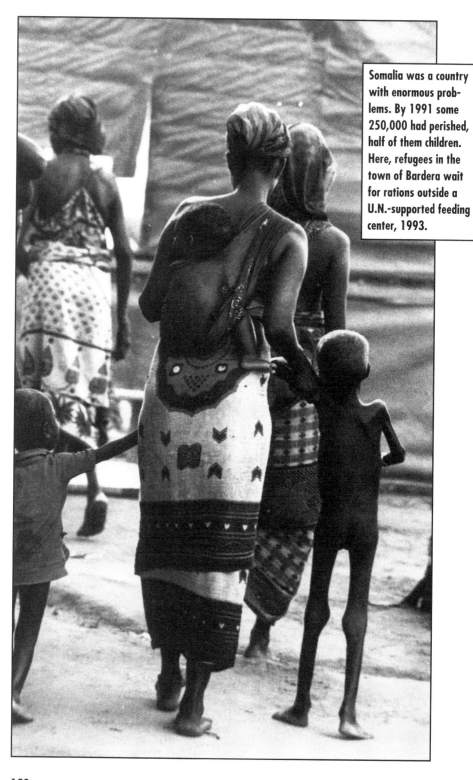

Somalia was a country with enormous problems. By 1991 some 250,000 had perished, half of them children. Here, refugees in the town of Bardera wait for rations outside a U.N.-supported feeding center, 1993.

Somalia: Frustration in a Failed Nation

by Jonathan T. Howe

U.N. peacekeeping soldiers went to starving Somalia on what was billed as a humanitarian-relief/nation-building mission—and came away bloodied. The secretary-general's special representative to the mission talks of the painful lessons learned there. If we are going to persist in peace-enforcement operations in broken countries, we need to field forces mandated and prepared to withstand armed opposition, even as they restore order.

Like many people around the world, I had seen the televised pictures of helpless refugees in the remote villages and towns of southern Somalia. But I was not prepared for what I saw upon my arrival in the capital city of Mogadishu on March 17, 1993. The extent of the destruction I witnessed on my initial tour that day was sobering. Once an attractive coastal city, Mogadishu had been totally destroyed by warring factions in Somalia's civil struggle. Buildings had not only been blown apart by weapons fire, their gutted hulks had been systematically looted of everything of value—from pipes to wires. Although the water system had been a high priority for early relief workers, it was only partially restored. Pipes and valves were stolen almost as soon as they were reinstalled. Electrical utility poles had been stripped bare. I wondered about the degree of greed and desperation that had motivated this utter despoliation of the very means of recovery.

The courtyards of many once-imposing buildings were crowded with tiny huts of sticks and burlap relief bags, which only partially sheltered thousands of displaced families from the sun and rain. Many of these families had fled to the city from small towns and villages, seeking security after their homes had been destroyed, their possessions and means of livelihood stolen. Trips to the countryside soon confirmed that the wanton destruction was widespread. It did seem that the battle with starvation, at least, was being won, although food convoys, wet-food distribution points, and malnutrition centers were still essential for survival.

Other enormous problems loomed: Orphanages were bursting. One-

159

legged victims of mines hobbled about. Restless hordes of idle young men roamed the streets. Anarchy and insecurity had reinforced a strong dependence on clan rather than nation. More than a million Somalis had fled to neighboring countries. The professional class had all but disappeared. Civil institutions had collapsed. There were no banks, postal services, or telephones. Only a remnant remained of a once-viable police force.

Somalia had ceased to exist as a nation. Its civilization and culture had hit bottom. Rebuilding would take years.

Although my assignment to Somalia had been totally unexpected, I was under no illusions that this first United Nations peace-enforcement operation was going to be anything but tough going. Our mandate was about to expand exponentially. What I did not anticipate was how unready our U.N. forces were for the added, complex responsibilities and how exceedingly difficult it would be for us to help Somalia. In trying to return this failed nation to a minimum standard of sustainability, we learned many painful lessons. Whatever the long-term outcome of our presence there, these lessons may be our most lasting legacy to future humanitarian peacekeeping missions.

Since the ouster of President Siad Barre in early 1991, an estimated 250,000 Somalis had died, half of them children under five. Without U.N. intervention some 1.5 million more were expected to perish in 1993. Notwithstanding the prolonged hardships they had already inflicted on their people, some political faction leaders continued to struggle for power, interfering with the flow of relief supplies and seizing substantial quantities for their supporters.

Conventional approaches to ending the suffering had been tried by the U.N. for more than a year with only limited success. These included: the assignment of military observers; attempts at negotiations; a U.S.-led military airlift of relief supplies to isolated towns in the interior; and deployment of the first increment of a U.N. force to guard relief supplies. This latter, a battalion of Pakistani troops, operating under traditional peacekeeping rules (Chapter VI of the U.N. Charter), was thwarted from carrying out its responsibilities by the faction leader who dominated much of southern Mogadishu, General Mohammed Farah Aideed.

As the desperate plight of starving Somalis continued to play across television sets throughout the world, the U.S. offered on November 25, 1992, to lead a military coalition to restore conditions that would permit the delivery of humanitarian relief. On December 3, 1992, the U.N. Security Council accepted this carefully circumscribed proposal.

Unprecedented peace-enforcement powers were granted to the coalition under Chapter VII of the Charter. The U.N. Pakistani battalion had had neither the authority nor the means to deal with General Aideed's Somali National Alliance (SNA) faction when they tried to stop U.N. soldiers from protecting food supplies in Mogadishu. Lead Marine elements landed on December 9, and the U.S. quickly established a force of nearly 30,000 troops. The U.S., however, planned to stay only long enough to restore the flow of relief and to turn the mission over to a traditional U.N. peacekeeping force.

By March 1993, pressures were already building for the U.N. to assume direction of military activities while keeping Chapter VII authority, which was considered essential for a U.N. force operating in the Somali environment. But Security Council Resolution 814, passed on March 26, 1993, also called for the United Nations Operation in Somalia (UNOSOM) to assume a much broader role. The U.N. would try to help Somalis put their nation back on its feet by assisting them to disarm, restore law and order, and rebuild their economy and institutions.

This ambitious mandate sought a more lasting recovery. It aimed to decrease the probability that eventual cessation of U.N.-protected emergency relief would simply lead to a collapse of order and a resumption of fighting, eventually returning Somalis to the abyss of disease and starvation. UNOSOM also was directed to facilitate recovery throughout the entire country—not just in the southern area where the American-led coalition had concentrated its operation.

The dramatic events that ensued during the United Nation's first year under this demanding mandate fell into three phases: transition from U.S. (Unified Task Force—UNITAF) to U.N. (UNOSOM) control (March to May 1993), organized hostilities against the U.N. (June to October 1993), and attempted reconciliation of the factions (November 1993 to March 1994). Strategies for each of these periods had to be adjusted to deal with changing local and international realities. In the four-month second phase, concerted guerrilla opposition brought into bold relief the political and practical vulnerabilities of a hastily-conceived United Nations force undertaking a humanitarian mission in a hostile atmosphere. Each phase demonstrated the mismatch between an ambitious mission and the means available to accomplish it.

Transition (March 26 to May 4, 1993)

Within several days of passage of Resolution 814, Somali leaders assembled in Addis Ababa, Ethiopia, signed an accord that called for, inter alia, a very ambitious political program: the establishment of interim government at the district, regional, and national levels and a two-year transition period to a democratically elected government. Two years appeared to be about as long as the U.N. could reasonably be expected to mount such a large recovery effort. Given competing world priorities, probabilities were low that the U.N. Security Council, troop-contributing countries, and nations donating humanitarian and economic assistance would be willing to sustain such a substantial program for a longer period. We were already seeing signs of "donor fatigue" as the immediate dangers of massive starvation began to subside. Traditional reconstruction projects under the United Nations Development Program (UNDP) would of course be needed for many years to come.

After examining each aspect of its mandate, UNOSOM concluded that significant progress could be made in two years. However, the ambitious multifaceted strategy adopted was dependent on having a relatively secure environment, good local cooperation, and adequate resources. During this two-year period UNOSOM would help Somalis to: (1) establish interim governance and prepare for an internationally supervised election; (2) progress from emergency relief to development and reconstruction, restoring basic services such as public health, water, electricity, telephones, schools, and a functioning agricultural economy; (3) rebuild the police, justice, and penal systems to a point where Somalis could replace most of the U.N. forces; and (4) return to their own towns and villages from refugee camps in neighboring countries and makeshift refuges in Somalia.

In UNOSOM senior staff meetings, some argued that only one program could be implemented at a time. For example, secure conditions were necessary before there could be local governance and control of law and order. Restoration of local services and the economy depended on political stability. While there was logic to a cautious step-by-step sequential approach, I was convinced this was a formula for never reaching any of the desired goals.

Success also depended on sustaining hope among the Somali people. Proceeding simultaneously with humanitarian, political, and security programs could produce benefits in a number of areas; and, realistically, it seemed to be the only way that a modest recovery could be achieved in a two-year period.

In organizing for this effort and in trying to establish a network of U.N. posts throughout the country, we were faced with antiquated U.N. procedures for identifying and moving qualified personnel into the field. U.N. headquarters in Mogadishu was dysfunctional. Messages from the field

Belgian members of UNITAF, the U.S.-led task force that preceded the full-blown U.N. operation, wait to join UNOSOM II reinforcements at Kismayo Airport, April 1993.

went unanswered; there was no civilian center for coordinating information and managing emergencies; and very few persons seemed to have the management skills necessary to organize and follow through on tasks. When I arrived in Mogadishu, the only phone was on my desk and could not be answered by my secretary, who was in another room out of sight. Many of these basic management inefficiencies were easily corrected. But as precious days to prepare flew by, we were unable to obtain enough of the talented civilians needed for the immense challenge we confronted. Both the UNOSOM staff and the U.N. agencies had only a small percentage of the people they required. For the overworked team in Somalia, which came from eighty different nations, each day seemed like a week.

Resources were equally scarce. Relief and development assistance depended on donations from nations to nongovernmental organizations (NGOs) or U.N. agencies. But most prospective donor nations were excessively cautious in fulfilling pledges made at the humanitarian conference in Addis Ababa in March 1993. In addition to lobbying nations to meet commitments already made, we tried to obtain extra funds that could be applied flexibly and rapidly to meet immediate Somali needs. Such expenditures would have especially high political impact. We wanted to spread programs throughout the country, with emphasis on neglected areas, like the north, that had established a degree of stability on their own without the benefit of international military presence. U.N. military contingents also wanted money to help them implement high-priority projects in areas where they were operating. Only a few nations responded.

Funds were even more difficult to obtain for restoration of the justice system. The Somali police force had had a long tradition of professionalism. It was one institution that had potential for rapid revitalization. But it needed an immediate infusion of assistance. Police buildings had been destroyed and nearly all of the equipment had disappeared. Most of the funds for this essential element of recovery had to come from voluntary donations of governments rather than being easily accessible in the U.N. peacekeeping budget. We wanted Somalis, rather than U.N. troops, to be able to deal with criminality as soon as possible. As I saw it, the Somali police represented the eventual ticket home for U.N. troops. Tragically, it took nearly a year of strenuous bureaucratic warfare in New York and numerous survey missions before we began to receive the equipment, training, and funding that police organizations desperately needed to begin to be effective. An opportunity had been lost.

The process of preparing to relieve the UNITAF military staff also began from scratch. Turkish lieutenant-general Bir, the first UNOSOM II commander, had to build a multinational staff from the ground up. For many weeks he did not have enough personnel to even estimate when he could relieve the American commander.

In late March the relentless pace of American withdrawal began to raise concerns. Promised U.N. replacement forces were way behind schedule; and two of the most effective units, the Australians and the Canadians, were expected to depart without relief shortly after a U.N. takeover. My first message to Secretary-General Boutros Boutros-Ghali upon arrival had been a plea to keep the Australians. They had done an outstanding job in the Baidoa region in all facets of their mission. A newly arrived Pakistani brigade was given the task of replacing the powerful American Marines in south Mogadishu. Nigerian, Zimbabwean, Botswanan and Moroccan forces had to be moved to the countryside from Mogadishu to help replace other departing forces, weakening the U.N.'s grip on the city.

Plans to move quickly into the central region and the northeast were postponed indefinitely with lengthy delays in the anticipated arrival of an Indian brigade. The Indians would be well supported by the Germans, who were making their first appearance as international peacekeepers after highly publicized internal debates. Because of their domestic controversy, the Germans were strictly limited to engineering and logistical assistance.

In late April 1993, I made my first visit outside the region to report to the secretary-general in New York on the impending transfer of responsibilities. Although U.S. and U.N. military commanders ultimately recommended a May 4 turnover date, the secretary-general, faced with the uncertainties in the situation, asked the U.S. to retain command responsibility for an additional month. The U.S. was unwilling to accept an additional delay in departure, apparently believing that its small Quick Reaction Force (QRF), which was remaining behind as an emergency reserve, provided sufficient insurance for unforeseen developments.

As a result, the early May change of command marked the transformation of the force from one dominated by a superpower with more than 20,000 troops of its own on the ground to one led by a weak organization of many small contingents, the largest being some 4,000 Pakistanis still waiting for a portion of their equipment. From a multinational force of some 30,000, the U.N. anticipated an initial dip to a low of 16,000 troops before replacements arrived. Although the U.N. with its smaller force had an expanded mission to work throughout the country, it had to stretch just to cover the gaps left by departing forces.

I don't know whether another month of U.S. command would have delayed or perhaps even prevented the vicious attacks against the U.N. in Mogadishu on June 5. As it happened, there was an attempt to challenge U.N. authority almost immediately following the May 4 change of command. On the evening of May 6–7, forces of faction-leader Ahmed Omar Jess, who were aligned with General Aideed, again attempted to retake the long-contested port city of Kismayo in the south from clans loyal to General Hersi Morgan. Belgian peacekeepers successfully beat back this blatant violation of the Somali-agreed cease-fire. If that aggression was intended to be the widely predicted test of the U.N., UNOSOM hoped that its credibility had been established.

Hostilities (June 5 to October 9, 1993)

It is still a matter of conjecture when plans were concocted by General Aideed for the brutal attack against United Nations forces on June 5, 1993. Schemes may have been: (1) engineered on the margins of the March Addis Reconciliation Conference; (2) developed in ensuing months as UNOSOM began working with Somalis to re-establish the justice system and to implement the Addis Accords; (3) hastily conceived as UNOSOM notified Aideed representatives of an impending inspection of authorized storage sites for weapons; or (4) prepared at some other time with different motives.

Some have theorized that a more proactive U.N. with a mandate to help Somalis restore representative government was perceived to be a threat to

The author, seated, second from right, meets with village elders in Baar shortly after his arrival.

Aideed's ambitions to hold onto power. Consistently opposed to U.N. peace efforts, Aideed had accepted a massive U.S. intervention force only on the eve of its December 9 arrival. He might have thought that if he embarrassed the U.N. he might force it to depart, or at least to abandon active implementation of its mandate. The U.N. did not have a worldwide reputation for staunch responses to attacks against it. But this was a different U.N. mission with unprecedented peace-enforcement powers.

The vicious attacks of June 5 were concentrated on lightly armed Pakistani forces returning from escorting U.N. arms inspectors and on Pakistani troops helping distribute food at a feeding station. These coordinated attacks represented a blatant challenge to the authority of the U N. Twenty-four brave Pakistani soldiers were killed and some fifty-seven others wounded as they fought their way out of well-laid traps, with assistance from other Pakistani, Italian, and American forces. Six Pakistanis were held captive for several days. One of them died. Roadblocks were established by Aideed supporters in a number of areas of the city, and civilian headquarters compounds were fired on throughout the day and into the early evening. This unprovoked attack on those who had come to help Somalia was an awful moment for us all. We lost many friends that day.

While UNOSOM concentrated on getting the violence halted in the city, determining what actually had happened, improving U.N. security, and obtaining release of those held captive, the Security Council's reaction was immediate. On Sunday, June 6, it passed Resolution 837 calling for the arrest of those responsible, curtailment of incitement to violence, and expeditious disarmament of Mogadishu.

Three objectives occupied UNOSOM over the next few hectic days. The first was to relocate the majority of international civilians to the relative safety of Kenya and to prepare to move a core staff into the U.N. military compound for better security and closer civilian-military coordination. Previous to these attacks an orderly combining of civilian and military headquarters had already been planned, but facilities were not yet ready to accommodate civilians. The second was to probe for any possibility of a dialogue that could lead to peaceful compliance with the provisions of Resolution 837. Several letters were exchanged over the next few days, but it became clear that Aideed was not then interested in negotiation. The third was to obtain improved equipment for the lightly armed UNOSOM military units and prepare plans to implement the provisions of the new Security Council mandate, with force if necessary.

International pressures for the immediate arrest of Aideed intensified. We felt we had to postpone arresting him, however, for a number of reasons: We first wanted to assess what actually had happened. Aideed initially had denied any involvement. Also, we needed to move the international civilians to safer locations, and we wanted the Pakistani prisoners back. The Pakistani contingent needed time to recover, to acquire better armament to deal with the heavier weapons used in the attack on June 5, and to be able to control the situation, including any violent reactions to Aideed's possible arrest.

Most importantly, we did not have the intelligence mechanisms for pinpointing Aideed's location or the trained professionals necessary to make an arrest while minimizing the risk to Somalis and U.N. troops involved. Such a force was requested within several days of the attack, but it was not until the American "Rangers" arrived more than two months later in late August that we finally had the appropriate means. By then, probabilities of capture had decreased.

On the morning of June 12, the U.N. military was ready to take an initial step in implementing Resolution 837. Attempts at political negotiations had failed, and the remaining U.N. civilians had been moved into the military compound. At this point we appeared to have no viable alternative to the use of force.

We knew of the dangers of a protracted struggle, but the consequences of not responding to these vicious attacks seemed worse than the risks of taking action. There was no future for a U.N. mission in Somalia that did not protect itself and failed to implement Security Council mandates. Implications for peacekeepers around the world were also a consideration. As I commented in a message to U.N. headquarters on the eve of the operation, "There are many risks and vulnerabilities in the course" being contemplated, but "the consequences of not acting have profound implications."

The first military action to implement the Security Council resolution commenced in the early morning hours of June 12. With great care to reduce the possibility of Somali casualties, precision fire from newly arrived U.S. AC-130 gunships silenced Aideed's radio, which had continued broadcasting provocative propaganda after the June 5 attacks. Weapons and ammunition were destroyed in each of the authorized SNA storage sites inspected on June 5. The Pakistanis were given the task of dismantling the largest site and did so very effectively. In some cases, ammunition was first removed to reduce collateral damage to Somali buildings in the vicinity. By late afternoon this well-executed first military initiative had been successfully completed.

We were very concerned about triggering a resumption of factional fighting. Letters were sent to all of the faction leaders sympathetic to the U.N. (at that time eleven of fifteen) urging them to maintain the peace and cautioning against taking advantage of a weakened SNA. We also urged Aideed to begin cooperating with the U.N.

The next morning the United Nations military began the first of a series of surgical strikes designed to eliminate systematically clandestine weapons stockpiles in Mogadishu, starting with a place near Aideed's compound, called "Atto's garage." This was not the voluntary disarmament campaign we had originally envisioned, but it was one way of rapidly reducing the huge amounts of weapons secretly stashed around the city.

In addition to sporadic attacks against U.N. positions and the newly combined civilian/military headquarters, Aideed's SNA responded with a carefully orchestrated demonstration designed to embarrass the Pakistanis and the U.N. Intentionally staged at a major U.N. strong point (at the K1-4 traffic circle) next to the only hotel used by the world press, the SNA action provoked the besieged Pakistanis into return fire at a threatening crowd with Somali women in front.

According to our information, Somali gunmen even shot their own people from behind in order to ensure there were substantial casualties for the television cameras to record. Although a diabolical propaganda scheme, it created some world opinion that a vengeful U.N. was out of control. Attempts to clarify what actually had happened never caught up with the first sensationalist images of Somali casualties being carted away from the scene of the demonstration. This action against his own people helped persuade us that an unrestrained Aideed had become a menace to the Somali people as well as to U.N. personnel.

It took us until June 17 to plan the next big U.N. operation, a multi-nation search of Aideed's headquarters complex. Lack of Pakistani armor made it imperative to bring French, Italian, and Moroccan forces from other areas of the city and countryside. The United States contributed air cover, Italian and Moroccan forces cordoned off the area, the Pakistanis conducted house-by-house searches of the compound, and the French provided a reserve. We did capture a number of weapons, documents, and command-and-control equipment, but occupants of the buildings had been given advance warning by our forces and time to escape. Aideed reportedly was among those who fled.

Heavy fighting ensued, however, as an SNA force attacked the Moroccan cordon. Again, they used a shield of women and children to close with our troops. (Aideed is said to have boasted about the success of this tactic.) Their use of hand grenades from close range caused the bulk of

Moroccan casualties. As the French reserve and the besieged Moroccans responded to the attacks, a battle erupted, flowing across several blocks of the city into the late afternoon. SNA forces firing from inside hospitals and several errant U.N. helicopter missiles complicated the U.N. counter-attack, but by late afternoon the SNA force had scattered.

As the day's battle concluded, we announced our intention to arrest General Aideed. Obviously, it would have been better to arrest him before announcing the intention to do so, but there was no telling when we might have the opportunity or the means. Though we still did not have the trained personnel to snatch Aideed cleanly, we thought it important at that juncture for the Somali people, and especially his own sub-clan, to realize that the U.N. did not consider him to have a political future in Somalia unless he was first cleared through a judicial process.

By focusing on Aideed and a few key SNA ringleaders, we hoped to encourage the rest of his followers to return to the political process under new interim leadership. Their place was assured by the Addis Accords. It also seemed specious to have conducted a disruptive sweep of Aideed's headquarters without acknowledging that he was one of those wanted under the terms of Resolution 837. In addition, although the investigation was far from complete, there were by then solid grounds for believing Aideed had orchestrated the attacks of June 5.

From his post at police headquarters, a member of the Nigerian contingent surveys Mogadishu. The capital city had been destroyed by warring factions in the Somali civil war.

171

Critics allege that we committed a fatal peacekeeping mistake on June 17 by publicly taking sides among competing factions. They tend to ignore that all Somali faction leaders had started with a clean slate. Although some had argued that certain warlords should be punished for past deeds, we considered it our mandate to look forward to the future—not backward to the past. We were determined to facilitate an even-handed political process in which the Somalis picked their future leaders. It would then be up to newly elected Somali authorities to deal with any accusations of past misdeeds. General Aideed had distinguished himself on June 5 from other Somali leaders by "taking sides" against the U.N. By brutally attacking Pakistani peacekeepers, he had demonstrated his hostility to the lawful actions of the international community.

Knowing that the timing of Aideed's arrest was problematic, our goal was to contain his assaults and to isolate him within his own community while we vigorously pursued multifaceted political, developmental and judicial programs throughout the country. We did not want the uncertain resolution of the Aideed issue to distract us from our main purpose, which was countrywide recovery. While the media painted the image of a mission consumed by the hunt for Aideed, we actually were expending most of our efforts on getting political, economic, and judicial programs under way.

In addition to trying to reduce the numbers of illegal arms and to better protect the U.N. mission from attacks in Mogadishu, we began to put in place our political strategy of implementing the first stages of the Addis Ababa Accords in areas of Somalia where this was feasible. Although still limited by personnel shortages, consultations were begun in the northeast and southern regions that would lead to local Somali selection of representatives to district councils.

The colorful nightly reports of the untiring efforts of my political division chief, Leonard Kapungu, and my deputy, Ambassador Lansana Kouyate, to form district and regional councils—and the enthusiastic ways they were received—were heartwarming. There were many local obstacles to this process but most were unrelated to events in distant Mogadishu. The Somali people seemed to relish the prospect of this fragile beginning of local self-rule. In ensuing months, while the media focussed on daily incidents in Mogadishu, more than fifty district councils were established and week-long training programs held for most of the new councilors, thanks to contributions from the Swedish Institute of Life and Peace.

UNOSOM tried hard to get programs of education, health, and basic services initiated in peaceful areas of the country. However, it was not easy to convince evacuated-aid organizations to begin operations in new areas.

Some, like UNICEF, eventually redistributed their programs to these relatively quiescent areas. We were determined to push the recovery throughout the country and not to let our efforts be held hostage to the failure to capture one individual in Mogadishu.

Progress in the rest of Somalia, where there was genuine support for the United Nations, was also a way to bring pressure on the relatively few members of Aideed's sub-clan who were still fanatically supporting him in Mogadishu. Many of his people feared they might miss out on the political process and the benefits of recovery if they did not cooperate with the us. However, Aideed seemed to have a facility for old-fashioned intimidation. It took great courage for clan members to urge reconciliation; those who did faced grave personal danger.

Within a month of commencement, the U.N. disarmament campaign in Mogadishu was running out of steam. For a variety of reasons, our military operations had become purely defensive: The number of easily accessible arms caches was diminishing. Some national military commanders were becoming reluctant to expose their men to potentially dangerous ground operations. Countries procrastinated in sending reinforcements considered necessary by U.N. commanders to conducting more comprehensive sweeps on the ground. Public reaction had been negative to a U.S. attack on the new Aideed command-and-control headquarters. The Americans did not like carrying the political burden of continuing such offensives with helicopters and AC-130 gunships.

A coordinated humanitarian, political, and disarmament campaign, called the "artichoke strategy" was developed for Mogadishu, beginning with a voluntary turn-in program. Political progress, humanitarian projects, and improvements to local police were to go hand-in-hand with arms control. We even began local consultations on the formation of councils in some of the city's fifteen districts.

Disarmament was never meant to make the city totally gun free. The objective was to remove major weapons and eventually reach a state in which the police had more power than the criminals. Repeated delays in the arrivals of replacement forces caused a steady slide in dates to begin this comprehensive plan. However, the principal impediment to unilateral disarmament of parts of the city was the understandable reluctance of cooperative clans to turn in weapons while there was still a threat from Aideed. They wanted to be able to defend themselves from encroachment.

The story was similar in the rest of the country. As the U.N. flexed its muscles in the aftermath of the June 5 incident, for example, many faction leaders around the country declared their readiness to turn in weapons. In

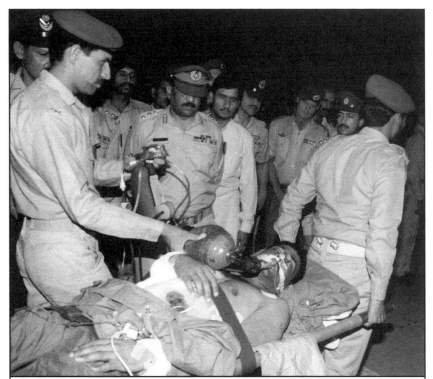

Pakistani army medical staff carry a wounded soldier to the Mogadishu airport for evacuation, June 1993. Twenty-four Pakistanis had been killed in a shootout with Somali gunmen.

exchange, however, they also wanted guarantees of protection for their people and, as a minimum, assistance in strengthening their police forces. They also wanted help in returning militia members to productive activity. Due to a lack of resources, the U.N. was neither ready to provide security nor a demobilization program that would help generate jobs for former militiamen. This opportunity for significant disarmament progress, which had been generated by forceful action in Mogadishu, eventually was lost.

In early July, in the aftermath of the ambush of an Italian unit searching for arms in their part of Mogadishu, allegations were made that the Italians had made a deal with Aideed's forces, effectively allowing SNA gunmen safe haven, putting certain arms caches off limits, and opening routes of access into the city and to certain areas within Mogadishu. This unsatisfactory situation for the rest of the force was ultimately resolved by moving Italian units out of the city and replacing them with Nigerians brought back from Belet Weyne in the west. But this time-consuming realignment was not accomplished until early September, leaving the force in an uncomfortable situation for over two months as the SNA increased the frequency of attempted ambushes and bombardment of United Nations areas in Mogadishu.

Initiatives against arms caches and command-and-control facilities had helped keep SNA gunmen off balance, but other factors also contributed to slackening protection for U.N. facilities in the city. Especially at night, weapons searches at checkpoints did not appear to be vigorously prosecuted, and patrols did not expand defensive perimeters to decrease the possibility of hit-and-run, short-range mortar attacks that routinely reached the port, airport, and headquarters. Ineffectual defense was partly a reflection of the disparity in training of the various contingents. A few were comfortable after dark; most were not.

Throughout the summer there had been periodic contacts with General Aideed's people and opposition groups within his clan. Ethiopian and Eritrean envoys made a concerted effort to find a formula for peacefully carrying out Security Council Resolution 837. However, it took arrival of the U.S. Rangers in late August to regenerate apparent SNA interest in finding a solution. The presence of specially trained troops and the real possibility that Aideed would be captured provided new leverage.

After some initial delay because of the unacceptable composition of the SNA delegation, secret preliminary meetings began. We considered that progress might even require curtailment of Ranger raids. However, substantive discussions were postponed almost as soon as they started. On the day scheduled for the first full meeting, September 5, 1993, a Nigerian unit was viciously ambushed while relieving Italian positions in the city. In addition, the Aideed group reneged on a pledge to allow a parallel meeting with clan leaders. Nonetheless, a week later we were ready to resume the dialogue. By this time, Aideed appeared to have lost interest, while the SNA made public professions to the contrary.

In the ensuing weeks the SNA seemed to shift tactics to larger ambushes and greater involvement of women and children. As U.N. soldiers tried to extricate themselves from these sorts of traps, more Somalis were killed. One such incident occurred on September 9. U.S. engineers escorted by Pakistani soldiers were trying to clear a large roadblock on a principal artery connecting UNOSOM facilities, "21 October Road." They were trapped by heavy fire from hundreds of Somalis behind walls and within buildings near the site of the June 5 ambush, and tank and helicopter gunship fire was necessary to extract the besieged peacekeepers. Although the helicopter gunners used great care with their protective fire, a large number of Somalis were killed or wounded, including some women who appeared to have been deliberately mixed into the crowd. While perhaps a sign of desperation, these costly tactics appeared to pay off for Aideed. As one astute observer later noted, it seemed that, the bigger Aideed's losses, the more his clansmen felt obligated to rally to his side.

International criticism of United Nations forces intensified, even though they were acting strictly in self-defense. Dissatisfaction also was growing in the U.S., as the media kept up a steady drumbeat of reports of ambushes and failed attempts to capture Aideed. "Nation building" championed in Security Council Resolution 814 became a pejorative term. Alternative policy approaches were being considered.

Political time was running out for the Rangers to accomplish their mission, but no one could predict how long it would take. With the exception of some unfortunate episodes of mistaken identity, they had conducted a series of very effective raids and captured a number of close Aideed associates. They were near another success in a very bad neighborhood during the afternoon of October 3, 1993, when two helicopters went down in an area crawling with Aideed sympathizers, ultimately causing the loss of some eighteen Americans, with one captured.

The delay in extricating the trapped Rangers has been bitterly criticized, but the combined force that came to the rescue could hardly have done more. While the Rangers were pinned down protecting the helicopter wreckage, the lightly armored U.S. Quick Reaction Force could not break through. Their call for assistance went out to U.N. contingents with armor. The Pakistanis by this time had a few old tanks and the Malaysians had armored personnel carriers. With their arrival on the scene, a plan was developed, and the hastily assembled combined rescue force moved out during the dark of night through a very dangerous area.

The Italians, who were now stationed outside Mogadishu, and the newly arrived Indians, who were restricted from operating in the city, were both asked to be ready to support a follow-on rescue operation if the first attempt at extraction was unsuccessful. Both nations responded positively.

Although there were some coordination problems with the rescue—language, lack of night equipment, and disorientation—by daybreak the remaining Rangers were all safely extracted. Both Pakistanis and Malaysians had suffered casualties. Rather than being a black-eye for the U.N., the rescue demonstrated what United Nations forces could do together in an emergency.

The Somalis who tried to kill the Rangers on that fateful day and evening took terrible losses. An estimated 300–500 were killed and hundreds more were wounded. This had a sobering impact within Aideed's sub-clan. Many expressed the view that they had paid any remaining blood debt to Aideed. They did not want any more killing, and they were ready to work for peace.

The shock of losing so many fine U.S. soldiers, the sickening mutilation and parading of bodies before television cameras, and the cruel exposure of a captured helicopter pilot caused outrage and revulsion in the U.S. The response might have been to crush any further interference with the U.N. mission. Instead, the tragedy intensified domestic criticism of prolonged participation in the mission. The rescue of the Somali people was deemed unworthy of another American life. Under heavy pressure from the Congress, President Bill Clinton decided to strengthen U.S. forces in the near term for additional protection, but to withdraw them by a certain date, March 31, 1994.

On October 9, as significant American reinforcements were en route, Aideed, at the urging of Ethiopian interlocutors, proposed to cease hostilities unilaterally against the U.N. UNOSOM welcomed this offer with certain provisions. The U.N. had begun a new phase of its effort to help the Somalis, but henceforth would have to deal from a much weaker position.

Reconciliation (October 9, 1993, to March 31, 1994, and beyond)

The new realities meant another U.N. strategy had to be formulated. Given the American decision to depart, reconciliation among the Aideed side and the twelve factions supporting the U.N. appeared to be the only feasible approach left that might salvage something for the Somalis. This strategy's fundamental weakness was its dependence on convincing Aideed and the "Group of Twelve" other faction leaders that settling differences peacefully was in their best long-term interests.

Reconciliation was imperative if the Somalis were going to be able to attract the assistance they needed for recovery. Donor nations were fed up with the internal squabbling. Cooperation was also essential to persuading enough troop-contributing nations to remain in Somalia to retain a viable force. The initial reaction by the other nations to the U.S. decision to depart was to try to beat the Americans out the door. If Americans were not willing to sacrifice any more, some governments reasoned, why should they? Other contingents worried about the absence of U.S. protection. A stampede seemed poised for March 31. Fortunately, enough troop contributing-countries ultimately decided to persevere and to give the Somalis a longer period to get their act together. But most Western nations joined the United States exodus.

Under this new strategy, UNOSOM slowed down efforts to create district councils in contentious areas where they might prove counterproductive to reconciliation efforts and instead concentrated on trying to persuade both sides to cooperate in moving toward a transitional government. There was even some concern that the "Group of Twelve" might decide to try immediately to resolve their "Aideed problem" by force, plunging the nation back into civil war.

In early December 1993, at an aid conference in Addis Ababa involving the factions (less SNA) and many of the impressive newly selected regional leaders from around the country, I stressed the new emphasis in the U.N.'s policy: Somali solutions to Somali problems, assistance prioritized for cooperative areas maintaining peaceful conditions, strengthening the Somali police to maintain law and order, and beginning disarmament with pilot programs for the rehabilitation of youth.

With the encouragement of Ethiopian president Meles Zenawi, faction leaders remained in Ethiopia for informal political discussions following the aid conference. Ali Mahdi, the leader of the "Group of Twelve," was convinced to join the group from Mogadishu, and finally his arch rival Aideed, with U.S. encouragement, also agreed to come. Aideed's flight from Mogadishu to Ethiopia in an American military aircraft (to ensure his safety) caused another furor in the U.S. In the end, however, the factions were not yet ready to make a deal, and the political discussions among Somalis in Ethiopia ended without a breakthrough.

In succeeding months, numerous other attempts to find a political formula for an interim government also proved unsuccessful. Political efforts made progress but never quite achieved their objective of establishing a transitional government. It would be months before Aideed, after unsuccessfully trying to find allies, returned to Somalia.

U.S. departure on March 31, 1994, did not bring the immediate unraveling that some had predicted, but in the ensuing months the U.N. became fatigued with countless false starts and promises and very little actual progress. A Security Council decision was made to shut down the mission by March 31, 1995, two years following the creation of UNOSOM II. Compared to the dire predictions of massive deaths in 1993 from disease and starvation, the Somalis had made a substantial turnaround. Hundreds of thousands of lives had been saved. Crops had been harvested. Animals were again being exported. Many children were attending school.

But the Somalian's opportunity to avoid bloodshed, to rejoin the community of nations, and to stand on their own feet with the generous assistance of the international community in a two-year time period had been squandered. The vast majority of Somalis, I am convinced, are tired of the tragedy and hardship of war and want only to live productive lives in

Secretary-General Boutros-Ghali, center, visits an orphanage operated by an Irish agency, October 1993. At left is General Maurice Quadri, commander of the French contingent.

peace. That day is now sometime in an unpredictable future.

The Next Somalia

The agonies of struggling to help Somalia spawned critical lessons for future peacekeeping. Dealing with a failed nation generates complexities for an organization designed to assist in resolving disputes between nations—not within one that has self-destructed. What does the world community do when institutions have ceased to exist and rampant lawlessness has led to massive starvation, genocide, or ethnic cleansing? Should the U.N. try to stabilize a country and facilitate the restoration of a modicum of civility. Or are such undertakings just too hard?

The alternatives to a concerted effort to help a nation get back on its feet are not very palatable. The world community can simply ignore the situation, it can wait until the warring parties exhaust themselves with killing or resolve differences on their own. Or it can restrict outside assistance to emergency relief. The consequences of these more limited approaches, however, are that many more innocents are likely to die.

In Somalia, the success of the different strategies undertaken by the U.N. depended on the readiness of the Somali people to work with the U.N. to find solutions. However, even though the majority of the people appeared to be supportive, the U.N. was unable politically to sustain its effort against the disruptive elements. Therefore, the tyranny of a few ulti-

On October 3, 1993, two Blackhawk helicopters were shot down in an area of Mogadishu controlled by followers of the Somali warlord Mohammed Farah Aideed. Eighteen Americans were killed and one captured. The photographs on these pages were taken from a television screen by Aideed's guerrillas and sent to Western media. In the larger, Somalis gather around the fuselage of one of the helicopters. In the inset, the mutilated body of a crewman is dragged through the streets. The propaganda was effective. A shocked American public demanded the return of its soldiers from what it regarded as a mission gone amok.

mately managed to deny international assistance to the majority. In the future, any U.N. peace-enforcement operation will need to have the strength, backed by the sustained resolve of participating nations, to stand up to the inevitable "spoilers," in whatever guise they take.

The U.N. approach historically is to monitor an agreed peace between sides in dispute, and to bend over backwards to avoid becoming involved. Its actions require agreement of all parties. Under Chapter VII, however, U.N. peace-enforcers must have an option to take sides if warranted. In the case of Somalia, many nations had no stomach for the consequences of peace-enforcement. For them, the injustice to Somalis appeared not to be worth the sacrifice necessary to correct it.

Whatever approach is mandated by the Security Council, a mission must be given the means to succeed from the beginning, and the nations involved must resolve to work together and to persevere. While force should be employed only as a last resort, it must then be applied effectively and in a reasonable period of time.

In the case of tough Chapter VII operations such as Somalia, an effective multifaceted civilian organization and a strong military force were essential at the inception of the operation. Inability to provide essential personnel and resources meant that the U.N. never fully realized its potential for dealing effectively with this unprecedented mandate.

Given the complexities of the Somali situation and the unsatisfied hunger of some political leaders for dominant power, there was no guarantee that the nation could have been restored even with an abundance of resources. Nonetheless, although success depended on highly problematic cooperation of faction leaders and a United Nations ready for tough challenges to peace-enforcement, Somalia should not be written off as a "mission impossible."

One thing is clear from the ambitious and well-intentioned effort undertaken in Somalia: If the U.N. is to be the instrument of choice for dealing with such situations in the future, it must be strengthened and given the resources with which to solve problems in a timely manner. Major reform is needed in the areas of personnel for the field, in resources for economic and judicial programs, and in constituting a multinational force able to withstand organized opposition. In addition, the support from U.N. headquarters in New York for missions in the field must be substantially strengthened and streamlined.

Most of the weaknesses experienced in Somalia are correctable if the goal of developing an effective peacekeeping organization is considered paramount, and nations are willing to invest the resources. Civilian personnel are critical to the effective implementation of policy. From media experts to lawyers, the U.N. needs to be able to rapidly assemble teams of individuals who can operate throughout a broken country. They must be skilled in coordinating humanitarian operations, reconstituting police and justice systems, working out political arrangements, communicating with the people, efficiently administering civilian personnel, and arranging logistical support for military forces. Trying to obtain the kinds of people who could put programs in place in Somalia took inordinate amounts of time with uneven results. The U.N. needs to study the lessons learned, train cadres of talented people, and maintain a ready pool of experienced volunteers all over the world.

United Nations programs must also be adequately funded. This means flexible humanitarian support and timely access to the wherewithal to develop a police and justice system. Because of the peculiar structure of U.N. bureaucracy and regulations, the bulk of funding for Somali police assistance had to be generated through voluntary contributions of interested nations rather than being drawn from the assessed money in the peacekeeping budget. Even though the Somali police were the ticket home for United Nations troops, endless meetings and surveys were a prerequisite for funding. By the time some help finally started to arrive, the United States was preparing to depart altogether. Clearly, funding for police programs needs to be an integral part of the assessed budget that is available from the beginning of a mission.

In the same way, the humanitarian division needed some flexible funding to support projects that would have immediate and positive impact. For example, funds could be used to initiate help to a peaceful area where the U.N. otherwise could not be present, perhaps allowing a newly formed district council to prioritize local needs and then carry out projects in a timely manner. When it comes to resources, timing is everything and resources are critical in the early stages.

There are relatively easy solutions to the above needs. But in one critical area—producing an effective multinational force comprised of small units from many nations—the challenge is particularly daunting and inherently difficult to correct. The complex problems of inoperability, uneven levels of training, inadequate equipment, and different languages do not compare with the difficulties caused by the nearly irresistible temptation for nations to interfere with the operations of their units, especially when facing dangerous circumstances. Local unit commanders inevitably want to check with headquarters thousands of miles away before participating in risky operations or a U.N. policy that might be considered controversial at

Under heavy pressure from Congress, President Bill Clinton agreed to end American participation in the mission in Somalia by March 1994. Here, U.S. marines board a navy hovercraft for redeployment to a ship offshore.

home. A U.N. force needs political as well as military cohesiveness.

For many nations it also will be difficult to sustain casualties when what happens in a far-off country that does not threaten critical national interests. This is the particular vulnerability of purely humanitarian operations in the post–Cold War period.

One alternative is to try to find a well-equipped nation, or, at a minimum, larger units from fewer nations, willing to contribute a dominant force and pledged to see the assignment through to conclusion. Another is to convince a regional organization such as NATO that has trained forces to undertake the assignment. Unfortunately, when considering volunteers for difficult humanitarian missions there are not many militarily viable regional alliances or prospects for large contributions from individual nations. Experiences in Somalia, Bosnia, Rwanda, and other recent adventures in peacekeeping are not likely to encourage nations to sign up for such undertakings.

Because of the understandable tendency of nations to put limits on national contingents and the other weaknesses of a hastily assembled international force, a more viable approach may be to develop, as others have proposed, an international volunteer force along the lines of the French Foreign Legion. Any U.N. standing force, of course, would have to begin as a pilot program with many phases of evaluation in its development. There are substantial downsides, and the cost would be high, but such a well-trained volunteer force would help solve the most intractable problem of peace-enforcement in desperate humanitarian situations—sustaining political integrity and commitment.

In reading Stanley Meisler's account (in the first edition of this work, and included in the present volume) of the U.N.'s chaotic four-year intervention in the Congo, I was struck by how similar the difficulties the U.N. experienced then were to those we encountered in Somalia some three decades later. Not much had been done in the interim to develop a credible peace-enforcement capability. If we are to expect so much of the U.N. in the post–Cold War period, then we need to give it the tools to do the job effectively. Unless we follow up hard on the lessons of Somalia and develop the capabilities needed for a peace-enforcement mission, the U.N. will be unprepared to cope with the inevitable next Somalia.

*Before serving as the special representative of the U.N. secretary-general in Somalia, from March 1993 to March 1994, **Admiral Jonathan T. Howe**, U.S. Navy, retired, was deputy assistant to the president for national security affairs. During his thirty-five year naval career, he was commander of NATO forces in southern Europe and director of the political-military bureau of the department of state. He is now executive director of the Arthur Vining Davis Foundations, Jacksonville, Fla.*

Nordic troops with UNPROFOR ration fuel and monitor traffic at a bridge on the border between Serbia and Macedonia, 1992. The U.N. mission in the Balkans was its biggest and costliest troop deployment.

Bosnia: Negotiation and Retreat

by Roy Gutman

The mission in Bosnia was a humiliating exercise in "how not to proceed," according to one U.N. ground commander. Even as massive war crimes were being committed, the superpowers of the U.N. Security Council looked the other way, refusing to take a consistent position, distorting historical precedent when convenient. Peacekeeping is not feasible in a raging war, nor is diplomacy, unless it is backed by military force. While U.N. personnel saved many lives, they also may have prolonged the conflict.

The narrow bridge across the Sava at Bosanska Gradiska is a bridge between two cultures, linking Bosnia–Herzegovina, a unique melting pot of nations and religions, with Croatia, which is mostly Roman Catholic. In the autumn of 1992, it was the gateway between a reign of terror and a region of relative calm, maintained by blue-helmeted U.N. troops from four continents.

Northern Bosnia was a nightmarish land of concentration camps, systematic rape, and daily massacres. To return to occupied Croatia, where Serbs had completed their conquests and the U.N. was present, was a relief. Yet there was anything but peace. From the bridge, I and my traveling companions, an interpreter and photographer, saw plumes of smoke rising over the town of Okucani. Soon, we were in front of two burning houses. I stopped the car and waved down a Nepalese soldier in U.N. uniform to ask what was going on.

"I think the houses are burning down," he replied.

It was a metaphor for the role of the U.N. in the former Yugoslavia. There was no sign of the fire brigade and no talk of culprits or victims. In this Croatian region known as Western Slavonia, Nepalese, Argentinians, Canadians, and Jordanians had their zones and camps, but the Serbian militias controlled the road and the land. The U.N. peacekeepers' job seemed to be to monitor the physical destruction of Serb-occupied Croatia.

Across the bridge, in Bosnia, U.N. troops had not yet arrived, except in

Sarajevo. The Serbs never let them deploy in the two-thirds of the country under their control. In Bosnia, U.N. troops were reduced to monitoring a mass slaughter.

The Balkans became the U.N.'s biggest and costliest troop deployment and perhaps the most damaging yet to the institution of peacekeeping. Some 22,000 troops were sent to Bosnia and 14,000 to Croatia in a force misleadingly named UNPROFOR, or United Nations Protection Force. Their mission was impossible. The mandate in Croatia did not envision the use of force, and in Bosnia a succession of mandates sidestepped both the causes and the effects of the conflict.

The U.N. military presence in Bosnia is largely a tale of wasted resources, squandered moral and political capital, and discredited processes and personnel. There were, however, notable exceptions. The war itself was a seminal event at the close of the twentieth century, a scene of shame and, occasionally, honor, for the world community. A critical look at the U.N.'s involvement is essential if the organization is to regain its compass at the start of the twenty-first.

Primary responsibility for the failure of the world community in Bosnia is borne by the superpowers that dominate the Security Council. Led by the United States, they deliberately looked away as massive war crimes were being committed, even as the crimes were being reported by the international news media. They maintained the arms embargo against the besieged state of Bosnia, in full knowledge that they were violating letter and spirit of the U.N. Charter, which recognizes self-defense by sovereign nations as an inherent right. These same powers set up a diplomatic process but, in defiance of experience and elementary logic, refused to back it by military force. There is ample evidence that this clumsy and contradictory response resulted in a longer and probably broader war. Yet, to blame major governments is no source of comfort to the U.N., an organization that has portrayed itself as the incorporation of mankind's hopes for peace and stability. The disappointment for so many in the public was that the U.N. structure turned out to be just another bureaucracy, more hidebound than most. It lacked any self-correcting mechanism. Its leadership failed to define the crisis in which it was engulfed, or to seize the initiative.

In August 1992, after the media broke the news that Serbs had set up death camps in northern Bosnia, President George Bush made no apologies for the obvious intelligence failure. He said the camps, where hundreds of Muslims and Croats died daily, were an illustration of a "a blood feud" and "a complex, convoluted conflict that grows out of age-old animosities." Two

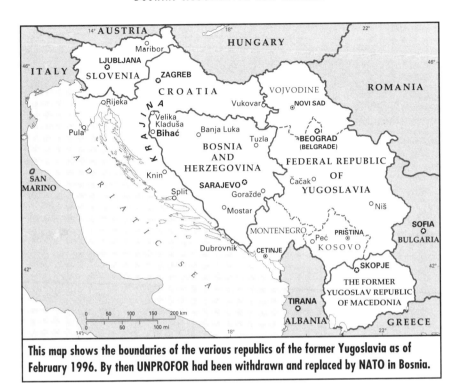

This map shows the boundaries of the various republics of the former Yugoslavia as of February 1996. By then UNPROFOR had been withdrawn and replaced by NATO in Bosnia.

months later, General Colin Powell, Chairman of the Joint Chiefs of Staff, justified his preferred "hand's off" policy by writing in a newspaper editorial that the conflict had "deep ethnic and religious roots that go back a thousand years." British prime minister John Major blamed the war on the removal of the "discipline" that the old Soviet Union had exerted "over the ancient hatreds" in the old Yugoslavia, forgetting that Yugoslavia had been an independent communist state since 1945. Republican senator John Warner topped them all when he told a Senate hearing: "My own research indicates that . . . these people have fought each other for not hundreds of years, but thousands of years for religious, ethnic, cultural differences."

The history was spurious. "These people" couldn't have been fighting since the dawn of time, for the Slavs did not appear in the Balkans until the sixth century. Even revenge-preaching Serbian nationalists did not claim any grievance before 1389, when a mainly Serb force was defeated by the Ottoman empire at Kosovo Polje. As for the image of unending conflict, Bosnia experienced mass carnage only once before, during the Yugoslav civil war that coincided with World War II. Unfortunately, all this ill-informed rhetoric by Western leaders confused the public, who would never have guessed that concentration camps had reappeared on European soil in a response to an obscure fourteenth-century battle.

189

In fact, the war that began in April 1992 was not the spontaneous eruption of an ancient struggle but a well-planned land-grab. The context for
the bloodbath in Bosnia was the breakup of Yugoslavia after Tito's death in
1980. Elsewhere in Eastern Europe, wherever the Red Army had installed
communist regimes, the West during the Cold War encouraged alternatives
to communism. But in Yugoslavia, which had been freed without much
Soviet help, the West gave political and financial backing to Tito, the independent communist. When communism collapsed there, as everywhere else
in Europe, the only alternative political force was nationalism.

The Serbs of Serbia, Yugoslavia's largest republic, led by Slobodan
Milosevic, stood to lose the most in the transformation. Serbs who dominated the army and secret police and Serbian intellectuals who had faithful-
ly served the communist regime feared the loss of privilege and wealth.
Nationalism was another ticket to staying in power.

In a 1986 memorandum, the Serbian Academy of Science complained
that Serbs had been shortchanged in Tito's Yugoslavia. They alleged that
there was "physical, political, legal and cultural genocide" against Serbs in
the autonomous region of Kosovo—a willful distortion of a long-term
demographic trend—and demanded the "complete national and cultural
integrity of the Serbian people . . . no matter in which republic or province
they might find themselves living." The document specifically urged Serbia
to take over the country's two autonomous provinces: the largely Hungarian
Vojvodina in the north of Serbia, and the overwhelmingly Albanian Kosovo
in the south.

Between 1961 and 1991, the Serbian proportion of the inhabitants of
Kosovo had dropped from 23.5 to 10 percent, while that of the Albanians
had risen from 67 to 90 percent. But the "genocide" claim had no factual
basis: Serbs were not being expelled but were emigrating from the poorest
of the Yugoslav regions to elsewhere in Serbia. The rhetoric concealed two
factual trends that in fact would threaten Serbian dominance in a democratic Yugoslavia. One was the shifting demographic balance, due to a falling
birthrate among Serbs and higher rates among other nationalities, Muslims
in particular. From 1961 to 1991, the Serbian proportion of the Yugoslav
population fell from 42 to 36.2 percent, while that of Muslims rose from
5.2 to 10 percent and of Albanians from 5 to 9.3 percent. Serbia proper
registered only 1.4 live births per thousand in 1990, compared to 7.7 in
Bosnia–Herzegovina and 23.1 in Kosovo. The second factor was that Serbs
stood to lose the most in the transformation to a market economy and
democratic political structure. The Serbs' influence over the security apparatus and their fear of losing their predominance furnished both the motive

Vukovar, in the eastern Slavonia region of Croatia, July 1992: At left, a British soldier surveys the effects of heavy shelling; at right, ambulances transport the wounded. Though the U.N. had its zones and camps in the area, Serb militias controlled the roads and the land.

and the means for aggression.

Slobodan Milosevic, who took power in Serbia as a communist in 1987, followed the academics' advice and his own ruthless instincts. He seized political control of Kosovo and Vojvodina, as well as the tiny republic of Montenegro, dominated by ethnic Serbs. Thus he acquired a blocking veto in the eight-member Yugoslav presidency and set off a constitutional crisis. Nationalism had already caught fire within the Orthodox Church, the academic community, and the army in Serbia. Milosevic poured on the fuel.

With Serbia setting the pattern, ethnic parties won elections in almost every republic and province, threatening the existence of the multiethnic state. Soon, fearing Serbian dominance, the advanced western republics of Croatia and Slovenia demanded a looser confederation. In response, Milosevic threatened to go to war. Early in 1991 he proclaimed that the Serbian people "want to live in one state." Dividing Yugoslavia and forcing Serbs to live in different states "is from our point of view, unacceptable, that is, let me emphasize, out of the question." The warning applied mainly to Croatia, which had a 10 percent Serbian population and Bosnia, where it

191

was one-third of the total.

The assault occurred in four stages: disarming the republic-level territorial defense forces, starting in May 1990; arming the local Serbs, starting later that year; organizing a political and constitutional process to set up Serbian states on Croatian and Bosnian territory; and then staging provocations to permit the federal army to intervene decisively on the Serbian side.

War began in June 1991 with the decision by Slovenia and Croatia to quit the Yugoslav federation. The Slovenes had strenuously resisted disarming their territorial defense units, were well prepared and won their war in ten days. But in Croatia, which had been largely disarmed, the Yugoslav army had the advantages of vast military superiority, proximity to Serbia, the ability to infiltrate "volunteers," and the presence of armed ethnic Serbs. One-third of Croatia soon fell to the Serbs.

By the time Alija Izetbegovic's Muslim Party of Democratic Action came to power in Bosnia in November and December 1990, nearly all arms had been collected in that republic. Some months later, the Bosnian government discovered while investigating a shooting incident in western Bosnia that arms had been distributed to twenty-two Serbian-majority districts. "This was the crucial turning point," commented Vladimir Velebit, a retired Yugoslav ambassador to several countries, who is of Serbian origin. "No single event compares with the arming of the local Serbs."

Meanwhile, to offset the shortage of Serbian manpower, Milosevic expanded the use of "volunteers," or "paramilitaries." Often soccer hooligans or jailed criminals who were rallied to the patriotic cause by state-controlled media, the irregular forces played an important—and lawful—role in the butchery during the Croatian war. In July 1991, Milosevic's home Serbian government issued a legal order placing Serbian paramilitary forces under the Serbs' territorial defense, a home guard officered by the regular army. In December 1991, as the Croatian war wound down and the war in Bosnia was still months away, the rump federal government under Milosevic's control took the next step, ordering all paramilitary forces under the command of the regular army.

To deal with the resistance anticipated from the far more numerous Muslims and Croats, Milosevic's security apparatus resorted to extraordinary means, including concentration camps. The army's classified 1987 Doctrine of Total National Defense permitted "political isolation" of domestic traitors "in combination with other measures and procedures, including physical liquidation." A secret 1989 state-of-emergency decree permitted authorities to "prohibit departure from certain places or order compulsory stay in a certain place for certain persons." On October 3,

1991, the federal government, under Milosevic's control, announced a "threat of imminent war," which Serbian media reported as a state of emergency. Finally, on April 8, 1992, the rump Yugoslav parliament extended all federal Yugoslav laws to Serbian-held areas of Bosnia and Croatia. Thus when Zeljko Raznjatovic, the "commander" of "Arkan's Tigers," demanded the surrender of Zvornik, in eastern Bosnia, at the start of the war in mid-April 1992, his force was fully integrated with the army of rump Yugoslavia and operating under Yugoslav law.

Months before the Bosnian state held a referendum and seceded from the Yugoslav federation, the Bosnian Serbs under the direction of Sarajevo psychiatrist Radovan Karadzic began drafting the documents that would lead to a declaration of independence. In October 1991, they held a founding "assembly of the Serbian nation," which invoked a right of self-determination, and decided to recognize only those republican laws that did not conflict with those of Serbian-dominated rump Yugoslavia. By December, the assembly voted to form the "Republika Srpska" (Serb Republic) as a state in Yugoslavia and declared independence. They approved a constitution on February 28, the eve of Bosnia's referendum, which Serbs boycotted.

In mid-March 1992, on the eve of the conflict, U.N. peacekeepers made their inauspicious debut in Bosnia. Their mission at the time was not to keep the peace in Bosnia, but to serve as the headquarters staff for the U.N. troops dispatched to keep the peace in Croatia. In June, Major General Lewis MacKenzie, a Canadian extrovert who had served on eight previous peacekeeping missions, was put in charge of Sarjevo headquarters. Under his command and that of his successors, UNPROFOR had at every stage to react to events, and never found its balance.

In mid-May, after Sarajevo came under Serbian bombardment, MacKenzie and the top U.N. staff left for Belgrade, the capital of Serbia and rump Yugoslavia. They returned on June 10 with their first, but limited, mandate for Bosnia, to organize the opening of Sarajevo airport for humanitarian airlifts. Even this limited mission put U. N. personnel at considerable risk in what had become a shooting gallery. His mere arrival in Sarajevo gave MacKenzie a hero's aura. In his memoir, *Peacekeeper, the Road to Sarajevo,* the Sarajevo commander noted in his diary for June 10: "I was really scared . . . . I wondered if I was losing my nerve. I went to sleep as the building shook every few minutes with concussions from mortar rounds."

By the time MacKenzie reappeared in Sarajevo, ethnic Serbs had set up a network of concentration camps throughout Bosnia, and reports emerged of the systematic torture and killing of men of military age and the rape of Bosnian women. From early June, the Bosnian government issued regular

English-language bulletins listing concentration camps that Serbian forces had established across the country, and the Bosnian U.N. liaison personally briefed U.N. officers. But MacKenzie took no notice, nor did the UNPRO-FOR commander for the region, Indian general Satish Nambiar. An internal U.N. investigation determined that they passed the lists to the U.N. Secretariat, but there the paper trail ended. No authority was given to those in the field to go out and look for the camps.

In ignoring the crimes, U.N. bureaucrats and military commanders overlooked practices that most citizens of Western countries believed unthinkable and intolerable in Europe after the Holocaust. U.N. officials apparently paid no attention to common sense but were guided by the judgment of

Western statesmen. When François Mitterrand paid a flying visit to Sarajevo on June 28, Bosnian president Izetbegovic privately and publicly begged the French president to investigate growing allegations of concentration camps and other atrocities by sending in independent human-rights monitors. Mitterrand returned to France and did not brief other western leaders on his trip, nor did he ask his own government to follow up.

The savior's aura faded as it became apparent that the token U.N. force had no means at its disposal to end the conflict and no interest even in documenting the crimes being committed. MacKenzie's memoir indicates almost no knowledge of the events preceding the war and little understanding of motives. He spent most of his time trying to arrange cease-fires,

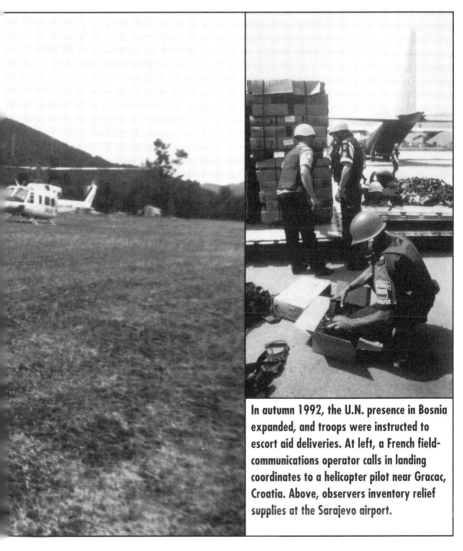

In autumn 1992, the U.N. presence in Bosnia expanded, and troops were instructed to escort aid deliveries. At left, a French field-communications operator calls in landing coordinates to a helicopter pilot near Gracac, Croatia. Above, observers inventory relief supplies at the Sarajevo airport.

which were invariably short-lived. His memoir passes over the war crimes. In this state of ignorance, U.N. personnel easily fell into traps that had been laid for them.

U.N. investigators later determined that U.N. personnel had frequented a hotel-restaurant in Vogosca, a Sarajevo suburb, where Serbs had set up a brothel supplied with Muslim and Croatian captives and, behind the hotel, a concentration camp in a partly buried bunker. The bunker was on the list the Bosnian government had handed to the U.N. command in Sarajevo. But no one from the U.N. ever reported on the existence of the camp or investigated its conditions.

"It was so blatant [a violation of humanitarian law] they should have seen it and reported it. And in fact if they had reported it, it is the sort of thing which would have gone public much earlier than it did," said Kofi Annan, the U.N. under-secretary for peace-keeping. But he went on to express sympathy for U.N. personnel reluctant to go beyond their mandates. "Soldiers like to have a clear mandate. They know if they go beyond their mandate, they will risk criticism from their own governments. They will not go out of their way to look for war crimes."

By design, the U.N. force was unsuited to the war that surrounded it. Peacekeeping forces avoid having an intelligence-gathering unit in order to allay any concern that they could become an offensive force, so individual battalions must rely on national resources, if they exist. UNPROFOR in Bosnia was thrown together without detailed advance planning, adequate means, or realistic mandates. Its commanders were sent into the theater without sufficient briefings, and, even worse, with the see-no-evil world view purveyed by their political masters. Yet once on the scene, they found themselves thrust instantly into the international spotlight, and called upon to make judgments for which they were ill prepared.

Some seized the opportunity to promote their mission in general and themselves in particular. MacKenzie, who became a master of the sound bite, helped confuse public perceptions of the war by playing down the aggression and suggesting it was all theater. "If I could convince both sides to stop killing their own people for CNN, perhaps we could have come to a cease-fire," he said at the end of his tour. MacKenzie did not substantiate his charge, because he had neither the technical equipment nor intelligence data to prove the case on either side. But such remarks enhanced his own importance, by portraying the U.N. commander as being evenhanded and above the fray.

He was not as detached as he pretended to be. After returning to Canada, MacKenzie capitalized on his new-found fame by giving speeches, interviews, and advice to the U.S. Congress and military establishment. His high profile drew criticism from within his own government, and he was forced to retire a year ahead of schedule, but he continued to give public speeches.

During the three-and-a-half-year war, about a quarter million people, mostly civilians, were killed or missing, and more than 2 million, or half the population of Bosnia–Herzegovina, were made homeless, most of them in 1992, in a process that began on MacKenzie's watch. A CIA study concluded that although all parties committed abuses of human rights, "ethnic Serbs are responsible for the overwhelming majority of the destruction, displacement, and loss of life associated with ethnic cleansing in Bosnia."

But MacKenzie put the blame for the war crimes on all parties, implying that there were no aggressors or victims: "Dealing with Bosnia is a little bit like dealing with three serial killers—one has killed fifteen, one has killed ten, one has killed five. Do we help the one that's only killed five?" he asked a House committee, citing no source for his judgment. A U.S–based Serbian nationalist group called Serbnet had paid him $15,000 for that appearance and others during a two-day visit to Washington.

In autumn 1992, the U.N. presence in Bosnia expanded with the deployment of British troops to central Bosnia and French Foreign Legion to Sarajevo. These were intended as an extension of the original show-the-flag mission in Sarajevo. Troops were instructed to escort aid deliveries, not to force their way through roadblocks or even protect aid workers unless U.N. forces were directly fired upon and their attackers could be targeted.

Yet some of these troops showed the real potential of peacekeeping. Operating out of Vitez in central Bosnia, British army colonel Bob Stewart and his Cheshire regiment working quietly and effectively opened routes to Tuzla in northeastern Bosnia, threw intense energy into dampening Croatian–Muslim enmities, kept lines of communication open to all sides, and undoubtedly saved many lives. What is so striking about the operation recounted in Stewart's *Broken Lives* (London: HarperCollins, 1993), was its seat-of-the-pants nature.

On his first reconnaissance mission in September 1992, Stewart tried to drive from Belgrade to Tuzla along a road that had been closed since May. After several false starts, he happened upon a Serbian military policeman who found the idea of taking that route "quite amusing." He "explained, as gently as possible, that we would have to cross the lines to do so and the overflowing graveyard on the hill in front of us was testament to how difficult such a plan was." They had wasted days in the attempt.

Yet once having reached Vitez, northwest of Sarajevo, by a 600-mile detour via Split, Stewart set up a completely professional shop, staying on top of the rapidly unfolding tensions that later exploded into a second Bosnian war, between Croats and Muslims. "Being where the action is taking place is probably one of the best lessons I learned in Bosnia on how to conduct peacekeeping," Stewart wrote in his memoir. He made this his maxim: "If there's trouble, get into the middle of it and calm things down by being there."

Stewart sent frequent and visible patrols into Turbe, a completely exposed Muslim village on the front lines north of Travnik in central Bosnia. It "in many ways represented what all our efforts were about. It was a major point of confrontation and as such was as dangerous a place as anywhere . . . . Patrolling and working in Turbe was obviously right at the edge of my mandate, and yet I considered it vital to be there. It was also the only place in my operational area where we were regularly to meet all three warring factions." His presence also made it possible to open briefly a new aid supply route through Serb-held territory for the United Nations High Commission for Refugees.

Simultaneously with the deployment of units such as Stewart's, the U.N. and European Community set up a diplomatic process. The United States had opted out of a leadership role during the series of wars over Yugoslav succession, turning the problem over to its European allies. Britain took on the leading role, through personalities such as Peter Lord Carrington, David Lord Owen, and U.N. ambassador, Sir David Hannay. In contrast to Stewart, whose every action seemed aimed at preserving a multiethnic Bosnia, Whitehall preferred to see Serbia as the *Ordnungsmacht* (bullyboy) of the region and to partition Bosnia along ethnic lines into Serbian, Croatian, and Muslim cantons. Stewart was the first on the scene at Ahmici, where Croats had slaughtered Muslims, and he carefully recorded the facts. But the focus in Whitehall was not on war crimes but on a draft of the partition. Paradoxically, Britain's diplomatic clout in pressing for partition was based on the deployment of Stewart's Cheshire regiment.

Between 1992 and 1994, a variety of diplomats, including Owen, Cyrus Vance of the United States, Thorvald Stoltenberg of Norway, and the five-nation "contact group" consisting of the United States, Britain, France, Germany, and Russia, produced three successive plans. All plans prescribe a territorial division along ethnic lines as the key to peace. The Bosnian government accepted each in turn, in the correct expectation it would be rejected by the Bosnian Serbs.

The diplomats made only one public attempt to deal with the mass slaughter that continued in plain view. On September 25, 1992, Vance and

In August 1993, U.N. soldiers evacuate a family from Sarajevo. Earlier that year many "safe areas" had been overrun by a Serb offensive. Diplomatic talks were bogged down.

Owen drove across the bridge at Bosanska Gradiska and spent a day in Banja Luka. After meeting local Muslim and Roman Catholic leaders and hearing firsthand of the details of "ethnic cleansing," they convinced the U.N. to set up a presence in Serb-conquered northern Bosnia. An advance unit of Dutch forces was sent, and Canadian troops were earmarked to join them. For a few remarkable months, the threat of a massive "cleansing" of this region receded. But the Bosnian Serbs gauged the world community's will to follow through, and balked. First they demanded large sums of money to provide even basic services; then in December 1992, the self-styled Bosnian Serb assembly rejected any U.N. military presence. Vance and Owen did not protest, but instead arranged for the designated troops to be sent to Macedonia, the southernmost former Yugoslavian republic, which had—so far, peacefully—also seceded. That was the end of the attempt. The murders, destruction, and devastation resumed.

Colonel Stewart felt the complete absence of coordination between his mission and the diplomacy in Geneva. Indeed, they seemed to be at cross-purposes. Stewart was aware of the Vance–Owen plan to create Croatian and Muslim-controlled cantons in his area of responsibility. Yet, he later wrote, "the instructions on how it might be carried out were never clear." Owens' memoir of the diplomacy, *Balkan Odyssey* (New York: Harcourt Brace & Company, 1995) makes no mention of Stewart or his regiment. From Stewart's ground-level vantage point, U.N. diplomacy probably exacerbated the war, a judgment with which many reporters who covered the events would agree. "Wherever we could we went into the fighting in an attempt to stop it by our presence," Stewart wrote. But in January 1993, "For the first time we seemed to be unable to influence events . . . . I felt sure it was related to the [just-published] Vance–Owen plan, which divided Bosnian cantons on ethnic lines, and attempts by all sides, particularly the Croats, to get control of as much land as possible."

The diplomatic process, besides leading to the unintended consequence of widening the war, took on a life of its own that kept the war going long after it could have been brought to an end. Serbian assaults picked up in pace early in 1993, but whenever Western public opinion called for a military response, Owen and top U.N. officials would deflect the pressures by citing the "delicate" diplomatic talks under way. The negotiations, conducted in the absence of military leverage, always ended in failure.

On repeated occasions, even with diplomacy in the doldrums, the diplomats thwarted any alternative to their efforts, most notably in May 1993, as Secretary of State Warren Christopher toured European capitals to discuss a new U.S. plan to end the war. Dubbed "lift and strike," the concept was to lift the embargo on arms to the Bosnian government and threaten air strikes against Serbian forces. However, Britain and France, using the presence of "peacekeeping" troops on the ground as diplomatic leverage against the United States, which had no troops in Bosnia, demanded that Christopher back down. Midway through his trip, President Bill Clinton abandoned the concept.

A few days later, at a conference in Athens, Owen and Vance, with Milosevic's help, strong-armed Karadzic into signing their plan. But the Bosnian Serb leader demanded a referendum, which killed the plan. Owen rejected force to back up the diplomacy, criticizing as a "delusion" the U.S. position that only force, starting with aerial bombardments, would convince the Serbs. "You will not solve the problem at 10,000 feet," he said. Just as the Vance–Owen plan collapsed, "lift and strike" died. Yet instead of stepping back and developing a new approach, the world community merely doubled its bets on peacekeeping.

Improvisation reigned supreme. After a Serbian offensive early in 1993 wiped out the tiny enclaves of Cerska and Konjevic Polje in eastern Bosnia, MacKenzie's successor, General Philippe Morillon of France, personally went to embattled Srebrenica. There, without previous authority, he promised U.N. protection to the city of 8,000 inhabitants, swollen by refugees to 60,000. "I will never abandon you," he said March 12. "You are now under the protection of the United Nations."

Morillon had uttered the words only when he had realized there was no other exit. In his 1993 account, *Croire et Oser*, he said that he had tried to escape Srebrenica earlier that night by claiming he had to relieve himself. "You join me," he said to Eric Dachy, a volunteer doctor with the aid organization Médecins sans Frontières (Doctors without Borders), as he departed, alone, at 10:00 P.M. A U.N. vehicle was to link up with him outside of town but failed to materialize. At about 5:00 AM Morillon returned alone, looking "frozen, cold, and really tired," Dachy later reported. He went to bed, and on waking up knew he was trapped. Only then did he bestride the porch of the post office to declare his fidelity to the town.

Soon after Morillon's eventual departure, Srebrenica came under renewed attack, and the U.N. Security Council, under pressure by non-aligned states, responded in mid-April by proclaiming the town a "U.N. safe area. " Three weeks later, the Security Council extended the concept to five other mostly Muslim cities: Tuzla, Gorazde, Zepa in the east, Bihac in the northwest, and Sarajevo. In June 1993, it authorized "necessary measures, including the use of force," to deter bombardment or armed incursion and to ensure the movement of humanitarian aid. This was classic "mission creep," with a vague statement of goals and no agreement on means. Secretary-General Boutros Boutros-Ghali said 34,000 troops would be needed to police the safe areas, but in the event, U.N. members promised 7,000, and only 3,400 were finally deployed, according to Human Rights Watch, quoting U.N. observers in the field. When foreign ministers met in Washington in late May, with diplomacy failed and the U.S. government backed off from its "lift and strike" option, they endorsed the plan to protect "safe areas" as the alternative.

But two years later, when Bosnian Serbs conquered Srebrenica, the "safe area" policy collapsed. All the flaws of the U.N. mission combined into a single disaster: the refusal to confront the Bosnian Serbs blocking food deliveries; the absence of military intelligence; the emphasis on diplomatic process and partition over the protection of the population; and the failure to implement the Geneva Conventions, or even to report on violations.

Sarajevo, winter 1994, above and opposite: U.N. soldiers inspect a surrendered Serbian

Other Western intelligence services picked up an advance warning of an offensive, and reportedly were aware of communications between Serbian and Bosnian-Serb military leaders during the offensive, but they never shared this data with the Dutch peacekeepers stationed in Srebrenica, according to Dutch officials. The U.N. later claimed to have had no advance intelligence of the Serbian offensive, and Dutch military officers said their army had failed to set up an adequate intelligence-gathering cell to monitor events that would affect Dutch troops. Thus, the offensive came as a surprise to U.N. forces on the ground. On July 6, after one observation post came under direct fire, the Dutch commander requested NATO air strikes to protect his troops, but Boutros-Ghali's senior envoy, Yasushi Akashi of Japan, and U.N. military commander for all of former Yugoslavia, General Bernard Janvier of France, rejected that option to avoid upsetting delicate diplomatic talks.

"The battalion commander discussed the possibilities of air support . . . with UNPROFOR. He was given to understand that, bearing in mind the negotiations being conducted by the EU [European Union] negotiator, Mr. [Carl] Bildt, and taking into account instructions concerning the restrictive use of force, he should not count on air support in this case," the Dutch government said in its investigation of the tragedy.

The enclave fell on July 11, and as the heavily outnumbered Dutch

anti-aircraft gun, and a tank that had been locked by its former occupants before fleeing.

troops looked on, the Serb forces separated the population into two groups. They loaded the women, children, and old people onto buses and trucks, and sent the men and boys to unknown locations. Bosnian Serbs also captured thousands of men and boys who tried to flee overland to government-held territory with the remnants of the Bosnian army force in Srebrenica.

The Dutch troops failed to defend the town or even to alert the world to the slaughter of which they were witnesses. Serb forces had captured fifty-five Dutch troops at their observation posts, stripped them of their weapons and equipment in defiance of international law, and taken them hostage. On July 15, they bused them out of Bosnia. En route to safety, the Dutch troops saw dozens of corpses piled on a truck-loading platform, and dozens more along the road near what turned out to be the main killing fields. Under the Geneva Conventions—and simple common sense—they should have reported such evidence of massive war crimes. But apart from answering questionnaires distributed by U.N. human-rights personnel, they kept their silence, waiting for 300 Dutch comrades to be released. They did not even inform Sarajevo headquarters. "The U.N. didn't ask for a debriefing," a Dutch spokesman said.

On July 19, with EU negotiator Bildt once again holding talks in Belgrade, the U.N. commander in Bosnia, General Rupert Smith of Britain, met the Bosnian-Serb commander, General Ratko Mladic, and asked him to give an account of the fall of Srebrenica. Mladic said the U.N. safe area had been "finished in a correct way. " According to a memo of the meeting, Smith did not reply. The agreement made no direct mention of the 6,000 to 8,000 missing men and boys of Srebrenica, and said only that the International Red Cross would have access to "reception points" within twenty-four hours. Mladic reneged on the commitment. The reception points turned out to be mass graves. The Serb takeover of Srebrenica brought the U.N. presence in Bosnia to an ignominious end.

Croatia had long before given up hope for a peaceful reintegration of Serbian-held territory with U.N. help. In April 1995, in a lightning strike, well-armed Croatian troops took back western Slavonia, destroying the bridge across the Sava at Bosanska Gradiska to prevent Serbs from removing their heavy weaponry. After the fall of Srebrenica, Serbian forces went on to attack two other enclaves, Zepa and Bihac, in clear preparation for an assault against Gorazde. With American backing, Bosnians and Croats made common cause. In August 1995, Croats recaptured the entire Krajina area in western Croatia, and expelled the U.N. peacekeepers. In mid-December the U.N. closed down its peacekeeping operation in Bosnia.

Future analysts will find many lessons in the three and a half years of Western humiliation in Bosnia. But some are already apparent. The first is that the West's management of the crisis was not a minor blip but a signal failure on a defining issue. Assistant Secretary of State Richard Holbrooke summarized Western policy in early 1995 as the worst collective security failure since the 1930s. He did not blame the atrocities on a "blood feud" or "serial killers."

It was Holbrooke who brought about a stable cease-fire following NATO's first serious bombing campaign against Serbian military installations in September 1995. He went on to negotiate the Dayton, Ohio, peace accords in November. President Clinton's subsequent decision to send 20,000 U.S. troops to Bosnia, as part of a 60,000-troop NATO deployment, opened a new era for NATO. The key factor in the U.S. transformation from passive critic to active leader was the agreement, at long last, to use significant force. The key to the initial success or failure of the Dayton agreement was the willingness to use force to back up its provisions.

By contrast, the U.N. deployment in Bosnia, with no military force to back it up, had been untenable. Peacekeeping is not feasible during a raging war, nor is diplomacy, unless it is backed by force. While U.N. personnel no doubt saved many lives, their presence probably also prolonged the conflict. While much about the U.N. presence in Bosnia was out of the control

A nearby U.N. checkpoint is visible from within a bombed-out building at Stari Vitez, Bosnia–Herzegovina, May 1994.

U.N. soldiers let Bosnian Muslim refugees through the Stari Vitez checkpoint, May 1994.

of the Department of Peacekeeping, the lack of direction to the troops on the ground is incomprehensible. As Colonel Stewart said of his mission, "Much as I appreciated being allowed to make almost all my own decisions in central Bosnia, that is certainly not the way to proceed."

This lack of direction led to confusing signals and uncoordinated improvisation that weakened U.N stature and raised the level of risks. "Overall, UNPROFOR often appeared to be ineffective . . . . Negotiation, followed by retreat, hardly inspired confidence," Stewart said. The fighting continued after the arrival of U.N. troops "much as before, with the U.N. forces simply regarded as an annoyance that was sometimes in the way." That "should not happen. When the U.N. goes into a country it should become a major player."

If the U.N. does find itself in a similar situation again, the very least its commanders can do to uphold the honor of their national battalions and the U.N. itself is to be aware of the rules of war and to demand compliance by other parties, as the Geneva Conventions require. This means raising the alarm on atrocities even if doing so places U.N. troops in danger.

The institution of peacekeeping, a Cold War invention, needs to be rethought in light of the failure in Bosnia. Peacekeepers have been effective in many places, although in reality their function is usually that of impartial cease-fire monitoring rather than peacekeeping. The pretension contained in the very designation raises unrealistic expectations. For by their nature, U.N. troops do nothing to resolve the underlying causes of conflict, and their deployment, as in Cyprus, can turn into an open-ended commitment.

Western leaders, it can only be hoped, will learn that any tactical advantage they gain by rewriting history sooner or later must be dispelled when the facts catch up with them. In the face of atrocity, they must act. In Bosnia–Herzegovina, they and their public participated in a replay of earlier European history, watching passively as a European state directed genocide.

Roy Gutman covers international security issues for Newsday *in Washington, D.C. Many of his articles on the "ethnic cleansing" in Bosnia—which won the Pulitzer Prize for international reporting in 1993, as well as other awards—are collected in his book,* A Witness to Genocide *(New York: Macmillan, 1993). He is also the author of* Banana Diplomacy, The Making of American Foreign Policy in Nicaragua 1981–87 *(New York: Simon and Schuster, 1988).*

An Australian peacekeeper evacuates a Hutu orphan whose mother was killed by the rival Tutsi faction, Rwanda, April 24, 1995. It is difficult, if not impossible, to keep peace in a region where the fighting continues.

The Changing Face of Peacekeeping

by Shashi Tharoor

The heady days of peacekeeping overstretch are gone. We're back to basics, but that need not mean a return to the brave old world of buffer zones and policing cease-fires, the nonthreatening application of military skills to defuse conflicts. We can find other alternatives to war.

In the late summer of 1995, the world's newspaper headlines and television screens bore eloquent testimony to the changing face of peacekeeping. Peacekeepers were pushed aside as Bosnian Serbs took the "safe areas" of Srebrenica and Zepa, and again as Croatian forces overran the former "United Nations Protected Area" of the Krajina. Blue Helmets were taken hostage or stood by in frustrated impotence as atrocities and human rights abuses were committed barely out of earshot. Then, the North Atlantic Council approved, and the secretary-general of the United Nations endorsed, new measures for decisive and disproportionate air strikes against Bosnian Serb military forces threatening or attacking the remaining safe areas, notably Sarajevo. These two sets of powerful images—one reflective of the limitations of peacekeeping in situations where there is no peace to keep, the other seemingly demonstrating the potential of the use of force to promote peace in the same situation—threw into question the basic assumptions underpinning United Nations peacekeeping.

This paradox describes the heart of the dilemma facing those of us who work in the peacekeeping field today. Early in 1995 the *New York Times* turned its magisterial gaze upon the future of United Nations peacekeeping, an activity that had earlier come in for considerable criticism in its editorial columns, particularly over Bosnia and Somalia. "Rethinking and retrenchment are in order . . . . There should be a shift back toward more limited objectives like policing cease-fires," it declared. "United Nations peacekeeping does what it can do very well. It makes no sense to continue eroding its credibility by asking it to do what it cannot."

This somewhat startling advocacy of a return to traditional verities gave pause to many of us who had been engaged in the practice of peacekeeping during its recent tumultuous history. Was the *Times* right, and if so, were we to contemplate a future of retreating headlong into the past?

At one level, there is something oddly comforting about the thought of seeking safety in well-worn practices; resting on old laurels is a good deal easier than wresting new ones. Yes, "traditional peacekeeping" is something the United Nations has done well and continues to know how to do. Our least problematic operations are always those where the parties agree to end their conflicts and only need our help to keep their word, where the consent and cooperation of the parties can be assumed and the impartiality of the peacekeepers is unchallenged, where the risks are low and the use of force largely unnecessary, the tasks assigned to the peacekeepers are those that are basic bread-and-butter skills for any army in the world, and the shoestring resources available to the United Nations are adequate for the job at hand. In these situations, the United Nations can bring a wealth of experience and precedent to bear in the successful conduct of such peacekeeping operations. Many of us in this business would like nothing more than to say: "Give us the buffer zones in Cyprus or Kuwait, the elections in Cambodia or Mozambique, the package deals in Namibia or El Salvador, and we'll deliver you an effective, efficient success story, on time and under budget." All professionals—and U.N. peacekeepers are no exception—are always happy to be asked to do what they can do best.

Sadly, however, this attractive formula has one thing wrong with it: It's a good answer, but only to part of the question. Traditional peacekeeping is all very well if the only crises confronting the United Nations are those that are ripe for the peacekeeping treatment. But classical, consensual peacekeeping does not respond fully to the nature of the world we live in and the challenges the new world disorder poses to the international community. If the nature of United Nations peacekeeping has acquired a certain elasticity in recent years, it is precisely because circumstances have led the world to make demands on the military capacity of the United Nations that vastly exceed anything we were called upon to do as recently as three or four years ago. We will not be able to face the twenty-first century by remaining firmly rooted in the twentieth.

At the same time, there is no question that the heady days of peacekeeping overstretch are over. "The number of United Nations operations, the scale of the operations, the money spent on operations cannot keep growing indefinitely," Secretary-General Boutros Boutros-Ghali recently declared. "The limits are being reached." At the end of the Cold War, an unprecedented degree of agreement within the Security Council in

The author, right, was photographed recently with two under-secretaries for peacekeeping: Kofi Annan, left, the present office holder, and the well-known Brian Urquart, center.

responding to international crises had plunged the United Nations into a dizzying series of peacekeeping operations that bore little or no resemblance in size, complexity, and function to those that had borne the peacekeeping label in the past. When I joined the peacekeeping staff at United Nations headquarters in October 1989, I was the sixth civilian officer (alongside three military officers) in a nine-person team. We had fewer than 8,000 soldiers in the field in five largely stable operations. The only new peacekeeping operation launched in the previous eleven years, that in Namibia, was coming to a successful end. Four years later, the United Nations deployed nearly 80,000 peacekeepers from eighty-two countries in seventeen operations around the world. Since statistics, like military uniforms, sometimes reveal more than they conceal, it is instructive that in the first eight years from the establishment of the United Nations in 1945, we had precisely two peacekeeping operations; in the last eight years, back to April 1988, there have been twenty-seven. That's not just a difference of degree, that's a difference of kind. In the last three years we have had three operations—Cambodia, Somalia, and the former Yugoslavia—that have vied for the distinction of being the largest peacekeeping operation in the history of the U.N. And the cost of sustaining these missions has risen from $626 million in 1986 to $3.8 billion in 1994, dropping to under $2 billion in 1995—but still greater than the United Nations' regular budget.

For years during the Cold War, peacekeeping had worked well, within the limitations imposed upon it by superpower contention—well enough, at any rate, to win the 1988 Nobel Peace Prize. Then, when these limitations evaporated, everything seemed possible. At the same time, the new transcendence of the global media added a sense of urgency to these crises: It is a striking coincidence that the reach and impact of CNN and its imitators peaked precisely at this time of post–Cold War concordance. Television showed that action was needed, and the end of the Cold War meant that action was possible. So "peacekeeping" became a catch-all term covering not merely the monitoring and implementation of cease-fire agreements, but an entire range of tasks including supervising and running elections, upholding human rights, overseeing land reform, delivering humanitarian aid under fire, rebuilding failed states and, as the *New York Times* put it in the same editorial, "ambitious attempts to impose peace on hostile forces determined to keep fighting." The widespread criticism, not all of it well-founded or fair, of United Nations efforts in situations where there was little peace to keep—particularly in Somalia, the former Yugoslavia, and Rwanda—lies directly behind the calls for retreat to a simpler era. Amidst so many voices urging the United Nations to go "back to basics," it is clear that it will be a long time before the Security Council again authorizes another of the hybrid operations whose ever-mounting scope spiralled seemingly out of control in a flurry of Council resolutions in 1992 and 1993.

But does this mean a return to the brave old world of buffer zones and policing cease-fires, the nonthreatening application of military skills to defuse conflicts? Not necessarily. The irony of the "back to basics" appeal is that the United Nations had already moved successfully beyond the basics before getting embroiled in the controversies of recent years. I have walked the "Green Line" that divides Nicosia between its Greek Cypriot and Turkish Cypriot residents, and seen how diligent patrolling by lightly armed soldiers can prevent conflict from reigniting between forces sometimes stationed literally a spitting distance across from each other. But the "basics" of Cyprus or the Golan Heights are by no means the only types of peacekeeping operation the United Nations has conducted without cavil or controversy. The operations that brought Namibia to independence, that transformed the society and politics of Cambodia and El Salvador, that restored hope in Mozambique, were all multidimensional efforts that demonstrated the effectiveness of a broader concept of peacekeeping—one that combined military functions with a variety of largely civilian undertakings to bring about change and so fulfil the objectives of the operation. The techniques involved worked; the world cannot do without them. In admitting, understandably, that we cannot afford to become part of the problem as we did by taking sides in Somalia; in acknowledging that we cannot easily find troop-contributing countries willing to commit forces to halt genocide, as we had hoped we might in Rwanda; in accepting that we can protect humanitarian-aid deliveries, but that we cannot force them through, as we discovered in Bosnia; in conceding all this, we do not need also to abandon the functions of policing the local police, of protecting ethnic minorities, of upholding human-rights standards, of running free and fair elections, of supervising mistrusted local administrations, of creating conditions conducive to political accommodation and national reconciliation, all of which we have done in recent years with success—takes us beyond the *New York Times'* prescription with which I began this article.

Yet that, too, is only a partial answer to the questions that confront us today. For "multidimensional peacekeeping" still rests on the traditional pillars of agreement and consent; the new functions identified above are usually reflected in the terms of a comprehensive settlement that both (or all) parties to a conflict wish the United Nations to implement; and none of them involve a threat to the United Nations' preference for the non-use of force. We can move beyond traditional peacekeeping and still find ourselves on familiar ground. The more difficult problems relate to situations in which agreements are nonexistent or short-lived; where the United Nations does not enjoy the formal consent or the practical cooperation of the parties amidst whom it is deployed; and when the nature of the ongoing conflict obliges us to confront searching questions about the need to use force in order to be effective, with the concomitant risk that doing so will jeopardize the U.N.'s impartiality and thus the very effectiveness we are trying to attain.

The thawing of the Cold War freeze has created the environment in which the world will be making its choices about the management of international conflict. The end of the Soviet Union loosened the straitjacket within which many potential conflicts had been confined. Many erupted amid the disinclination of the big powers to intervene; during the Cold War, both sides had sought to prevent conflicts arising that might engage their interests. Today, the stakes are lower; Somalia is not seen as threatening to lead to a Stalingrad, and Sarajevo 1992, for all its emotional impact, did not carry the globe-threatening resonance of Sarajevo 1914. In this climate warring factions, unfettered by bondage to one superpower or another, pursue their ambitions without regard to an outside world that clearly cannot summon the will or the resources to intercede decisively. A post-ideological world stokes its frenzies in the flames of nationalism, ethnicity,

At Ndosha Camp, Zaire, across the border with Rwanda, children whose parents had been massacred, July 1994, are fed. Along with malnourishment, cholera was taking its toll.

and tribal triumphalism. Old injustices and older enmities are revived and intensified; history becomes a whip with which to flail those who are inclined to compromise. Few rules are observed in these wars, fewer still in the tenuous moments of peace that punctuate them. The techniques of a calmer era, peacekeeping included, seem inadequate to the moment.

And yet, where the political circumstances permit action, abstention is not a morally acceptable option. For most of the crises that thrust themselves on the United Nations agenda, indifference is impossible. This is not just a moral matter, though the suffering caused by these conflicts—in many of which the infliction of agony on innocent civilians is a direct aim, rather than a by-product, of war—remains an affront to the world's conscience. In a world of instant satellite communications, with television images of suffering broadcast as they occur, few democratic governments are immune to the public clamor to "don't just stand there, do something." (This is particularly ironic since some of our "classical" successes were based on the principle, "don't do something, just stand there"!) For a couple of years, the international community, pressed to respond and unready with an alternative international security mechanism, found in United Nations peacekeeping the "something" it could "do." Peacekeepers took unprecedented risks, made foreseeable mistakes, suffered an intolerable level of casualties; governments, accountable politically for the safety of their soldiers, cut their losses and proved unwilling to risk additional ones. In the process we have all learned what peacekeeping cannot do; and yet we cannot afford to do nothing. The challenge of the future is to define that "something" in terms of what is do-able—in other words, to identify how the United Nations can be enabled to respond to future Somalias and Rwandas while retaining the support of member states.

It is important to remember that a consistent body of practice and doctrine on peacekeeping had evolved over the years: Peacekeepers functioned under the command and control of the secretary-general; they represented moral authority rather than the force of arms; they reflected the universality of the United Nations in their composition; they were deployed with the consent and cooperation of the parties; they were impartial and functioned without prejudice to the rights and aspirations of any side; they did not use force or the threat of force except in self-defense; they took few risks and suffered a minimal number of casualties; they did not seek to impose their will on any of the parties. As the Security Council proclaimed "no-fly zones" and "safe areas," declared punitive actions against warlords, and acquiesced in NATO-declared "exclusion zones"; as member states established command arrangements that did not in all cases terminate in New York; as peacekeepers mounted anti-sniping patrols and called in air strikes—all these principles have been strained to the breaking point.

We at the United Nations believe that peacekeeping is not peace-*enforcement,* and that the two activities do not mix very well; that, in other words, enforcement action proceeds from different premises and is not merely one more stage in a "peacekeeping continuum." But events in Bosnia have reopened the question, and we have again begun to hear about "peace-enforcement," which had fallen out of fashion after the disasters of Somalia. The same soldiers on the ground were expected, under eighty-one Security Council resolutions and a further eighty-one Presidential Statements of the Council, to perform humanitarian functions that required the daily ongoing cooperation of all parties, while serving to limit their recourse to certain military means (maintaining a "no-fly zone" that disallowed the use of aircraft for combat purposes) or to attacks upon certain towns (the so-called safe areas). For years the United Nations force coped with the contradiction of the international community threatening air strikes on a party without whose consent and cooperation United Nations soldiers could not function, move, or be resupplied. Finally, the air strikes occurred, and helped bring about a peace agreement—but only after the U.N.'s "failure" had guaranteed this success, since the loss of two "safe areas" (Srebrenica and Zepa) and our inability to find governments willing to provide troops for a third (Gorazde) reduced our dependence on the Bosnian Serbs, and our vulnerability to Serb retaliation. As long as United Nations peacekeepers were deployed amongst, and worked with the cooperation of, the Bosnian Serbs, they were trapped in the basic conundrum that you can't make war and peace with the same people on the same territory at the same time.

If the objective of the international community was the firm and secure establishment of a viable sovereign state of Bosnia and Herzegovina, as many Security Council resolutions implied, then peacekeeping was not a direct means to that end; rather, it was a means of containing the situation while others—diplomats and negotiators—pursued that end. We must not let the success of the NATO airstrikes in September 1995 mislead us into believing that force is a peacekeeping panacea. (Air power, as Eliot Cohen memorably put it, "is an unusually seductive form of military strength because, like modern courtship, it appears to offer gratification without commitment.") In Somalia, UNOSOM's attempts to impose peace led to the loss of political support and its eventual withdrawal; UNPROFOR was blamed for failing to do things it was never mandated, staffed, financed, equipped, or deployed to do. For a long time, the United Nations was criticized for *not* doing in Bosnia what it was criticized *for* doing in Somalia. Public opinion and political rhetoric have tended to outstrip both the mandate and means given to the U.N. Most of UNPROFOR's critics, for instance, seemed to think that UNPROFOR ought to be resisting or repelling "aggression." But the answer to aggression is not a peacekeeping operation; it is Desert Storm. In responding to the complex origins of the Yugoslav tragedy, the Security Council chose not to take military sides in the conflict, but rather to use a peacekeeping operation as a means to alleviate the consequences of the conflict—feeding and protecting civilians, delivering humanitarian relief, and helping create conditions conducive to promoting a peace settlement. As a result a large number of people are alive, and housed, and safe today who would have been killed, or displaced, or in peril had UNPROFOR not been deployed.

Should UNPROFOR have jeopardized these achievements by using more force, sooner? Such a question points to a central dilemma in those situations where the United Nations deploys peacekeepers when there is no peace to keep. Impartiality is the oxygen of peacekeeping: The only way peacekeepers can work is by being trusted by both sides, being clear and transparent in their dealings, keeping lines of communication open. I will never forget one of the most surreal experiences of my United Nations career, standing alongside the secretary-general's special representative, Yasushi Akashi, in the office of the Bosnian Serb leader, Radovan Karadzic, while Karadzic screamed at his army commander General Mladic, on the telephone about an ongoing assault on Gorazde that had hit United Nations observers there. Akashi was in Karadzic's office to threaten air strikes on his host's forces if they did not permit the immediate evacuation of the wounded United Nations soldiers. The U.N. commander, General Michael Rose, was on the walkie-talkie to Akashi as we stood in the office, asking for air action: Each side could hear the other's conversation. One can scarcely imagine an approach more removed from the assumptions of warfare. But that is precisely the point: Peacekeeping is not war making; peacekeepers have no enemies, only partners in the common quest for peace. They moment they lose the trust of the parties, the moment they are seen by one side or the other as the "enemy," they become part of the problem they were sent to solve. This was reflected in UNPROFOR's pattern of deployment in a variety of dispersed locations, loosely configured across all the battle lines, full of unarmed or lightly armed observers and relief workers, and traveling in highly visible white-painted vehicles. For such a vulnerable force to take sides through the use of force might have been morally gratifying—at least briefly—but it would also be militarily

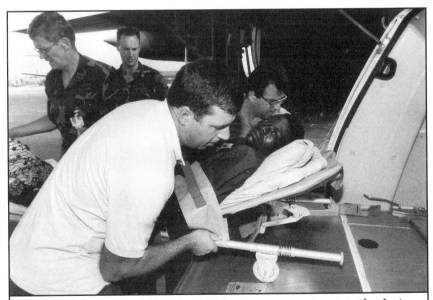

In 1992, U.N. helicopters airlifted Angolans from remote areas to vote in the elections. A survivor of a crash that killed four peacekeepers is transferred from a rescue plane.

irresponsible. The purpose of any U.N. peacekeeping deployment is, in the last analysis, to help extinguish the flames of war, not to fan them.

The experience of the United Nations in Angola, Somalia, and the former Yugoslavia has made it clear that those who are convinced they have more to gain on the battlefield than at the negotiating table are not the right partners for United Nations peacekeeping. In any case, as the secretary-general has pointed out, the imposition of peace requires military, financial, and political resources that member states are simply not willing to provide for operations other than war; and these resources require a capacity to manage them that the United Nations Secretariat does not possess and is unlikely to be granted. The conditions imposed by the Security Council on the deployment of U.N. peacekeeping troops in Angola under UNAVEM–III, and in particular the requirement that both parties show a tangible commitment to peace and take concrete steps toward honoring their undertakings before the U.N. operation is fully deployed, are far more typical of the attitude of the international community. Bosnia 1995 is the exception.

At the same time it is essential to find alternatives to war when traditional peacekeeping is not appropriate. The United Nations is redoubling its efforts to forestall conflicts before they erupt. Early warning and preventive diplomacy are activities with a mixed track record. It is fair to say that no one hears of the wars that did not occur because the United Nations was able to head them off, but it is also true that early warning is of little use in and of itself, unless it is accompanied by the political will to act on the warnings received. There has been no shortage of early warning on Burundi, and indefatigable efforts by the United Nations Secretary-General Boutros Boutros-Ghali, but clear limits on the extent of preventive action that governments are prepared to undertake. Any international intervention to prevent a conflict would have to be credible; in other words, the governments declaring their determination not to permit another genocidal civil war would have to be prepared to back up their statements of resolve with action if the parties on the ground decided to ignore them. This implies that effective preventive action requires the same degree of political commitment and agreement as post-conflict peacekeeping. Sadly, governments reluctant to send in troops after a conflict has broken out are usually also reluctant to do the same before. Yet there is no doubt that preventive deployment would be cheaper in lives and resources than anything that might follow.

The one current functioning example of preventive deployment, UNPREDEP (formerly UNPROFOR) in the former Yugoslav republic of

Macedonia (FYROM), has contributed immensely to the stability of the government and the state of FYROM. But the catch with any preventive deployment is that it is impossible to prove a negative: Any such force is a success only until it fails. Preventive deployment may not always, and indefinitely, deter conflict, but there is no doubt that at the very least it raises the political price of any aggression and increases the international community's stake in a peaceful outcome for any conflict that may occur in its area of operations.

If conflict does occur despite the best efforts of the diplomats and peacemakers, it is vital that it be nipped in the bud. The future of United Nations peacekeeping demands a rapid-response capacity; we at the Secretariat are largely agnostic as to how we acquire this. At the moment, the only tool available to us in this domain, the Stand-By Forces Arrangement, is yet to prove itself. In that dreadful summer of 1994, when the United Nations needed 5,500 soldiers for Rwanda, we turned to the nineteen governments that at that time had pledged a total of 31,000 troops for future U.N. peacekeeping operations; all declined to participate. The "arrangement" thus turned out to be one for obtaining negative answers more rapidly than in the past, rather than generating forces more rapidly than in the past. Currently, the number of countries enrolled in the scheme has gone up to fifty-three; it is not yet clear whether this implies a parallel increase in the viability of the Stand-By Forces Arrangement when the proverbial crunch comes.

Secretary-General Boutros Boutros-Ghali has, in his *Agenda for Peace* and subsequently, suggested the establishment of a rapid-deployment force to serve as the Security Council's strategic reserve whenever emergency situations require peacekeepers to be deployed at short notice. This idea has not so far found favor with member states. A somewhat more ambitious idea that has gained currency in recent years is that of a permanent United Nations force—a "standing army" or "United Nations legion"—consisting of individuals recruited, paid, and managed by the U.N. as a sort of military counterpart to the international civil service. The principal advantage of this idea is that such a force could immediately be deployed upon the Security Council's authorization; it would not require further governmental decisions, since the soldiers would belong to the United Nations, not to their national armies. The principal disadvantages, however, relate to cost, size limitations (how many "legionnaires" would one need to maintain effective rotations? What would happen if a new crisis found the available forces already deployed in an earlier one?), and the political unreadiness of certain member states to contemplate the existence of what could be seen

219

British soldiers patrol Stari Vitez, Bosnia, May 1994. Though criticized by the press for inaction, UNPROFOR soldiers were never mandated to use force except in self-defense.

as a supranational military entity under the command of the secretary-general of the United Nations.

Whichever solution is eventually retained, it is clear that if the world wants the United Nations to serve, even occasionally, as a fire brigade, it will have to do better than the present system, under which the fire breaks out, the aldermen on the Security Council agree it needs to be put out, and the fire chief is then sent out to hire firemen, rent fire trucks, find hoses of the right length, and look for sources of water to put into them— while hoping that, by the time he has what he needs, the house will not have burned down and there will still be enough survivors to rescue.

But in all that it is asked to do, the United Nations can be only as good as it is allowed to be. We have worked for too long on a shoestring: The only reconnaissance we did before issuing the Vance plan for Croatia in December 1991, for instance, consisted of a Finnish colonel and me, neither a Yugoslavia expert, driving through the battle lines in the midst of the fighting for four days to get a sense of the "lay of the land" and meet the fighters on both sides. This "two-men-in-a-jeep" approach is now well behind us: We are developing the capacity to plan, mount, support, and manage peacekeeping operations better than ever before, and to combine the "gifted amateurism" and inventive idealism of the traditional days of peacekeeping with the technological sophistication, the modern communi-

U.N. observers travel about Sarajevo, a "safe area," in the relative security of an armored vehicle. By war's end, the Serbs had reduced the city to virtual rubble.

cations and logistics, and the planning skills and response capacity of the military professionals. But we cannot do this without surmounting the endemic problem of the enormous gap between mandates and means. As we learned from Rwanda in 1994 and from the Bosnian "safe areas" in 1993, the Security Council may well pass resolutions without having the obligation to provide the troops to implement them; but when the troops are found, they too often need to be equipped (usually with unfamiliar equipment) and trained, tasks for which the United Nations has no infrastructure and which it performs by improvisation. And when troops are finally found, equipped, and deployed, their governments have to be paid, an obligation that the United Nations is falling increasingly behind in fulfilling.

The General Assembly routinely exhorts member states to pay their assessed contributions for peacekeeping operations "on time and in full," but in practice only a handful of states send in their contributions within the stipulated thirty days after the issuance of a letter of assessment (which itself comes at the end of a lengthy process of budget preparation and review by two different governmental bodies, and a vote by the General Assembly). Recent experience has been that, three months after assessments are levied, barely fifty percent of the required funds have come in. The result is to tie the operational hands of the United Nations—which frequently has to deal with commercial contractors, and in some cases government providers, who want cash "up front" for goods and services—and, equally troubling, to limit the ability of the Secretariat to reimburse troop-contributing countries. The secretary-general has often been obliged by a severe shortage of cash to suspend all reimbursements to troop- and equipment-contributing countries. In the case of developing countries, this can cause serious hardship, particularly since governments with hard-currency problems tend to await United Nations reimbursement *before* paying their troops. The resulting problems of morale in missions—where soldiers subsisting on the United Nations' daily allowance of $1.25 a day serve side-by-side with Western troops earning hardship bonuses in addition to their much higher regular salaries—have contributed to serious operational difficulties on the ground.

The problem is all the more ironic when seen against the comparative costs of other military activities—two days of Operation Desert Storm, for instance, would have paid for all of the United Nations peacekeeping operations that calendar year (1991)—and even against the kinds of military expenditures national governments are usually willing to allocate from their defense budgets. (The world spends $250 on war and defense for every dollar it spends on peacekeeping). An instructive indication of this came in 1993 when NATO planners, asked to prepare for a possible operation to implement a peace settlement in Bosnia and Herzegovina, estimated its annual cost at $8.3 billion—by ironic coincidence the exact figure, at that point, of the United Nations' cumulative expenditure on all peacekeeping operations since 1948. If peacekeeping is to have a future, governments will have to find ways to overcome their legislators' proclivity to pay for war, but not for peace. The annual cost of the peacekeeping operation on the Iran–Iraq border at the end of the brutal eight-year war between those countries amounted to less than the value of the crude oil carried in two supertankers—and if you remember how many oil tankers were at threat during that conflict, the operation that prevented the war from resuming was very good value for money.

Peacekeeping today is therefore in flux, if not in crisis. If it is to serve as a useful instrument in the maintenance of international peace and security, it needs conceptual clarity, political support, and financial resources. Peacekeeping has served the world well; the Blue Helmets can point to a Nobel Peace Prize to prove it. For peacekeeping to remain effective in a changing world, its credibility must not be jeopardized by the application of peacekeeping to inappropriate situations, by the issuance of mandates unsupported by doctrinal consistency or military means, or by the undermining of its authority by attempts to reconcile peacekeeping with war making under the rubric of peace-enforcement. Perhaps, as the whirling currents of the confused present subside, the day will come when we can stop talking about the "changing face of peacekeeping" and survey instead, with satisfaction, an instrument whose capacity and limitations are understood by all—and are clearly seen in a face that has stopped changing.

Shashi Tharoor is the special assistant to the United Nations under-secretary-general for peacekeeping operations. The views expressed here, however, are personal and do not necessarily reflect those of the organization. He is also the author of The Great Indian Novel *(New York: Arcade Publishing, Inc., 1993) and other works of fiction and scholarship.*

A Gazetteer of Peacekeeping Operations

The following is adapted from the booklet, *United Nations Peace-Keeping*.
Data is current as of March 31, 1996, except where noted.

Peacekeeping was pioneered and developed by the United Nations as one of the means for maintaining international peace and security. Since 1948, over 750,000 military and civilian police personnel and thousands of other civilians have served in United Nations peacekeeping operations. And more than 1,440 have died while supervising peace agreements, monitoring cease-fires, patrolling demilitarized zones, creating buffers between opposing forces, and defusing local conflicts that risk wider war. Most United Nations peacekeepers have been soldiers, volunteered by their governments in national contingents to apply military discipline and training to the task of restoring and maintaining the peace. They received the Nobel Peace Prize for their work in 1988.

Since Cold War tensions have subsided, peace has been threatened by resurgent ethnic and nationalist conflicts in many regions. Consequently, United Nations peacekeeping operations have grown rapidly in number and complexity in recent years. While thirteen operations were established in the first forty years of United Nations peacekeeping, twenty-eight new operations have been launched since 1988. At its peak in 1995, the total deploy-

I. MIDDLE EAST

■ UNTSO
United Nations Truce Supervision Organization

HEADQUARTERS:
Government House, Jerusalem
DURATION:
June 1948 to present
STRENGTH:
178 military observers, supported by international and locally recruited civilian staff

FATALITIES (January 31, 1996):
38 (12 military observers, 17 other military personnel, 6 international civilian staff and 3 local staff)
CHIEF OF STAFF:
Major-General Rufus Modupe Kupolati (Nigeria)
CURRENT CONTRIBUTORS:
Argentina, Australia, Austria, Belgium, Canada, Chile, China, Denmark, Finland, France,

ment of United Nations military and civilian personnel reached almost 70,000 from seventy-seven countries. "Traditional" peacekeeping has given way to complex, integrated operations that require a combination of political, military, and humanitarian action. Police officers, electoral observers, human rights monitors, and other civilians have joined military personnel under the United Nations flag to help implement negotiated settlements of conflicts between previously hostile parties, encouraging former opponents to build a peaceful future together.

As the world has increasingly turned to the United Nations to deal with the conflicts, the cost of United Nations peacekeeping has risen accordingly. The annual cost of all operations in 1995 amounted to approximately $3.0 billion. This investment in peacekeeping must be seen in perspective, however. Global military expenditures at the beginning of the 1990s amounted to about $1 trillion a year, or $2 million per minute. In other words, preparing for war costs in just over a day what keeping the peace costs in a year. The real cost of peacekeeping must ultimately be measured against the cost of the alternative—war.

Peacekeeping operations are set up by the Security Council—the United Nations principal organ vested with the primary responsibility for maintaining international peace and security. These operations must have the consent of the host governments, and usually of the other parties involved, and must not be used in any way to favor one party against another. The success of a peacekeeping operation also requires a clear and practicable mandate, the cooperation of the parties in implementing it, effective command at headquarters in New York and in the field, and adequate logistic and financial support.

United Nations troops carry light arms and are allowed to use minimum force only in self-defense, or if armed persons try to stop them from carrying out the orders of their commanders. United Nations military observers are unarmed. Only in exceptional circumstances may United Nations troops be authorized to use force in carrying out their responsibilities.

Ireland, Italy, Netherlands, New Zealand, Norway, Russian Federation, Sweden, Switzerland and, United States

FUNCTION:
Established to assist the Mediator and the Truce Commission in supervising the observance of the truce in Palestine. Since then, UNTSO has performed various tasks entrusted to it by the Security Council, including the supervision of the General

Armistice Agreements of 1949 and the observation of the cease-fire in the Suez Canal area and the Golan Heights following the Arab-Israeli war of June 1967. At present, UNTSO assists and cooperates with UNDOF on the Golan Heights in the Israel-Syria sector, and UNIFIL in the Israel-Lebanon sector. UNTSO also has a presence in the Egypt-Israel sector in the Sinai. In addition, UNTSO maintains offices in Beirut and Gaza.

■ UNEF I
First United Nations Emergency Force

LOCATION:
First the Suez Canal sector and the Sinai peninsula. Later along the Armistice Demarcation Line in the Gaza area and the international frontier in the Sinai peninsula (on the Egyptian side)
HEADQUARTERS:
Gaza
DURATION:
November 1956–June 1967
STRENGTH:
6,073 military personnel, supported by international and locally recruited civilian staff
FATALITIES:
107 (106 military personnel and 1 local civilian staff)

FUNCTION:
Established to secure and supervise the cessation of hostilities, including the withdrawal of the armed forces of France, Israel and the United Kingdom from Egyptian territory and, after the withdrawal, to serve as a buffer between the Egyptian and Israeli forces. In May 1967, Egypt compels UNEF I to withdraw.

■ UNEF II
Second United Nations Emergency Force

LOCATION:
Suez Canal sector and later the Sinai peninsula
HEADQUARTERS:
Ismailia

DURATION:
October 1973–July 1979
STRENGTH:
6,973 military personnel, supported by international and locally recruited civilian staff
FATALITIES:
55 (53 military personnel and 2 international civilian staff)

FUNCTION:
Established to supervise the cease-fire between Egyptian and Israeli forces and, following the conclusion of the agreements of January 18, 1974, and September 4, 1975, to supervise the redeployment of Egyptian and Israeli forces and to man and control the buffer zones established under those agreements

■ UNDOF
United Nations Disengagement Observer Force

LOCATION:
Syrian Golan Heights
HEADQUARTERS:
Damascus
DURATION:
June 1974 to present
CURRENT STRENGTH:
1,054 troops assisted by approximately 80 military observers of UNTSO's Observer Group Golan; they are supported by approximately 35 international and 80 locally recruited civilian staff
FATALITIES (January 31, 1996):
36 (35 military personnel and 1

international civilian staff)
FORCE COMMANDER:
Major-General Johannes C.
Kosters (Netherlands)
CURRENT CONTRIBUTORS:
Austria, Canada, Japan, and
Poland

FUNCTION:
Established after 1973 Middle
East war to maintain the cease-fire
between Israel and Syria, to supervise the disengagement of Israeli
and Syrian forces, and to supervise the areas of separation and
limitation, as provided in the
Agreement on Disengagement of
May 31, 1974. Since its establishment, UNDOF has continued to
perform its functions effectively
with the cooperation of the parties. The situation in the Israeli-
Syria sector has remained quiet
and there have been no serious
incidents

■ UNIFIL
United Nations Interim Force In Lebanon

LOCATION:
Southern Lebanon
HEADQUARTERS:
Naqoura
DURATION:
March 1978 to present
CURRENT STRENGTH:
4,568 troops assisted by approxi-
mately 60 military observers of
UNTSO's Observer Group
Lebanon; there are also approxi-
mately 140 international and 190
local civilian staff
FATALITIES (January 31, 1996):
209 (207 military personnel,
1 international civilian staff and
1 local staff)

FORCE COMMANDER:
Major-General Stanislaw
Franciszek Wozniak (Poland)
CURRENT CONTRIBUTORS:
Fiji, Finland, France, Ghana,
Ireland, Italy, Nepal, Norway, and
Poland

FUNCTION:
Established to confirm the withdrawal of Israeli forces from
southern Lebanon, to restore
international peace and security
and to assist the government of
Lebanon in ensuring the return of
its effective authority in the area.
UNIFIL has, however, been prevented from fully implementing
its mandate. Israel has maintained
its occupation of parts of south
Lebanon, where the Israeli forces
and their local auxiliary continued
to be targets of attacks by groups
that have proclaimed their resistance to the occupation. UNIFIL
does its best to limit the conflict
and protect the inhabitants from
the fighting. In doing so, it con-
tributes to stability in the area.

■ UNOGIL
United Nations Observation Group In Lebanon

LOCATION:
Lebanese-Syrian border areas and
vicinity of zones held by opposing
forces
HEADQUARTERS:
Beirut, Lebanon
DURATION:
June–December 1958

STRENGTH:
591 military observers, supported
by international and locally
recruited civilian staff
FATALITIES:
None

FUNCTION:
Established to ensure that there
was no illegal infiltration of personnel or supply of arms or other
matériel across the Lebanese borders. After the conflict had been
settled, tensions eased and
UNOGIL was withdrawn.

■ **UNYOM**
**United Nations Yemen Observation
Mission**

LOCATION:
Yemen
HEADQUARTERS:
Sana'a
DURATION:
July 1963–September 1964
STRENGTH:
25 military observers and 164
military personnel of reconnais-
sance and air units, supported by
international and locally recruited
civilian staff
FATALITIES:
None

FUNCTION:
Established to observe and certify
the implementation of the disen-
gagement agreement between
Saudi Arabia and the United Arab
Republic

II. INDIA AND PAKISTAN

■ **UNMOGIP**
**United Nations Military Observer
Group In India and Pakistan**

LOCATION:
The cease-fire line between India
and Pakistan in the State of
Jammu and Kashmir
HEADQUARTERS:
Rawalpindi (November–April);
Srinagar (May–October)
DURATION:
January 1949 to present
STRENGTH:
44 military observers, supported
by international and locally
recruited civilian staff
FATALITIES (January 31, 1996):
9 (1 military observer, 5 other
military personnel, 1 international
civilian staff and 2 local staff)
CHIEF MILITARY OBSERVER:
Major-General Alfonso Pessolano
(Italy)
CURRENT CONTRIBUTORS:
Belgium, Chile, Denmark,
Finland, Italy, Republic of Korea,
Sweden, and Uruguay

FUNCTION:
Established to supervise, in the
State of Jammu and Kashmir, the
cease-fire between India and
Pakistan. Following the 1972
India-Pakistan agreement defining
a Line of Control in Kashmir,
India took the position that the
mandate of UNMOGIP had
lapsed. Pakistan, however, did not
accept this position. Given that
disagreement, the Secretary-
General's position has been that
UNMOGIP can be terminated
only by a decision of the Security
Council. In the absence of such a

decision, UNMOGIP has been maintained with the same mandate and functions.

■ UNIPOM
United Nations India–Pakistan Observation Mission

LOCATION:
Along the India-Pakistan border between Kashmir and the Arabian Sea
HEADQUARTERS:
Lahore (Pakistan)/Amritsar (India)
DURATION:
September 1965–March 1966
STRENGTH:
96 military observers, supported by international and locally recruited civilian staff
FATALITIES:
None

FUNCTION:
Established to supervise the cease-fire along the India-Pakistan border except in the State of Jammu and Kashmir, where UNMOGIP operated, and the withdrawal of all armed personnel to the positions held by them before August 5, 1965. After the withdrawal of the troops by India and Pakistan had been completed on schedule, UNIPOM was terminated.

III. CYPRUS

■ UNFICYP
United Nations Peacekeeping Force In Cyprus

LOCATION:
Cyprus
HEADQUARTERS:
Nicosia

DURATION:
March 1964 to present
CURRENT STRENGTH:
1,165 troops and support personnel, and 35 civilian police; there is also a provision for some 370 internationally and locally recruited civilian staff
FATALITIES (January 31, 1996):
167 (161 military personnel, 3 civilian police, and 1 international civilian staff)
SPECIAL REPRESENTATIVE OF THE SECRETARY-GENERAL AND CHIEF OF MISSION:
Mr. Joe Clark (Canada)
DEPUTY SPECIAL REPRESENTATIVE RESIDENT IN CYPRUS:
Mr. Gustave Feissel (United States)
FORCE COMMANDER:
Brigadier General Ahti Vartiainen (Finland)
CURRENT CONTRIBUTORS:
Argentina, Australia, Austria, Canada, Finland, Hungary, Ireland, and United Kingdom

FUNCTION:
Established to prevent a recurrence of fighting between the Greek Cypriot and Turkish Cypriot communities and to contribute to the maintenance and restoration of law and order and a return to normal conditions. After the hostilities of 1974, UNFICYP's mandate was expanded. Following a de facto cease-fire, which came into effect on August 16, 1974, UNFICYP has supervised the cease-fire and maintained a buffer zone between the lines of the Cyprus National Guard and of the Turkish and Turkish Cypriot forces. In the absence of a political settlement to

the Cyprus problem, UNFICYP
continues its presence on the
island.

IV. AFRICA

■ ONUC
United Nations Operation In The Congo

LOCATION:
Republic of the Congo (now
Zaire)
HEADQUARTERS:
Léopoldville (now Kinshasa)
DURATION:
July 1960–June 1964
STRENGTH:
19,828 military personnel, sup-
ported by international and local-
ly recruited civilian staff
FATALITIES:
250 (245 military personnel and 5
international civilian staff)

FUNCTION:
Initially established to ensure the
withdrawal of Belgian forces, to
assist the government in maintaining law and order and to provide technical assistance. The
function of ONUC was subsequently modified to include
maintaining the territorial integrity and political independence of
the Congo, preventing the occurrence of civil war and securing the
removal from the Congo of all
foreign military, paramilitary and
advisory personnel not under the
United Nations Command, and
all mercenaries.

■ UNTAG
United Nations Transition Assistance Group

LOCATION:
Namibia and Angola
HEADQUARTERS:
Windhoek, Namibia
DURATION:
April 1989–March 1990
STRENGTH:
At maximum deployment,
UNTAG's overall strength was
approximately 8,000, consisting
of some 4,500 military personnel,
1,500 police and 2,000 civilians
FATALITIES:
19 (11 military personnel, 4 civil-
ian police, 3 international civilian
staff and 1 local staff)

FUNCTION:
Established to assist the Special
Representative of the secretary-
general to ensure the early independence of Namibia through free
and fair elections under the supervision and control of the United
Nations. UNTAG was also to
help the Special Representative to
ensure that: all hostile acts were
ended; troops were confined to
base, and, in the case of the South
Africans, ultimately withdrawn
from Namibia; all discriminatory
laws were repealed, political prisoners were released, Namibian
refugees were permitted to return,
intimidation of any kind was prevented, law and order were impar-

tially maintained. Independent Namibia joined the United Nations in April 1990.

■ UNAVEM I
United Nations Angola Verification Mission I

LOCATION:
Angola
HEADQUARTERS:
Luanda
DURATION:
January 1989–May 1991
STRENGTH:
70 military observers, supported by international and locally recruited civilian staff
FATALITIES:
None

FUNCTION:
Established on December 20, 1988, to verify the redeployment of Cuban troops northward and their phased and total withdrawal from the territory of Angola in accordance with the timetable agreed between Angola and Cuba. The withdrawal was completed by May 25, 1991—more than one month before the scheduled date. On June 6, the secretary-general reported to the Council that UNAVEM I had carried out, fully and effectively, the mandate entrusted to it.

■ UNAVEM II
United Nations Angola Verification Mission II

LOCATION:
Angola
HEADQUARTERS:
Luanda
DURATION:
May 1991–February 1995
STRENGTH:
350 military observers, 126 police monitors; there were also some 80 international civilian staff and 155 local staff, and up to 400 electoral observers
FATALITIES:
5 (2 military observers, 1 other military personnel, 1 police observer, and 1 international civilian staff)

FUNCTION:
Established on May 30, 1991, to verify the arrangements agreed by the Angolan parties for the monitoring of the cease-fire and for the monitoring of the Angolan police during the cease-fire period and to observe and verify the elections in that country, in accordance with the Peace Accords for Angola, signed by the Angolan government and the União Nacional para a Independência Total de Angola (UNITA). Despite the United Nations verification that the elections—held in September 1992—had been generally free and fair, their results were contested by UNITA. After renewed fighting in October 1992 between the government and UNITA forces, UNAVEM II's mandate was adjusted in order to help the two sides reach agreement on modalities for completing the peace process and, at the same time, to broker and help imple-

ment cease-fires at the national or local level. Following the signing on November 20, 1994, by the government of Angola and UNITA of the Lusaka Protocol, UNAVEM II verified the initial stages of the peace agreement. In February 1995, the Security Council set up a new mission— UNAVEM III—to monitor and verify the implementation of the Protocol.

◼ UNAVEM III
United Nations Angola Verification Mission III

LOCATION:
Angola
HEADQUARTERS:
Luanda
DURATION:
February 1995 to present
AUTHORIZED STRENGTH:
350 military observers, 7,000 other military personnel, 260 police observers; there is also a provision for 336 international civilian staff, 343 locally recruited staff and 68 United Nations Volunteers
CURRENT STRENGTH:
336 military observers, 6,576 troops and other military personnel and 226 civilian police
FATALITIES (January 31, 1996):
8 (7 military personnel and 1 civilian police)
SPECIAL REPRESENTATIVE OF THE SECRETARY-GENERAL AND CHIEF OF MISSION:
Mr. Alioune Blondin Beye (Mali)
FORCE COMMANDER:
Major-General Phillip Valerio Sibanda (Zimbabwe)
CIVILIAN POLICE:
Chief Superintendent Iqbal (Bangladesh)

CURRENT CONTRIBUTORS:
Algeria, Bangladesh, Brazil, Bulgaria, Congo, Egypt, Fiji, France, Guinea Bissau, Hungary, India, Italy, Jordan, Kenya, Malaysia, Mali, Namibia, Netherlands, New Zealand, Nigeria, Norway, Pakistan, Poland, Portugal, Republic of Korea, Romania, Russian Federation, Senegal, Slovak Republic, Sweden, Tanzania, Ukraine, United Kingdom, Uruguay, Zambia, and Zimbabwe

FUNCTION:
Established to assist the government of Angola and the União Nacional para a Independência Total de Angola (UNITA) in restoring peace and achieving national reconciliation on the basis of the "Accordos de Paz" signed on May 31, 1991, the Lusaka Protocol signed on November 20, 1994, and relevant Security Council resolutions. Among the main features of UNAVEM III's mandate are the following: to provide good offices and meditation to the Angolan parties; to monitor and verify the extension of State administration throughout the country and the process of national reconciliation; to supervise, control and verify the disengagement of forces and to monitor the cease-fire; to verify information received from the government and UNITA regarding their forces, as well as all troop movements; to assist in the establishment of quartering areas; to

verify the withdrawal, quartering and demobilization of UNITA forces; to supervise the collection and storage of UNITA armaments; to verify the movement of government forces (FAA) to barracks and the completion of the formation of FAA; to verify the free circulation of persons and goods; to verify and monitor the neutrality of the Angolan National Police, the disarming of civilians, the quartering of the rapid reaction police, and security arrangements for UNITA leaders; to coordinate, facilitate and support humanitarian activities directly linked to the peace process, as well as participating in mine-clearance activities; to declare formally that all essential requirements for the holding of the second round of presidential elections have been fulfilled, and to support, verify and monitor the electoral process.

■ MINURSO
United Nations Mission For The Referendum In Western Sahara

LOCATION:
Western Sahara
HEADQUARTERS:
Laayoune
DURATION:
April 1991 to present
AUTHORIZED STRENGTH:
Approximately 1,700 military observers and troops, 300 police officers and about 800 to 1,000 civilian personnel
CURRENT STRENGTH:
240 military observers, 48 military support personnel, 64 police officers; there is also a provision for approximately 250 international and local civilian staff

FATALITIES (January 31, 1996):
7 (1 military observer, 3 other military personnel, 1 civilian police and 2 international civilian staff)
ACTING SPECIAL REPRESENTATIVE OF THE SECRETARY-GENERAL:
Erik Jensen (Malaysia)
FORCE COMMANDER:
Major-General José Leandro (Portugal)
CIVILIAN POLICE COMMISSIONER:
Brigadier-General Walter Fallmann (Austria)
CURRENT CONTRIBUTORS:
Argentina, Austria, Bangladesh, Belgium, China, Egypt, El Salvador, France, Germany, Ghana, Greece, Guinea, Honduras, Hungary, Ireland, Italy, Kenya, Malaysia, Nigeria, Norway, Pakistan, Poland, Portugal, Republic of Korea, Russian Federation, Togo, Tunisia, United States, Uruguay, and Venezuela

FUNCTION:
Established in accordance with "the settlement proposals", as accepted by Morocco and the Frente Popular para la Liberación de Saguia el-Hamra y de Río de Oro (Frente POLISÁRIO) on August 30, 1988, to monitor a cease-fire, verify the reduction of Moroccan troops in the Territory, monitor the confinement of Moroccan and Frente POLISARIO troops to designated locations, ensure the release of all Western Saharan political prisoners or detainees, oversee the exchange of prisoners of war, implement the repatriation pro-

gram, identify and register qualified voters, organize and ensure a
free referendum and proclaim the
results. However, due to the parties' divergent views on some of
the key elements of the settlement
plan, in particular with regard to
the criteria for eligibility to vote,
it has not been possible to implement the plan in conformity with
the repeatedly revised timetable.
The primary function of MIN-
URSO in its present limited
deployment is restricted to complementing the identification
process, verifying the cease-fire
and cessation of hostilities, and
monitoring local police and
ensuring security and order at
identification and registration
sites. In January 1996, the
Security Council extended the
mandate of MINURSO for only
four months. The Council made
it clear that, unless meaningful
progress was made towards the
completion of the settlement
plan, the secretary-general would
have to submit a detailed program
for the phased withdrawal of the
United Nations operation.

■ UNOSOM I
United Nations Operation In Somalia I

LOCATION:
Somalia
HEADQUARTERS:
Mogadishu
DURATION:
April 1992–April 1993
STRENGTH:

50 military observers, 3,500 security personnel, up to 719 logistic
support personnel; there were also
some 200 international civilian
staff.
FATALITIES:
8 (military personnel)

FUNCTION:
Established to monitor the cease-
fire in Mogadishu, the capital of
Somalia, and to provide protection and security for United
Nations personnel, equipment
and supplies at the sea- and airports in Mogadishu and escort
deliveries of humanitarian supplies from there to distribution
centers in the city and its immediate environs. In August 1992,
UNOSOM's mandate and
strength were enlarged to enable it
to protect the humanitarian convoys and distribution centers
throughout Somalia. In December
1992, after the situation in
Somalia had further deteriorated,
the Security Council authorized
Member States to form the
Unified Task Force (UNITAF) to
establish a safe environment for
the delivery of humanitarian assistance. UNITAF worked in coordination with UNOSOM I to
secure major population centers
and ensure that humanitarian
assistance was delivered and distributed. UNOSOM I's mandate
came to an end in April 1993
with UNOSOM II taking over
from UNITAF.

■ UNOSOM II
United Nations Operation In Somalia II

LOCATION:
Somalia

HEADQUARTERS:
Mogadishu
DURATION:
May 1993–March 1995
STRENGTH:
Approximately 28,000 military and police personnel; there were also some 2,800 international and locally recruited staff
FATALITIES:
147 (143 military personnel, 3 international civilian staff and 1 local staff)

FUNCTION:
Established to take over from the Unified Task Force (UNITAF)—a multinational force, organized and led by the United States, which, in December 1992, had been authorized by the Security Council to use "all necessary means" to establish a secure environment for humanitarian relief operations in Somalia. The mandate of UNOSOM II was to take appropriate action, including enforcement measures, to establish throughout Somalia a secure environment for humanitarian assistance. To that end, UNOSOM II was to complete, through disarmament and reconciliation, the task begun by UNITAF for the restoration of peace, stability, law and order. Its main responsibilities included monitoring the cessation of hostilities, preventing resumption of violence, seizing unauthorized small arms, maintaining security at ports, airports and lines of communication required for delivery of humanitarian assistance, continuing mine-clearing, and assisting in repatriation of refugees in Somalia. UNOSOM II was also entrusted with assisting the

Somali people in rebuilding their economy and social and political life, re-establishing the country's institutional structure, achieving national political reconciliation, recreating a Somali State based on democratic governance, and rehabilitating the country's economy and infrastructure. In February 1994, after several violent incidents and attacks on United Nations soldiers, the Security Council revised UNOSOM II's mandate to exclude the use of coercive methods. UNOSOM II was withdrawn in early March 1995.

■ ONUMOZ
United Nations Operation In Mozambique

LOCATION:
Mozambique
HEADQUARTERS:
Maputo
DURATION:
December 1992–December 1994
AUTHORIZED STRENGTH:
Between 7,000 and 8,000 military and civilian personnel, and 1,114 civilian police
FATALITIES:
24 (21 military personnel, 2 civilian police and 1 international civilian staff)

FUNCTION:
Established to help implement the General Peace Agreement, signed on 4 October 1992 in

Rome by the President of the Republic of Mozambique and the President of the Resistência Nacional Moçambicana (REN-AMO). The mandate of ONU-MOZ was: to facilitate impartially the implementation of the agreement; to monitor and verify the cease-fire, the separation and concentration of forces, their demobilization and the collection, storage and destruction of weapons; to monitor and verify the complete withdrawal of foreign forces and to provide security in the transport corridors; to monitor and verify the disbanding of private and irregular armed groups; to authorize security arrangements for vital infrastructures; and to provide security for United Nations and other international activities in support of the peace process; to provide technical assistance and monitor the entire electoral process; to coordinate and monitor humanitarian assistance operations, in particular those relating to refugees, internally displaced persons, demobilized military personnel and the affected local population. After successful presidential and legislative elections in October 1994, and the installation of the Mozambique's new Parliament and the inauguration of the President of Mozambique in early December, ONUMOZ's mandate formally came to an end at midnight on December 9, 1994. The mission was formally liquidated at the end of January 1995.

■ UNOMUR
United Nations Observer Mission Uganda-Rwanda

LOCATION:
Ugandan side of the Uganda-Rwanda border
HEADQUARTERS:
Kabale, Uganda
DURATION:
June 1993–September 1994
STRENGTH:
81 military observers, supported by international and locally recruited civilian staff
FATALITIES:
None

FUNCTION:
Established to monitor the border between Uganda and Rwanda and verify that no military assistance — lethal weapons, ammunition and other material of possible military use — was being provided across it. While the tragic turn of events in Rwanda in April 1994 prevented UNOMUR from fully implementing its mandate, the observer mission played a useful role as a confidence-building mechanism in the months following the conclusion of the Arusha Peace Agreement and during UNAMIR's initial efforts to defuse tensions between the Rwandese parties and to facilitate the implementation of that agreement. UNOMUR was officially closed on September 21, 1994.

■ UNAMIR
United Nations Assistance Mission For Rwanda

LOCATION:
Rwanda

HEADQUARTERS:
Kigali
DURATION:
October 1993–March 1996
AUTHORIZED STRENGTH:
Almost 5,400 military personnel, 50 military police and 120 civilian police personnel; there is also a provision for international and locally recruited civilian staff.
FATALITIES (January 31, 1996):
26 (3 military observers, 22 other military personnel and 1 civilian police)

FUNCTION:
Originally established to help implement the Arusha Peace Agreement signed by the Rwandese parties on August 4, 1993. UNAMIR's mandate was: to assist in ensuring the security of the capital city of Kigali; monitor the cease-fire agreement, including establishment of an expanded demilitarized zone and demobilization procedures; monitor the security situation during the final period of the transitional government's mandate leading up to elections; assist with mine-clearance; and assist in the coordination of humanitarian assistance activities in conjunction with relief operations. After renewed fighting in April 1994, the mandate of UNAMIR was adjusted so that it could act as an intermediary between the warring Rwandese parties in an attempt to secure their agreement to a cease-fire; assist in the resumption of humanitarian relief operations to the extent feasible; and monitor developments in Rwanda, including the safety and security of civilians who sought refuge with UNAMIR. After the situation in Rwanda deteriorated further,

UNAMIR's mandate was expanded to enable it to contribute to the security and protection of refugees and civilians at risk, through means including the establishment and maintenance of secure humanitarian areas, and the provision of security for relief operations to the degree possible. Following the cease-fire and the installation of the new government, the tasks of UNAMIR were further adjusted: to ensure stability and security in the north-western and south-western regions of Rwanda; to stabilize and monitor the situation in all regions of Rwanda to encourage the return of the displaced population; to provide security and support for humanitarian assistance operations inside Rwanda; and to promote, through mediation and good offices, national reconciliation in Rwanda. UNAMIR also contributed to the security in Rwanda of personnel of the International Tribunal for Rwanda and of human rights officers, and assisted in the establishment and training of a new, integrated, national police force. In December 1995, the Security Council further adjusted UNAMIR's mandate to focus primarily on facilitating the safe and voluntary return of refugees. UNAMIR's mandate came to an end on March 8, 1996. The withdrawal of the mission was completed in April.

■ UNOMIL
United Nations Observer Mission In Liberia

LOCATION:
Liberia
HEADQUARTERS:
Monrovia
DURATION:
September 1993 to present
AUTHORIZED STRENGTH:
160 military observers; they are supported by military support personnel, United Nations Volunteers, international civilian and local civilian staff
CURRENT STRENGTH:
85 military observers and 8 military support personnel
FATALITIES:
None
SPECIAL REPRESENTATIVE OF THE SECRETARY-GENERAL:
Mr. Anthony B. Nyakyi (Tanzania)
CHIEF MILITARY OBSERVER:
Major-General Mahmoud Talha (Egypt)
CURRENT CONTRIBUTORS:
Bangladesh, China, Czech Republic, Egypt, Guinea Bissau, India, Jordan, Kenya, Malaysia, Pakistan, and Uruguay

FUNCTION:
Established to supervise and monitor, in cooperation with the Military Observer Group (ECO-MOG) of the Economic

Community of West African States (ECOWAS), the Cotonou Peace Agreement signed by the Liberian parties on July 25, 1993. In accordance with the agreement, ECOMOG had primary responsibility for ensuring the implementation of the agreement's provisions, and UNOMIL's role was to monitor the implementation procedures in order to verify their impartial application. Delays in the implementation of the Peace Agreement and resumed fighting among Liberian factions made it impossible to hold elections in February-March 1994, as scheduled. In the following months, a number of supplementary peace agreements, amending and clarifying the Cotonou Agreement, were negotiated—the Akosombo Agreement of September 12, 1994, the Accra Agreement of December 21, 1994, and the Abuja Agreement of August 19, 1995. In accordance with the peace agreements, ECOWAS is to continue to play the lead role in the peace process in Liberia, while ECOMOG retains the primary responsibility for assisting in the implementation of the military provisions of the agreements. For its part, UNOMIL is to continue to observe and monitor the implementation of the peace agreements. Its main functions are to exercise its good offices to support the efforts of ECOWAS and the Liberian National Transitional government to implement the peace agreements; investigate allegations of reported cease-fire violations; recommend measures to prevent their recurrence and report to the secretary-general accordingly; monitor compliance with the other military provisions of the agreements and verify their impartial application, especially disarming and demobilization of combatants; and assist in the maintenance of assembly sites and in the implementation of a program for demobilization of combatants. UNOMIL has also been requested to support humanitarian assistance activities; investigate and report to the secretary-general on violations of human rights; assist local human rights groups in raising voluntary assistance for training and logistic support; observe and verify the election process, including the legislative and presidential elections, scheduled to take place on August 20, 1996.

■ UNASOG
United Nations Aouzou Strip Observer Group

LOCATION:
Aouzou Strip, Republic of Chad
DURATION:
May 1994–June 1994
STRENGTH:
9 military observers
FATALITIES:
None

FUNCTION:
Established to verify the withdrawal of the Libyan administration and forces from the Aouzou Strip in accordance with the decision of the International Court of Justice. UNASOG accomplished its mandate after both sides–the

Republic of Chad and the Libyan Arab Jamahiriya–declared withdrawal to be complete

V. CENTRAL AMERICA

■ ONUCA
United Nations Observer Group In Central America

LOCATION:
Costa Rica, El Salvador, Guatemala, Honduras and Nicaragua
HEADQUARTERS:
Tegucigalpa, Honduras
DURATION:
December 1989–January 1992
AUTHORIZED STRENGTH:
260 military observers, infantry battalion of approximately 800 all ranks, and crews and support personnel for an air wing and naval unit; the mission also included international and locally recruited civilian staff
FATALITIES:
None

FUNCTION:
Established to verify compliance by the governments of Costa Rica, El Salvador, Guatemala, Honduras and Nicaragua with their undertakings to cease aid to irregular forces and insurrectionist movements in the region and not to allow their territory to be used for attacks on other States. In addition, ONUCA played a part in the voluntary demobilization of the Nicaraguan Resistance and monitored a cease-fire and the separation of forces agreed by the Nicaraguan parties as part of the demobilization process

■ ONUSAL
United Nations Observer Mission In El Salvador

LOCATION:
El Salvador
HEADQUARTERS:
San Salvador
DURATION:
July 1991–April 1995
AUTHORIZED STRENGTH:
380 military observers; 8 medical officers; and 631 police observers; there was also a provision for some 140 civilian international staff and 180 local staff
FATALITIES:
5 (3 police observers and 2 local civilian staff)

FUNCTION:
Established to verify the implementation of all agreements between the government of El Salvador government and Frente Farabundo Martí para la Liberación Nacional aimed at ending decade-long civil war. The agreements involved a cease-fire and related measures, reform and reduction of the armed forces, creation of a new police force, reform of the judicial and electoral systems, human rights, land tenure and other economic and social issues. After the armed conflict had been formally brought to an end in December 1992, ONUSAL verified elections which were carried out successfully in March and April 1994. After completion of ONUSAL's mandate on April 30, 1995, a small group of United Nations civilian personnel—known as the United Nations Mission in El Salvador (MINUSAL)—has remained in El Salvador to provide good offices to the parties, to verify implemen-tation of the outstanding points of the agreements and to provide a continuing flow of accurate and reliable information.

VI. CAMBODIA

■ UNAMIC
United Nations Advance Mission In Cambodia

LOCATION:
Cambodia
HEADQUARTERS:
Phnom Penh
DURATION:
November 1991–March 1992
STRENGTH:
1,504 military and civilian personnel
FATALITIES:
None

FUNCTION:
Established to assist the four Cambodian parties to maintain their cease-fire during the period prior to the establishment and deployment of the United Nations Transitional Authority in Cambodia, and to initiate mine-awareness training of civilian populations. Later, the mandate was enlarged to include a major training program for Cambodians in mine-detection and mine-clearance and the mine-clearing of repatriation routes, reception centers and resettlement areas. UNAMIC was absorbed by UNTAC in March 1992.

▪ UNTAC
United Nations Transitional Authority In Cambodia

LOCATION:
Cambodia
HEADQUARTERS:
Phnom Penh
DURATION:
March 1992–September 1993
STRENGTH:
Approximately 22,000 military and civilian personnel
FATALITIES:
78 (4 military observers, 41 other military personnel, 14 civilian police, 5 international civilian staff and 14 local staff)

FUNCTION:
Established to ensure the implementation of the Comprehensive Political Settlement of the Cambodia Conflict, signed in Paris on October 23, 1991. Under the agreement, the Supreme National Council of Cambodia (SNC) was "the unique legitimate body and source of authority in which, throughout the transitional period, the sovereignty, independence and unity of Cambodia are enshrined". The SNC, which was made up of the four Cambodian factions, delegated to the United Nations "all powers necessary" to ensure the implementation of the agreement. The mandate given to UNTAC included aspects relating to human rights, the organization and conduct of free and fair general elections, military arrangements, civil administration, the maintenance of law and order, the repatriation and resettlement of the Cambodian refugees and displaced persons and the rehabilitation of essential Cambodian infrastructure during the transitional period. Upon becoming operational on March 15, 1992, UNTAC absorbed UNAMIC, which had been established immediately after the signing of the agreement in October 1991. UNTAC's mandate ended in September 1993 with the promulgation of the Constitution for the Kingdom of Cambodia and the formation of the new government.

VII. THE FORMER YUGOSLAVIA

▪ UNPROFOR
United Nations Protection Force

February 1992–March 1995

LOCATION:
Bosnia and Herzegovina, Croatia, the Federal Republic of Yugoslavia (Serbia and Montenegro), and the former Yugoslav Republic of Macedonia.
HEADQUARTERS:
Zagreb, Croatia
STRENGTH (March 1995):
38,599 military personnel, including 684 United Nations military observers; the Force also included 803 civilian police, 2,017 other international civilian staff and 2,615 local staff.
FATALITIES:
167 (3 military observers, 159 other military personnel, 1 civilian police, 2 international civilian staff and 2 local staff)

FUNCTION:
Initially, established in Croatia in

241

February 1992 as an interim arrangement to create the conditions of peace and security required for the negotiation of an overall settlement of the Yugoslav crisis. UNPROFOR's mandate was to ensure that the three "United Nations Protected Areas" (UNPAs) in Croatia were demilitarized and that all persons residing in them were protected from fear of armed attack. In the course of 1992, UNPROFOR's mandate was enlarged to include monitoring functions in certain other areas of Croatia ("pink zones"); to enable the Force to control the entry of civilians into the UNPAs and to perform immigration and customs functions at the UNPA borders at international frontiers; and to include monitoring of the demilitarization of the Prevlaka Peninsula and to ensure control of the Peruca dam, situated in one of the "pink zones". In addition, UNPROFOR monitored implementation of a cease-fire agreement signed by the Croatian government and local Serb authorities in March 1994 following a flare-up of fighting in January and September 1993. In June 1992, as the conflict intensified and extended to Bosnia and Herzegovina, UNPROFOR's mandate and strength were enlarged in order to ensure the security and functioning of the airport at Sarajevo, and the delivery of humanitarian assistance to that city and its environs. In September 1992, UNPROFOR's mandate was further enlarged to enable it to support efforts by the United Nations High Commissioner for Refugees to deliver humanitarian relief throughout Bosnia and Herzegovina, and to protect convoys of released civilian detainees if the International Committee of the Red Cross so requested. In addition, the Force monitored "no-fly" zone, banning all military flights in Bosnia and Herzegovina, and the United Nations "safe areas" established by the Security Council around five Bosnian towns and the city of Sarajevo. UNPROFOR was authorized to use force in self-defense in reply to attacks against these areas, and to coordinate with the North Atlantic Treaty Organization (NATO) the use of air power in support of its activities. Similar arrangements were subsequently extended to the territory of Croatia. UNPROFOR also monitored the implementation of a cease-fire agreement signed by the Bosnian government and Bosnian Croat forces in February 1994. In addition, UNPROFOR monitored cease-fire arrangements negotiated between Bosnian government and Bosnian Serbs forces, which entered into force on 1 January 1995. In December 1992, UNPROFOR was also deployed in the former Yugoslav Republic of Macedonia, to monitor and report any developments in its border areas that could undermine confidence and stability in that republic and threaten its territory.

■ UNPF
United Nations Peace Forces

On March 31, 1995, the Security Council decided to restructure UNPROFOR, replacing it with three separate but interlinked peacekeeping operations. The Council extended the mandate of UNPROFOR in Bosnia and Herzegovina, established the United Nations Confidence Restoration Operation in Croatia (UNCRO), and decided that UNPROFOR within the former Yugoslav Republic of Macedonia should be known as the United Nations Preventive Deployment Force (UNPREDEP). Their joint theatre headquarters, known as United Nations Peace Forces headquarters (UNPF-HQ), was established in Zagreb, the capital of Croatia. UNPF-HQ was also responsible for liaison with the government of the Federal Republic of Yugoslavia (Serbia and Montenegro), other concerned Governments and NATO. Each of the three operations was headed by a civilian Chief of Mission and had its own military commander. Overall command and control of the three operations was exercised by the Special Representative of the secretary-general and a Theatre Force Commander. The total authorized strength of United Nations Peace Forces in the former Yugoslavia was 57,370 all ranks. Eventually, following positive developments in the former Yugoslavia, the termination of the mandates of UNCRO, and UNPROFOR and the establishment of two new United Nations missions in Bosnia and Herzegovina and

Croatia, UNPF-HQ was phased out.

LOCATION:
Bosnia and Herzegovina, Croatia, the Federal Republic of Yugoslavia (Serbia and Montenegro), and the former Yugoslav Republic of Macedonia
HEADQUARTERS:
Zagreb
DURATION:
March 31, 1995 – January 31, 1996
AUTHORIZED STRENGTH (UNPROFOR, UNCRO, UNPREDEP and UNPF-HQ):
57,370 all ranks; supported by the international and local civilian staff [see UNPROFOR above]
FATALITIES (UNPF-HQ):
9 (1 military observer, 2 other military personnel, 2 civilian police, 3 international United Nations staff and 1 local staff)

■ UNPROFOR
United Nations Protection Force

March 1995–December 1995
LOCATION:
Bosnia and Herzegovina
HEADQUARTERS:
Zagreb, Croatia
STRENGTH (November 1995):
24,178 troops, 311 military observers and 45 civilian police; they were supported by international and locally recruited civilian staff
FATALITIES:
40 (38 military personnel, 1 civilian police and 1 local staff)

[Grand total UNPROFOR February 21, 1992—December 20, 1995: 207]

FUNCTION:
Following the collapse of the December 1994 cease-fire at the end of April 1995, a cycle of violence escalated in Bosnia and Herzegovina. The continued shelling of the safe area of Sarajevo led to the NATO bombing of some Bosnian Serb targets, which in turn created a hostage crisis for the UN peacekeeping force. Over 400 peacekeepers were either detained or severely restricted in movement. NATO air strikes were halted and these peacekeepers were eventually released. This event led to the creation of the heavily armed combat-ready United Nations Rapid Reaction Force. The fall of the safe areas of Srebrenica and Zepa in July and the resumed shelling of Sarajevo led to a punitive air campaign by NATO against the key military targets of Bosnian Serbs. In the meantime, in August-September, the Bosnian government and Croatian forces, supported by the Croatian Army, launched a successful offensive in north-western and western Bosnia and Herzegovina, which changed dramatically the military situation in the country. In November, a United States initiative led to the peace agreement initialed and subsequently signed by the leaders of Bosnia and Herzegovina, Croatia, and the Federal Republic of Yugoslavia. As requested by the agreement, the Security Council authorized Member States to establish a NATO-led multinational Implementation Force (IFOR) to help ensure compliance with the provisions of the agreement. After IFOR took over from UNPROFOR on December 20, 1995, the latter's mandate was terminated.

■ UNCRO
United Nations Confidence Restoration Operation

LOCATION:
Croatia
HEADQUARTERS:
Zagreb, Croatia
DURATION:
March 1995–January 1996
STRENGTH (November 1995):
6,581 troops, 194 military observers and 296 civilian police; they were supported by international and locally recruited civilian staff
FATALITIES:
16 (military personnel)

FUNCTION:
Established on March 31, 1995, to replace UNPROFOR in Croatia. The troops and observers were deployed in Serb-controlled Western Slavonia, the Krajina region and Eastern Slavonia. Observers were also stationed in the Prevlaka peninsula. The new mandate included: (a) performing the functions envisaged in the cease-fire agreement of March 29, 1994; (b) facilitating implementation of the economic agreement of December 2, 1994; (c) facilitating implementation of all relevant Security Council resolutions; (d) assisting in controlling, by moni-

toring and reporting, the crossing of military personnel, equipment, supplies and weapons, over the international borders between Croatia and Bosnia and Herzegovina, and Croatia and the Federal Republic of Yugoslavia (Serbia and Montenegro) at the border crossings; (e) facilitating the delivery of international humanitarian assistance to Bosnia and Herzegovina through the territory of Croatia; and (f) monitoring the demilitarization of the Prevlaka peninsula. It was decided that UNCRO should be an interim arrangement to create the conditions that would facilitate a negotiated settlement consistent with the territorial integrity of Croatia and which would guarantee the security and rights of all communities living in Croatia. Croatia's reintegration by force of Western Slavonia and the Krajina region in May and August 1995 effectively eliminated the need for United Nations troops in those areas and their withdrawal was initiated. However, in Eastern Slavonia–the last Serb-controlled territory in Croatia–the mandate of UNCRO remained essentially unchanged. The government of Croatia and the Croatian Serb leadership agreed to resolve the issue of Eastern Slavonia through negotiation. UN-sponsored talks concluded with the signing of the Basic Agreement on the Region of Eastern Slavonia, Baranja and Western Sirmium on November 12. The agreement provided for the peaceful integration into

Croatia of that region and requested the Security Council to establish a transitional administration to govern the region during the transitional period. Following the establishment of the United Nations administration, the mandate of UNCRO was terminated on January 15, 1996.

■ UNPREDEP
United Nations Preventive Deployment Force

LOCATION:
The former Yugoslav Republic of Macedonia
HEADQUARTERS:
Skopje
DURATION:
March 1995 to present
AUTHORIZED STRENGTH:
1,050 troops, 35 military observers, 26 civilian police; there is also a provision for 73 international civilian staff, and 127 locally recruited staff
FATALITIES:
None
CHIEF OF MISSION:
Mr. Henryk J. Sokalski (Poland)
FORCE COMMANDER:
Brigadier-General Bo Lennart Wranker (Sweden)
CURRENT CONTRIBUTORS:
Argentina, Bangladesh, Belgium, Brazil, Canada, Czech Republic, Denmark, Egypt, Finland, France, Ghana, Indonesia, Ireland, Jordan, Kenya, Nepal, New Zealand, Nigeria, Norway, Pakistan, Poland, Portugal, Russian Federation, Sweden, Switzerland, Turkey, Ukraine, United Kingdom, and United States

FUNCTION:
Established on March 31, 1995,
to replace UNPROFOR in the
former Yugoslav Republic of
Macedonia. The mandate of
UNPREDEP remained essentially
the same: to monitor and report
any developments in the border
areas which could undermine
confidence and stability in the
former Yugoslav Republic of
Macedonia and threaten its territory. Effective February 1, 1996,
following the termination of the
mandates of UNCRO, UNPRO-
FOR, and UNPF-HQ, UNPRE-
DEP became an independent
mission, reporting directly to
United Nations Headquarters in
New York. Despite its new status,
the operation has maintained
basically the same mandate,
strength and composition of
troops.

■ UNMIBH
United Nations Mission In Bosnia and Herzegovina

LOCATION:
Bosnia and Herzegovina
HEADQUARTERS:
Sarajevo
DURATION:
December 1995 to present
AUTHORIZED STRENGTH:
1,721 police monitors; there is
also a provision for 252 interna-
tional staff and 905 locally
recruited staff
CURRENT STRENGTH:
1,222 police monitors
FATALITIES:
None

**SPECIAL REPRESENTATIVE OF THE SECRE-
TARY-GENERAL AND COORDINATOR OF
UNITED NATIONS OPERATIONS IN BOSNIA
AND HERZEGOVINA:**
Mr. Iqbal Riza (Pakistan)
COMMISSIONER OF IPTF:
Mr. Peter FitzGerald (Ireland)
CURRENT CONTRIBUTORS:
Argentina, Austria, Bangladesh,
Denmark, Fiji, Finland, France,
Germany, Ghana, Greece,
Hungary, India, Indonesia,
Ireland, Jordan, Kenya, Malaysia,
Nepal, Netherlands, Pakistan,
Poland, Portugal, Russian
Federation, Senegal, Spain,
Sweden, Switzerland, Tunisia,
Turkey, Ukraine, and United
States

FUNCTION:
On December 21, the Security
Council established, for a period
of one year, the United Nations
International Police Task Force
(IPTF) and a United Nations
civilian office. This was done in
accordance with the peace agreement signed by the leaders of
Bosnia and Herzegovina, Croatia
and the Federal Republic of
Yugoslavia (Serbia and
Montenegro) on December 14,
1995. The operation has come to
be known as the United Nations
Mission in Bosnia and
Herzegovina (UNMIBH). IPTF
tasks include: (a) monitoring,
observing and inspecting law
enforcement activities and facilities, including associated judicial
organizations, structures and proceedings; (b) advising law
enforcement personnel and
forces; (c) training law enforcement personnel; (d) facilitating,
within the IPTF mission of assistance, the parties' law enforce-

ment activities; (e) assessing threats to public order and advising on the capability of law enforcement agencies to deal with such threats; (f) advising government authorities in Bosnia and Herzegovina on the organization of effective civilian law enforcement agencies; and (g) assisting by accompanying the parties' law enforcement personnel as they carry out their responsibilities, as the Task Force deems appropriate. In addition, the Task Force is to consider requests from the parties or law enforcement agencies in Bosnia and Herzegovina for assistance, with priority being given to ensuring the existence of conditions for free and fair elections. The United Nations Coordinator, acting under the secretary-general's authority, exercises authority over the IPTF Commissioner and coordinates other United Nations activities in Bosnia and Herzegovina relating to humanitarian relief and refugees; de-mining, human rights, elections, and rehabilitation of infrastructure and economic reconstruction. UNMIBH closely cooperates with a NATO-led multinational Implementation Force (IFOR), authorized by the Security Council to help ensure compliance with the provisions of the peace agreement, and with the High Representative, appointed by the Peace Implementation Conference and approved by the Security Council, and whose task

is to mobilize and coordinate the activities of organizations and agencies involved in civilian aspects of the peace settlement in Bosnia and Herzegovina, and monitor the implementation of that settlement.

■ UNTAES
United Nations Transitional Administration For Eastern Slavonia, Baranja and Western Sirmium

LOCATION:
Croatia
HEADQUARTERS:
Vukovar
DURATION:
January 1996 to present
AUTHORIZED STRENGTH:
5,000 troops, 100 military observers and 600 civilian police; there is also a provision for 317 international civilian staff and 686 locally recruited staff
CURRENT STRENGTH:
3,113 troops, 100 military observers and 223 civilian police
FATALITIES:
None
TRANSITIONAL ADMINISTRATOR:
Mr. Jacques Paul Klein (United States)
FORCE COMMANDER:
Major-General Jozef Schoups (Belgium)
CURRENT CONTRIBUTORS:
Argentina, Bangladesh, Belgium, Brazil, Czech Republic, Denmark, Egypt, Finland, Ghana, Indonesia, Ireland, Jordan, Kenya, Nepal, New Zealand, Nigeria, Norway, Pakistan, Poland, Russian Federation, Senegal,

Slovak Republic, Sweden,
Switzerland, Tunisia, Turkey,
Ukraine, and United Kingdom

FUNCTION:
The November 12, 1995, Basic
Agreement on the Region of
Eastern Slavonia, Baranja and
Western Sirmium provides for the
peaceful integration of that region
into Croatia. The agreement
requested the Security Council to
establish a transitional administration to govern the region during the transitional period of 12
months, which might be extended
by up to a further 12 months and
to authorize an international force
to maintain peace and security
during that period and to otherwise assist in the implementation
of the agreement. UNTAES was
set up on January 15, 1996, for
an initial period of 12 months,
with both military and civilian
components. The military component is to supervise and facilitate the demilitarization of the
Region; monitor the voluntary
and safe return of refugees and
displaced persons to their home
of origin in cooperation with
UNHCR; contribute, by its presence, to the maintenance of peace
and security in the region; and
otherwise assist in implementation of the Basic Agreement. The
civilian component is to establish
a temporary police force, define
its structure and size, develop a

training program and oversee its
implementation, and monitor
treatment of offenders and the
prison system; undertake tasks
relating to civil administration
and to the functioning of public
services; facilitate the return of
refugees; organize elections, assist
in their conduct, and certify the
results. The component has also
been requested to undertake other
activities relevant to the Basic
Agreement, including assistance
in the coordination of plans for
the development and economic
reconstruction of the Region; and
monitoring of the parties' compliance with their commitments to
respect the highest standards of
human rights and fundamental
freedoms, promote an atmosphere
of confidence among all local residents irrespective of their ethnic
origin, monitor and facilitate the
de-mining of territory within the
Region, and maintain an active
public affairs element. UNTAES
is also to cooperate with the
International Criminal Tribunal
for the Former Yugoslavia in performing its mandate. Member
States are authorized, acting
nationally or through regional
organizations, to take all necessary
measures, including close air support to defend or help withdraw
UNTAES, and that such actions
would be based on UNTAES's
request and procedures communicated to the United Nations.

■ UNMOP
United Nations Mission Of Observers In Prevlaka

LOCATION:
Prevlaka peninsula, Croatia

DURATION:
January 1996 to present
AUTHORIZED STRENGTH:
28 military observers
FATALITIES:
None
CHIEF MILITARY OBSERVER:
Colonel Göran Gunnarsson
(Sweden)
CURRENT CONTRIBUTORS:
Argentina, Bangladesh, Belgium, Brazil, Canada, Czech Republic, Denmark, Egypt, Finland, France, Ghana, Indonesia, Ireland, Jordan, Kenya, Nepal, Nepal, New Zealand, Nigeria, Norway, Pakistan, Poland, Portugal, Russian Federation, Sweden, Switzerland, Ukraine and, United Kingdom

FUNCTION:
United Nations military observers have been deployed in the strategically-important Prevlaka peninsula since October 1992, when the Security Council authorized UNPROFOR to assume responsibility for monitoring the demilitarization of that area. Following the restructuring of UNPROFOR in March 1995, those functions were carried out by UNCRO. With the termination of UNCRO's mandate in January 1996, the Council authorized United Nations military observers to continue monitoring the demilitarization of the peninsula for a period of three months, to be extended for an additional three months upon a report by the secretary-general that an extension would continue to help decrease tension there. United Nations military observers are under the command and direction of a Chief Military Observer,

who reports directly to United Nations Headquarters in New York.

VIII. THE REPUBLICS OF THE FORMER SOVIET UNION

■ UNOMIG
United Nations Observer Mission In Georgia

LOCATION:
Georgia
HEADQUARTERS:
Sukhumi
DURATION:
August 1993 to present
AUTHORIZED STRENGTH:
136 military observers; there was also a provision for 64 international civilian staff and 75 locally recruited staff
CURRENT STRENGTH:
128 military observers, supported by 55 international and 75 local civilian staff
FATALITIES:
2 (military observers)
SPECIAL ENVOY OF THE SECRETARY-GENERAL:
Mr. Edouard Brunner
(Switzerland)
RESIDENT DEPUTY TO THE SPECIAL ENVOY AND HEAD OF MISSION:
Mr. Liviu Bota (Romania)
CHIEF MILITARY OBSERVER:
Major-General Per Källström
(Sweden)
CURRENT CONTRIBUTORS:
Albania, Austria, Bangladesh, Cuba, Czech Republic, Denmark, Egypt, France, Germany, Hungary, Indonesia, Jordan,

Pakistan, Poland, Republic of Korea, Russian Federation, Sweden, Switzerland, Turkey, United Kingdom, United States, and Uruguay

FUNCTION:
Originally established to verify compliance with the July 27, 1993, cease-fire agreement between the government of Georgia and the Abkhaz authorities in Georgia with special attention to the situation in the city of Sukhumi; to investigate reports of cease-fire violations and to attempt to resolve such incidents with the parties involved; and to report to the secretary-general on the implementation of its mandate, including, in particular, violations of the cease-fire agreement. After UNOMIG's original mandate had been invalidated by the resumed fighting in Abkhazia in September 1993, the mission had an interim mandate to maintain contacts with both sides to the conflict and with Russian military contingents, and to monitor and report on the situation, with particular reference to developments relevant to United Nations efforts to promote a comprehensive political settlement. Following the signing, in May 1994, by the Georgian and Abkhaz sides of the agreement on a Cease-fire and Separation of Forces, UNOMIG's tasks are: to monitor and verify the implementation of the agreement; to observe the operation of the peacekeeping force of the Commonwealth of Independent

States; to verify that troops do not remain in or re-enter the security zone and that heavy military equipment does not remain or is not reintroduced in the security zone or the restricted weapons zone; to monitor the storage areas for heavy military equipment withdrawn from the security zone and restricted weapons zone; to monitor the withdrawal of Georgian troops from the Kodori valley to places beyond the frontiers of Abkhazia; to patrol regularly the Kodori valley; and to investigate reported or alleged violations of the agreement and attempt to resolve such incidents.

■ UNMOT
United Nations Mission Of Observers In Tajikistan

LOCATION:
Tajikistan
HEADQUARTERS:
Dushanbe
DURATION:
December 1994 to present
AUTHORIZED STRENGTH:
45 military observers
CURRENT STRENGTH:
45 military observers, supported by 18 international and 26 local civilian staff
FATALITIES (January 31, 1996):
1 (military observer)
SPECIAL ENVOY OF THE SECRETARY-GENERAL:
to be announced
DEPUTY SPECIAL ENVOY AND HEAD OF MISSION:
Mr. Darko Silovic (Croatia)
CHIEF MILITARY OBSERVER:
Brigadier-General Hasan Abaza (Jordan)
CURRENT CONTRIBUTORS:
Austria, Bangladesh, Bulgaria,

Denmark, Jordan, Poland,
Switzerland, Ukraine, and
Uruguay

FUNCTION:
Established with a mandate to
assist the Joint Commission, composed of representatives of the
Tajik government and of the Tajik
opposition, to monitor the implementation of the agreement on a
Temporary Cease-fire and the
Cessation of Other Hostile Acts
on the Tajik-Afghan Border and
within the Country for the
Duration of the Talks; to investigate reports of cease-fire violations and to report on them to
the United Nations and to the
Joint Commission; to provide its
good offices as stipulated in the
agreement; to maintain close contact with the parties to the conflict, as well as close liaison with
the mission of the Conference on
Security and Cooperation in
Europe and with the Collective
Peacekeeping Forces of the
Commonwealth of Independent
States in Tajikistan and with the
border forces; to provide support
for the efforts of the secretary-
general's Special Envoy; and to
provide political liaison and coordination services, which could
facilitate expeditious humanitarian assistance by the international
community.

IX. HAITI

■ UNMIH
United Nations Mission In Haiti

LOCATION:
Haiti
HEADQUARTERS:
Port-au-Prince
DURATION:
September 1993 to present
CURRENT AUTHORIZED STRENGTH:
1,200 troops and 300 civilian
police, supported by international
and locally recruited civilian staff
FATALITIES (January 31, 1996):
6 (4 military personnel and 2
civilian police)
SPECIAL REPRESENTATIVE OF THE SECRE-
TARY-GENERAL AND CHIEF OF MISSION:
Mr. Enrique ter Horst
(Venezuela)
FORCE COMMANDER:
Brigadier-General J. R. P. Daigle
(Canada)
POLICE COMMISSIONER:
Colonel Philippe Balladur
(France)
CURRENT CONTRIBUTORS:
Algeria, Bangladesh, Canada,
Djibouti, France, Mali,
Netherlands, Pakistan, Russian
Federation, Togo, Trinidad and
Tobago, and United States

FUNCTION:
Originally established to help
implement certain provisions of
the Governors Island Agreement
signed by the Haitian parties on
July 3, 1993. In 1993, UNMIH's
mandate was to assist in modern-
izing the armed forces of Haiti
and establishing a new police
force. However, due to non-coop-
eration of the Haitian military
authorities, UNMIH could not
be fully deployed at that time and
carry out that mandate. After the

restoration, in October 1994, of the Haitian Constitutional government with the help of a multinational force led by the United States and authorized by the Security Council, UNMIH's mandate was revised to enable the mission to assist the democratic government of Haiti in fulfilling its responsibilities in connection with: sustaining a secure and stable environment established during the multinational phase and protecting international personnel and key installations; and the professionalization of the Haitian armed forces and the creation of a separate police force. UNMIH was also to assist the legitimate constitutional authorities of Haiti in establishing an environment conducive to the organization of free and fair legislative elections to be called by those authorities. UNMIH assumed its functions in full on March 31, 1995. Haiti has remained safe and secure since then. Democratic legislative elections were held in summer 1995, despite some logistical difficulties. The Presidential elections were held successfully on December 17, 1995, and the transfer of power to the new President took place on February 7, 1996. Upon the receipt of the request of the President of Haiti, UNMIH's mandate has been extended until the end of June 1996.

X. OTHER PEACEKEEPING MISSIONS

■ UNSF
United Nations Security Force In West New Guinea (West Irian)

LOCATION:
West New Guinea (West Irian)
HEADQUARTERS:
Hollandia (now Jayaphra)
DURATION:
October 1962–April 1963
STRENGTH:
1,576 military personnel, supported by international and locally recruited civilian staff
FATALITIES:
None

FUNCTION:
Established to maintain peace and security in the territory under the United Nations Temporary Executive Authority (UNTEA), established by agreement between Indonesia and the Netherlands. UNSF monitored the cease-fire and helped ensure law and order during the transition period, pending transfer to Indonesia.

■ DOMREP
Mission of the Representative of the Secretary-General in the Dominican Republic

LOCATION:
Dominican Republic
HEADQUARTERS:
Santo Domingo
DURATION:
May 1965–October 1966
STRENGTH:
The Military Adviser to the Representative of the Secretary-General was provided with a staff of 2 military observers

FATALITIES:
None

FUNCTION:
Established to observe the situation and to report on breaches of the cease-fire between the two de facto authorities in the Dominican Republic. Following the agreement on a new government, DOMREP was withdrawn.

■ UNGOMAP
United Nations Good Offices Mission In Afghanistan and Pakistan

LOCATION:
Afghanistan and Pakistan
HEADQUARTERS:
Kabul and Islamabad
DURATION:
May 1988–March 1990
STRENGTH:
50 military observers, supported by international and locally recruited civilian staff
FATALITIES:
None

FUNCTION:
Established to assist the Personal Representative of the secretary-general to lend his good offices to the parties in ensuring the implementation of the Agreements on the Settlement of the Situation Relating to Afghanistan and in this context to investigate and report possible violations of any of the provisions of the Agreements. When UNGOMAP's mandate ended,

the Personal Representative remained in the country and served as head of the Office of the secretary-general in Afghanistan and Pakistan, established on March 15, 1990, as well as Coordinator of the United Nations Office for the Coordination of Humanitarian Assistance to Afghanistan. In December 1994, the secretary-general discontinued the function of the personal representative, creating in its place the Office of the Secretary-General in Afghanistan.

■ UNIIMOG
United Nations Iran-Iraq Military Observer Group

LOCATION:
Iran and Iraq
HEADQUARTERS:
Tehran and Baghdad
DURATION:
August 1988–February 1991
STRENGTH:
400 military personnel, supported by international and locally recruited civilian staff
FATALITIES:
1 (military personnel)

FUNCTION:
Established to verify, confirm and supervise the cease-fire and the withdrawal of all forces to the internationally recognized boundaries, pending a comprehensive settlement. UNIIMOG was terminated after Iran and Iraq had withdrawn fully their forces to the internationally recognized boundaries. Small civilian offices were established in Tehran and Baghdad to implement the remaining tasks which were essentially political. By the end of

1992, those offices were phased out.

■ UNIKOM
United Nations Iraq-Kuwait Observation Mission

LOCATION:
The demilitarized zone along the boundary between Iraq and Kuwait
HEADQUARTERS:
Umm Qasr, Iraq
DURATION:
April 1991 to present
CURRENT STRENGTH:
245 military observers, 900 troops and military support personnel; there was also approximately 70 international and 140 local civilian staff
FATALITIES (January 31, 1996):
5 (1 military observer, 3 military personnel and 1 international civilian staff)
FORCE COMMANDER:
Major-General Gian Giuseppe Santillo (Italy)
CURRENT CONTRIBUTORS:
Argentina, Austria, Bangladesh, Canada, China, Denmark, Fiji, Finland, France, Germany, Ghana, Greece, Hungary, India, Indonesia, Ireland, Italy, Kenya, Malaysia, Nigeria, Pakistan, Poland, Romania, Russian Federation, Senegal, Singapore, Sweden, Thailand, Turkey, United Kingdom, United States, Uruguay and, Venezuela

FUNCTION:
Established following the withdrawal of Iraq's forces from the territory of Kuwait. UNIKOM, set up initially as an unarmed observation mission, was to monitor a demilitarized zone (DMZ) along the boundary between Iraq and Kuwait and the Khawr 'Abd Allah waterway, to deter violations of the boundary, and to observe any hostile action mounted from the territory of one State against the other. In February 1993, following a series of incidents on the border, the Security Council decided to increase UNIKOM's strength and to extend its terms of reference to include the capacity to take physical action to prevent violations of the DMZ and of the newly demarcated boundary between Iraq and Kuwait.

A World Map of Peacekeeping

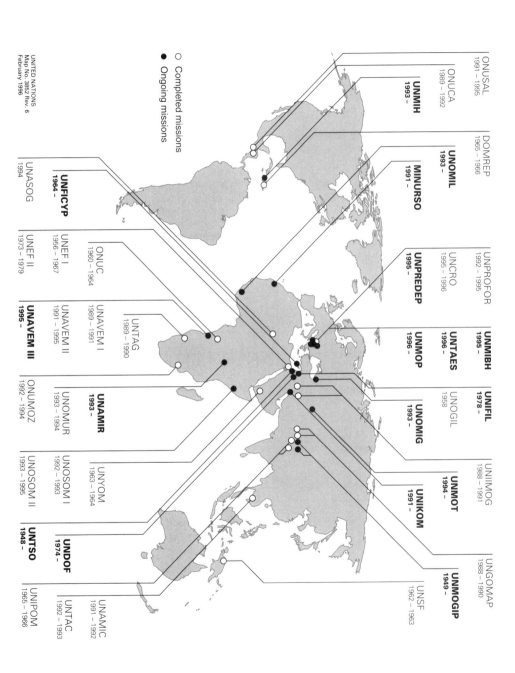

UNITED NATIONS
Map No. 3852 Rev. 6
February 1996

○ Completed missions
● Ongoing missions

ONUSAL
1991 – 1995

ONUCA
1989 – 1992

UNMIH
1993 –

DOMREP
1965 – 1966

UNOMIL
1993 –

MINURSO
1991 –

UNASOG
1994

UNFICYP
1964 –

UNEF II
1973 – 1979

UNEF I
1956 – 1967

ONUC
1960 – 1964

UNAVEM I
1989 – 1991

UNTAG
1989 – 1990

UNPROFOR
1992 – 1995

UNCRO
1995 – 1996

UNPREDEP
1995 –

UNMIBH
1995 –

UNTAES
1996 –

UNMOP
1996 –

UNIFIL
1978 –

UNOGIL
1958

UNAVEM III
1995 –

UNAVEM II
1991 – 1995

UNAMIR
1993 –

UNOMUR
1993 – 1994

ONUMOZ
1992 – 1994

UNOMIG
1993 –

UNOSOM II
1993 – 1995

UNOSOM I
1992 – 1993

UNYOM
1963 – 1964

UNMOT
1994 –

UNIKOM
1991 –

UNIIMOG
1988 – 1991

UNTSO
1948 –

UNDOF
1974 –

UNMOGIP
1949 –

UNGOMAP
1988 – 1990

UNIPOM
1965 – 1966

UNTAC
1992 – 1993

UNAMIC
1991 – 1992

UNSF
1962 – 1963

255

Chapter Six and a Half

Nowhere in the United Nations Charter is peacekeeping policy actually specified. It is a constantly evolving enterprise, existing somewhere between Chapter VI and Chapter VII. Former secretary-general Dag Hammarskjöld dubbed it "Chapter Six and a Half."

CHAPTER VI
PACIFIC SETTLEMENT OF DISPUTES

Article 33
1. The parties to any dispute, the continuance of which is likely to endanger the maintenance of international peace and security, shall, first of all, seek a solution by negotiation, enquiry, mediation, conciliation, arbitration, judicial settlement, resort to regional agencies or arrangements, or other peaceful means of their own choice.
2. The Security Council shall, when it deems necessary, call upon the parties to settle their dispute by such means.

Article 34
The Security Council may investigate any dispute, or any situation which might lead to international friction or give rise to a dispute, in order to determine whether the continuance of the dispute or situation is likely to endanger the maintenance of international peace and security.

Article 35
1. Any Member of the United Nations may bring any dispute, or any situation of the nature referred to in Article 34, to the attention of the Security Council or of the General Assembly.
2. A state which is not a Member of the United Nations may bring to the attention of the Security Council or of the General Assembly any dispute to which it is a party if it accepts in advance, for the purposes of the dispute, the obligations of pacific settlement provided in the present Charter.
3. The proceedings of the General Assembly in respect of matters brought to its attention under this Article will be subject to the provisions of Articles 11 and 12.

Article 36
1. The Security Council may, at any stage of a dispute of the nature referred to in Article 33 or of a situation of like nature, recommend appropriate procedures or methods of adjustment.
2. The Security Council should take into consideration any procedures for the settlement of the dispute which have already been adopted by the parties.
3. In making recommendations under this Article the Security Council should also take into consideration that legal disputes should as a general rule be referred by the parties to the International Court of Justice in accordance with the provisions of the Statute of the Court.

Article 37
1. Should the parties to a dispute of the nature referred to in Article 33 fail to settle it by the means indicated in that Article, they shall refer it to the Security Council.
2. If the Security Council deems that the continuance of the dispute is in fact likely to endanger the maintenance of international peace and security, it shall decide whether to take action under Article 36 or to recommend such terms of settlement as it may consider appropriate.

Article 38
Without prejudice to the provisions of Articles 33 to 37, the Security Council may, if all the parties to any dispute so request, make recommendations to the parties with a view to a pacific settlement of the dispute.

Chapter VII
ACTION WITH RESPECT TO THREATS TO THE PEACE, BREACHES OF THE PEACE, AND ACTS OF AGGRESSION

Article 39
The Security Council shall determine the existence of any threat to the peace, breach of the peace, or act of aggression and shall make recommendations, or decide what measures shall be taken in accordance with Articles 41 and 42, to maintain or restore international peace and security.

Article 40
In order to prevent an aggravation of the situation, the Security Council may, before making the recommendations or deciding upon the measures provided for in Article 39, call upon the parties concerned to comply with such provisional measures as it deems necessary or desirable. Such provisional measures shall be without prejudice to the rights claims, or position of the parties concerned. The Security Council shall duly take account of failure to comply with such provisional measures.

Article 41
The Security Council may decide what measures not involving the use of armed force are to be employed to give effect to its decisions, and it may call upon the Members of the United Nations to apply such measures. These may include complete or partial interruption of economic relations and of rail, sea, air, postal, telegraphic, radio, and other means of communication, and the severance of diplomatic relations.

Article 42
Should the Security Council consider that measures provided for in Article 41 would be inadequate or have proved to be inadequate, it may take such action by air, sea, or land forces as may be necessary to maintain or restore interna-

tional peace and security. Such action may include demonstrations, blockade, and other operations by air, sea, or land forces of Members of the United Nations.

Article 43

1. All Members of the United Nations, in order to contribute to the maintenance of international peace and security, undertake to make available to the Security Council, on its call and in accordance with a special agreement or agreements, armed forces, assistance, and facilities, including rights of passage, necessary for the purpose of maintaining international peace and security.

2. Such agreement or agreements shall govern the numbers and types of forces, their degree of readiness and general location, and the nature of the facilities and assistance to be provided.

3. The agreement or agreements shall be negotiated as soon as possible on the initiative of the Security Council. They shall be concluded between the Security Council and Members or between the Security Council and groups of Members and shall be subject to ratification by the signatory states in accordance with their respective constitutional processes.

Article 44

When the Security Council has decided to use force it shall, before calling upon a Member not represented on it to provide armed forces in fulfillment of the obligations assumed under Article 43, invite that Member, if the Member so desires, to participate in the decisions of the Security Council concerning the employment of contingents of that Member's armed forces.

Article 45

In order to enable the United Nations to take urgent military measures, Members shall hold immediately available national air-force contingents for combined international enforcement action. The strength and degree of readiness of these contingents and plans for their combined action shall be determined, within the limits laid down in the special agreement or agreements referred to in Article 43, by the Security Council with the assistance of the Military Staff Committee.

Article 46

Plans for the application of armed force shall be made by the Security Council with the assistance of the Military Staff Committee.

Article 47

1. There shall be established a Military Staff Committee to advise and assist the Security Council on all questions relating to the Security Council's military requirements for the maintenance of international peace and security, the employment and command of forces placed at its disposal, the regulation of armaments, and possible disarmament.

2. The Military Staff Committee shall consist of the Chiefs of Staff of the permanent members of the Security Council or their representatives. Any Member of the United Nations not permanently represented on the Committee shall be invited by the Committee to be associated with it when the efficient discharge of the Committee's responsibilities requires the participation of that Member in its work.

3. The Military Staff Committee shall be responsible under the Security Council for the strategic direction of any armed forces placed at the disposal of the Security Council. Questions relating to the command of such forces shall be worked out subsequently.

4. The Military Staff Committee, with the authorization of the Security Council and after consultation with appropriate regional agencies, may establish regional sub- committees.

Article 48

1. The action required to carry out the decisions of the Security Council for the maintenance of international peace and security shall be taken by all the Members of the United Nations or by some of them, as the Security Council may determine.

2. Such decisions shall be carried out by the Members of the United Nations directly and through their action in the appropriate international agencies of which they are members.

Article 49

The Members of the United Nations shall join in affording mutual assistance in carrying out the measure decided upon by the Security Council.

Article 50

If preventive or enforcement measures against any state are taken by the Security Council, any other state, whether a Member of the United Nations or not, which finds itself confronted with special economic problems arising from the carrying out of those measures shall have the right to consult the Security Council with regard to a solution of those problems.

Article 51

Nothing in the present Charter shall impair the inherent right of individual or collective self-defense if an armed attack occurs against a Member of the United Nations, until the Security Council has taken measures necessary to maintain international peace and security. Measures taken by Members in the exercise of this right of self-defense shall be immediately reported to the Security Council and shall not in any way affect the authority and responsibility of the Security Council under the present Charter to take at any time such action as it deems necessary in order to maintain or restore international peace and security.

Suggested Further Reading

Alexander, Maj. Gen. H.T. *African Tightrope.* London: Pall Mall Press, 1966.

Ali, Rabia, & Lawrence Lifschultz (eds.). *Why Bosnia?* Stony Creek, Conn., 1993.

Allan, James H. *Peacekeeping: Outspoken Observations by a Field Officer.* Westport, Conn., & London: Praeger, 1996.

Boutros-Ghali, Boutros. *An Agenda for Peace.* New York: United Nations, 1995.

—*Confronting New Challenges: Fourth Annual Report to the General Assembly.* New York: United Nations, 1995.

Cigar, Norman. *Genocide in Bosnia.* College Station: Texas A&M Press, 1995.

Clark, Walter & Jeffrey Herbst. "Somalia and the Future of Humanitarian Intervention." Center of International Studies Monograph Series No. 9, Princeton Univ., 1995.

Clarke, Walter S. "Humanitarian Intervention in Somalia." Bibliography. Carlisle Barracks, Penn: Center for Strategic Leadership, U.S. Army War College, March 1995.

Cohen, Ben, & George Stamkowski (eds.) *With No Peace to Keep: United Nations Peacekeeping and the War in Former Yugoslavia.* London: Grainpress Ltd., 1995.

"Comprehensive Report on Lessons Learned From United Nations Operation in Somalia, April 1992–March 1995." Friedrich E. Stiftung, Germany; Life and Peace Institute, Sweden; Norwegian Institute of International Affairs; in cooperation with the Lessons Learned Unit of the Department of Peace-Keeping Operations, December 1995.

Cushman, Thomas, & Stjepan Mestrovic (eds.). *This Time They Knew.* New York: New York University Press, 1996.

Dizdarevic, Zlatko. *Sarajevo.* New York: Henry Holt & Co., 1994.

Donia, Robert, & John Fline. *Bosnia and Hercegovina: Tradition Betrayed.* New York: Columbia Univ. Press, 1994.

Erskine, Emmanuel A., Lt. Gen. *UNFIL: An African Soldier's Reflections.* New York: St. Martin's Press, 1989.

Evans, Gareth. "Cooperation for Peace, the Global Agenda for the 1990s and Beyond." Canberra: Department of Foreign Affairs and Trade, June 1994.

Freye, William R. *A United Nations Peace Force.* Oceana Publications, 1957.

Guest, Iain. *Behind the Disappearances: Argentina's Dirty War Against Human Rights and the United Nations.* Philadelphia: Univ. of Pennsylvania Press, 1990.

Gutman, Roy. *A Witness to Genocide.* New York: Macmillan, 1993.

Harbottle, Michael. *The Blue Berets.* Harrisburg, Penn: Stackpole Books, 1971.

Head, Thomas. "The Judgment of God: Andrew of Fleury's Account of the Peace League of Bourges." In Thomas Head and Richard Landes (eds.), *The Peace of God.* Ithaca, New York: Cornell Univ. Press, 1992.

Hemleben, Sylvester John. *Plans for World Peace Through Six Centuries.* Chicago: Univ. of Chicago Press, 1943.

Howe, Jonathan T. "The U. S. and U.N. in Somalia: The Limits of Involvement." *The Washington Quarterly,* Vol. 18, Number 3.

—"UNISOM II: Could Technology Have Made a Difference?" Background Paper: "Improving the Prospects for Future International Peace Operations—Workshop

Proceedings." Washington, D.C: U.S. Cong., Off. of Technology Assessment, U.S. Gov. Printing Off., September 1995.

International Peace Academy. *Peacekeeper's Handbook.* New York: Pergamon Press, 1984.

James, Alan. *Peacekeeping in International Politics.* London: Macmillan, 1990.

Joyce, James Avery. *Broken Star: The Story of the League of Nations, 1919–1939.* Swansea: Christopher Davies, 1918.

Kalb, Madelein. *The Congo Cables.* New York: Macmillan, 1982.

Little, Allen, & Laura Silber. *Yugoslavia: Death of a Nation.* N.Y: TV Books, 1996.

Mackinley, John. *The Peacekeepers.* London: Unwin Hyman, 1989.

Maass, Pete. *Love Thy Neighbor.* New York: Alfred A. Knopf, Inc., 1996.

Malcolm, Noel. *Bosnia: A Short History.* London: Macmillan, 1994.

McCallum, R. B. *Public Opinion and the Last Peace.* London: Oxford Univ. Press, 1944.

McNeil, William. *The Pursuit of Power.* Chicago: Univ. of Chicago Press, 1982.

Margueritte, Victor. *The League Fiasco, 1920–1936.* London: William Hodge & Co., Ltd., 1936.

Meisler, Stanley. *The U.N.: The First Fifty Years.* N.Y: Atlantic Monthly Press, 1995.

Oakley, Robert and John Hirsch. *Somalia and Operation Restore Hope: Reflections on Peacemaking and Peacekeeping.* Washington, D.C: U.S. Institute of Peace Press, 1995.

O'Brien, Conor Cruise. *To Katanga and Back.* New York: Simon & Schuster, 1962.

O'Connor, Richard. *The Spirit Soldiers.* New York: G.P. Putnam's Sons, 1973.

O'Shea, J.D. "New Zealand and the Italo–Ethiopian Dispute." Unpublished war narrative, 1947.

Rieff, David. *Slaughterhouse.* New York: Simon & Schuster, 1995

Rikhye, Maj. Gen. Indar Jit. *The Theory and Practice of Peacekeeping.* New York: St. Martin's Press, 1984.

—"Peacekeeping and Peacemaking," In

Peacekeeping, Henry Wiseman (ed.). New York: Pergamon, 1983.

Russell, Ruth B. *A History of the United Nations Charter.* Washington, D.C: The Brookings Institution, 1958.

Scott, George. *The Rise and Fall of the League of Nations.* New York: Macmillan Publishing Co., Inc. 1973.

Sells, Michael. *A Bridge Betrayed.* Univ. of California Press, 1996.

Senn, Alfred E. *The Great Powers, Lithuania, and the Vilna Question, 1920–1928.* Leiden, Netherlands: E.J. Brill, 1966.

Souleyman, Elizabeth V. *The Vision of World Peace in Seventeenth and Eighteenth Century France.* New York: G.P. Putnam's Sons, 1941.

Stewart, Bob. *Broken Lives.* London: HarperCollins, 1994.

U.N. Dept. of Pub. Inform. *Basic Facts about the United Nations,* 1995.

—*The United Nations and Cambodia (1991–1995).* Blue Books, Vol. II, 1995.

—*The United Nations and El Salvador (1990–1995).* Blue Books, Vol. IV, 1995.

—*The United Nations and Mozambique (1992–1995).* Blue Books, Vol. V., 1995.

—*The United Nations and Somalia (1992–1996).* Blue Books. Vol. VIII, 1996.

—*The United Nations and the Iraq–Kuwait Conflict (1990–1996).* Blue Books, Vol. XI, 1996.

—*United Nations Peace-keeping: Information Notes,* 1995.

—"The United Nations and the Situation in Somalia." Reference paper, April 1995.

Urquhart, Brian. *A Life in Peace and War.* New York: Harper & Row, 1987.

—*Hammarskjöld.* New York: Alfred A. Knopf, Inc., 1973.

Vulliamy, Ed. *Seasons in Hell.* London: Simon & Schuster, 1994.

Walters, F.P. *A History of the League of Nations.* Westport, Conn: Greenwood Press, 1986.

Woodhouse, C.M. *The Battle of Navarino.* London: Hodder and Stoughton. l965.

Index

About MHQ Magazine

Since 1988, *MHQ: The Quarterly Journal of Military History* has published narrative writing on military history. Articles range from ancient times to the present day, around the world, and illuminate common themes of drama, tragedy, bravery and folly, war's impact on society and culture, and how conflicts begin and end. Contributing writers include today's leading historians, biographers, journalists, and memoirists. *MHQ* is owned by American Historical Publications. Its offices are located in New York City.

Barbara Benton is special-projects editor for *MHQ*. Marleen Adlerblum is art director.